The Philosophy of Robert Boyle

This book presents the first integrated treatment of the mechanical or corpuscular philosophy of Robert Boyle, one of the leading English natural philosophers of the Scientific Revolution. It focuses on the concepts central to Boyle's philosophy, including the theory of matter and its qualities, causation, laws of nature, motion and the incorporeal.

The book is divided into two parts – the first examining the manner in which Boyle distinguished between various types of qualities, his view on the perception of these qualities and the ontological status of the sensible qualities. The second part examines Boyle's mechanism in general. Through detailed examination of Boyle's conceptions of motion, laws and space, it is argued that Boyle upholds a unique view of the causal interaction of natural bodies.

Boyle wrote as a natural philosopher and a committed experimentalist. This book is the first ever that is entirely given over to an exposition of his philosophy. It will therefore be of vital interest to any serious scholar of the history and the philosophy of science.

Peter R. Anstey is a postdoctoral fellow in the School of Philosophy at the University of Sydney. He has had a long-term interest in the natural philosophy of Robert Boyle and is co-editor of the Boyle newsletter.

Routledge Studies in Seventeenth-Century Philosophy

The Philosophy of
Robert Boyle

Peter R. Anstey

London and New York

First published 2000
by Routledge
11 New Fetter Lane, London EC4P 4EE

Simultaneously published in the USA and Canada
by Routledge
29 West 35th Street, New York, NY 10001

Routledge is an imprint of the Taylor & Francis Group

Typeset in Garamond 3 by
Keystroke, Jacaranda Lodge, Wolverhampton
Printed and bound in Great Britain by
St Edmundsbury Press, Bury St Edmunds, Suffolk

British Library Cataloguing in Publication Data
A catalogue record for this book is available from the British Library

Library of Congress Cataloging-in-Publication Data
Anstey, Peter R., 1962–
    The philosophy of Robert Boyle / Peter R. Anstey.
        p.   cm. — (Routledge studies in seventeenth-century philosophy; 5)
    Includes bibliographical references and index.
    1. Boyle, Robert, 1627–1691. I. Title. II. Series.

    B1201.B434 A57 2000
    192–dc21   99–059382

ISBN 0–415–22429–2

for Julia

Ex rerum Causis Supremam noscere Causam

Contents

Preface

A close friend of Robert Boyle's once said of him that 'he was a corpuscularian without Epicurus'. I believe this to be a particularly apt description of his philosophy, but its real import will not be immediately obvious to all. Boyle is not known as a philosopher. Most of us first encountered him in high school science when we learnt Boyle's Law. Most philosophers know at least that he was a champion of the mechanical philosophy and of his impact on John Locke. But few know Boyle as a philosopher. Yet write philosophy he did. Though he did not write it in the distilled form of his contemporaries Hobbes and Locke. Instead he wrote as a natural philosopher, a committed experimentalist. This book is the first ever that is entirely given over to an exposition of that philosophy. It is my hope that it will not be the last.

The issues that most drew me to philosophy as an undergraduate were of a rather distilled metaphysical variety: laws of nature, causation and properties. The seminal influence here was (and still is) my teacher David Armstrong. It was only as I began seriously to read Boyle, with an eye on the secondary literature, that I began to realise that there is much work to be done in correctly articulating Boyle's views on the very metaphysical issues which had so captivated me as an undergraduate. With the encouragement of Stephen Gaukroger, I began to chart Boyle's intellectual context and to gain familiarity with Boyle's vast *oeuvre*. It was at this point that I discovered that a renaissance in Boyle studies was well under way. Yet to my surprise I found that there are few studies, if any, that attempt to give a systematic interpretation of his corpuscular philosophy.

This study is an attempt, albeit a partial one, to fill that lacuna. It presents an exposition of how the various components of Boyle's mechanical philosophy fit together. The primary focus is on the metaphysics of his natural philosophy: his theory of qualities, of motion and of laws and his integration of the various components of his ontology into a coherent world-view. And an attempt is made to interpret these in a way that is sensitive to the very fertile intellectual context with which Boyle was fully engaged. As such, this is a study in the history of philosophy, one which has hopefully been enriched by my earlier philosophical preoccupations.

Having discussed the scope and nature of the study in the Introduction, I proceed to treat of Boyle's natural philosophy under two general heads. Part I deals with the theory of qualities and Part II with matter in motion. In expounding Boyle's theory of qualities, I first detail the various distinctions that he made among the qualities and then discuss the criteria Boyle employs in order to distinguish between the mechanical and 'non-mechanical' affections of matter. From there I proceed to the problem of the sensible qualities, examining first his views on perception and then the ontological status of the sensibles. Once the theory of qualities is set out, I turn to the theory of matter in motion. Much of what Boyle says about motion can be found stated, often more eloquently and accurately, in the writings of other mechanical philosophers. Yet there is one issue about which he wrote which has hitherto, to my knowledge, received scant treatment but which is of considerable interest. It is his role in the evolution of the notion of the *state* of a body. I use an analysis of this issue in Boyle as a way into a study of his 'mechanism', proceeding on to his understanding of space, laws of nature and concurrence. The final chapter deals with mind/body interaction.

The book is a revised version of my doctoral dissertation on Robert Boyle completed at the University of Sydney. The research would not have been possible without an Australian Postgraduate Research Award. The transcription from the *Boyle Papers* in Appendix 2 is reprinted here with the kind permission of the Johns Hopkins University Press. It first appeared in Peter Anstey, 'Boyle on Occasionalism: An Unexamined Source', *Journal of the History of Ideas*, 60, (1), 1999, pp. 59–62.

It may be a little clichéd to say that the debts accrued in undertaking a project such as this are too many to list. But it is true. The conversations, offhand suggestions, referrals to sources, the practical help, not to mention the general goodwill and encouragement that keeps one going, for all these things I am more than grateful. A special debt is owed to Stephen Gaukroger whose astute judgment and extensive knowledge of seventeenth-century ideas have helped me avoid numerous pitfalls and diversions. Michael Hunter has helped in many ways, not least through his technical knowledge of the Boyle archive. Thanks too go to those who have read and commented on various parts of the book in draft form: Eugenio Benitez, Keith Campbell, Alan Chalmers, Brian Ellis, Alan Gabbey, Keith Hutchison, the late George Molnar, John Schuster, M. A. Stewart and John Sutton. I would like to give special thanks to my friend Robert Urquhart whose unfailing support, particularly in bibliographic matters, has been an inspiration. Veronica Leahy, Barry and Jill Anstey and Rod and Janet West have given practical support; and Peter Alexander and Andrew Pyle kindly gave of their time to direct me in the very early stages of the project. Above all, however, I acknowledge the support and love of my wife Julia. I dedicate the book to her.

Abbreviations

General

AT	*Œuvres de Descartes*, revised edn, 11 vols, (eds) C. Adam and P. Tannery, Paris: Vrin (1996)
Barnes	*The Complete Works of Aristotle: The Revised Oxford Translation*, 2 vols, (ed.) J. Barnes, Princeton: Princeton University Press (1984)
BP	*Royal Society Boyle Papers*, University Publications of America, Bethesda: Bethesda, MD (1992)
Brush	*The Selected Works of Pierre Gassendi*, trans., C. B. Brush, New York: Johnson Reprint Corporation (1972)
CSM	*The Philosophical Writings of Descartes*, 2 vols, trans., J. G. Cottingham, R. Stoothoff and D. Murdoch, Cambridge: Cambridge University Press (1984–5)
CSMK	*The Philosophical Writings of Descartes*, 3rd vol, trans., J. G. Cottingham, R. Stoothoff, D. Murdoch and A. Kenny, Cambridge: Cambridge University Press (1991)
English Works	*The English Works of Thomas Hobbes*, (ed.) Sir W. Molesworth, 11 vols, London: John Bohn (1839–1845)
Essay	*An Essay concerning Human Understanding*, by John Locke, 4th edn, (1700), (ed.) Peter H. Nidditch, Oxford: Oxford University Press (1975)
OED	*Oxford English Dictionary*, 2nd edn, Oxford: Oxford University Press (1989)
Oldenburg	*The Correspondence of Henry Oldenburg*, 13 vols, (eds) A. R. and M. B. Hall, Madison, Milwaukee and London: University of Wisconsin Press, Mansell and Taylor & Francis (1965–86)

Phil. Trans.	*Philosophical Transactions of the Royal Society*
Physiologia	*Physiologia Epicuro-Gassendo-Charltoniana*, by Walter Charleton, London (1654)
Principia	*The Mathematical Principles of Natural Philosophy*, by Isaac Newton (1729), trans., A. Motte and F. Cajori, Los Angeles and Berkeley: University of California Press (1966)
Royal Society MSS	*Royal Society Manuscripts*
S.	*Selected Philosophical Papers of Robert Boyle*, (ed.) M. A. Stewart, Indianapolis: Hackett (1991)
Works (1744)	*The Works of the Honourable Robert Boyle*, (ed.) Thomas Birch, 1st edn, 5 vols, London (1744)
Works	*The Works of the Honourable Robert Boyle*, (ed.) Thomas Birch, 2nd edn, 6 vols, London (1772)
Works (1999–)	*The Works of Robert Boyle*, (eds) Michael Hunter and Edward B. Davis, London: Pickering and Chatto, 14 vols, vols 1–7, 1999

Short-titles used for Boyle's works

'A Paradox'   *A Paradox of the Natural and Preternatural State of Bodies, Especially of the Air,* in *Tracts Consisting of Observations About the Saltness of the Sea* [etc.] (1673)

'Advices'   *Some Advices About Judging of Things Said to Transcend Reason,* appended to *Things above Reason* (1681)

Certain Physiological Essays   *Certain Physiological Essays, Written at Distant Times, and on Several Occasions* (1661; 2nd edn, 1669)

'Chemists' Doctrine of Qualities'   'Of the Imperfections of the Chemists' Doctrine of Qualities', in *Mechanical Qualities* (1675)

Christian Virtuoso, I   *The Christian Virtuoso: Shewing, That by Being Addicted to Experimental Philosophy, a Man is Rather Assisted, than Indisposed, to be a Good Christian* (1690–1)

Christian Virtuoso, I, Appendix   *Appendix* to *The Christian Virtuoso*, (ed.) Henry Miles, first published in *Works (1744)*

Christian Virtuoso, II   *The Christian Virtuoso, Part II*, (ed.) Henry Miles, first published in *Works (1744)*

'Chymical Paradox'   'A Chymical Paradox, grounded upon New Experiments, making it probable, that Chymical Principles are transmutable; so that, out of one of them, others may be produced', published with *The Aerial Noctiluca: Or Some New Phenomena, and a Process of a Factitious Self-shining Substance* (1680)

Cold New Experiments and Observations Touching Cold, or an Experimental History of Cold, Begun (1665)

Colours Experiments and Considerations Touching Colours (1664)

Cosmical Qualities Tracts Written by the Honourable Robert Boyle About the Cosmicall Qualities of Things [etc.] (1670)

'Cosmical Suspicions' 'Cosmicall Suspicions (Subjoyned as an Appendix to the Discourse of the Cosmicall Qualities of Things)' in *Cosmical Qualities* (1670)

Defence A Defence of the Doctrine Touching the Spring and Weight of the Air (1662)

Effluviums Essays of the Strange Subtilty, Great Efficacy [and] Determinate Nature of Effluviums (1673)

Examen An Examen of Mr. T. Hobbes his Dialogus Physicus De Natura Aeris (1662)

'Excellency of the Mechanical Hypothesis' 'About the Excellency and Grounds of the Mechanical Hypothesis', annexed to *Excellency of Theology* (1674)

Excellency of Theology The Excellency of Theology, Compar'd with Natural Philosophy (1674)

Experimenta et Observationes Physicae Experimenta et Observationes Physicae: Wherein are Briefly Treated of Several Subjects Relating to Natural Philosophy in an Experimental Way (1691)

Final Causes A Disquisition about the Final Causes of Natural Things (1688)

'Fluidity and Firmness' 'The History of Fluidity and Firmness', in *Certain Physiological Essays* (1661)

Forms and Qualities The Origine of Forms and Qualities, (According to the Corpuscular Philosophy) . . . (1666–7)

Gems An Essay about the Origine & Virtues of Gems (1672)

General History of Air The General History of the Air, Designed and Begun by the Honourable Robert Boyle Esq. (1692)

Hidden Qualities Tracts: Containing Suspicions about Some Hidden Qualities of the Air [etc.] (1674)

High Veneration Of the High Veneration Man's Intellect Owes to God; Peculiarly for his Wisedome and Power (1685)

'History of Particular Qualities' 'The History of Particular Qualities', in *Cosmical Qualities* (1670)

'Hydrostatical Discourse'   'An Hydrostatical Discourse Occasion'd by some Objections of Dr *Henry More*, against Some Explications of New Experiments' in *Tracts Written by the Honourable Robert Boyle Containing New Experiments, touching the Relation betwixt Flame and Air* (1672)

Hydrostatical Paradoxes   Hydrostatical Paradoxes, Made out by New Experiments, (For the Most Part Physical and Easie) (1666)

'Intestine Motions'   'An Essay of the intestine Motions of the Particles of Quiescent Solids', appended to *Certain Physiological Essays*, 2nd edn (1669)

Languid Motion   An Essay Of the Great Effects of Even Languid and Unheeded Motion (1685)

Mechanical Qualities   Experiments, Notes, &c. about the Mechanical Origine or Production of Divers Particular Qualities (1675)

'Nature of Cold'   'Of the Positive or Privative Nature of Cold', in *Tracts Consisting of Observations About the Saltness of the Sea* [etc.] (1673)

Notion of Nature   A Free Enquiry Into the Vulgarly Receiv'd Notion of Nature; Made in an Essay, Address'd to a Friend (1686)

Philaretus   An Account of Philaretus, {i.e. Mr. R. Boyle,} during his Minority, first published in *Works (1744)*

Porosity   Experiments and Considerations About the Porosity of Bodies, in Two Essays (1684)

'Possibility of the Resurrection'   'Some Physico-theological Considerations about the Possibility of the Resurrection', in *Reason and Religion* (1675)

'Proëmial Essay'   'A Proëmial Essay, wherein, with some Considerations touching Experimental Essays in general . . .', in *Certain Physiological Essays* (1661)

Reason and Religion   Some Considerations about the Reconcileableness of Reason and Religion (1675)

'Requisite Digression'   'A requisite Digression concerning those, that would exclude the Deity from intermeddling with Matter', Essay IV, in *Usefulness, I* (1663)

'Salt-Petre'   'A Physico-Chymical Essay, Containing an Experiment, with some Considerations touching the differing parts and redintegration of Salt-Petre', in *Certain Physiological Essays* (1661)

Sceptical Chymist   The Sceptical Chymist: or Chymico-Physical Doubts & Paradoxes . . . (1661)

'Some Specimens'   'Some Specimens of an Attempt to Make Chymical Experiments Useful to Illustrate the Notions of the Corpuscular Philosophy', in *Certain Physiological Essays* (1661)

Specific Medicines   *Of the Reconcileableness of Specific Medicines to the Corpuscular Philosophy* (1685)

Spring of the Air   *New Experiments Physico-Mechanicall, Touching the Spring of the Air, and its Effects* (1660)

'Theological Distinction'   'Reflections upon a Theological Distinction' appended to *Christian Virtuoso, I* (1690)

Things Above Reason   *A Discourse of Things above Reason. Inquiring Whether a Philosopher Should Admit There Are Any Such* (1681)

Usefulness, I   *Some Considerations touching the Usefulness of Experimentall Naturall Philosophy. The First Part* (1663)

Usefulness, II, sect. 1   *Some Considerations touching the Usefulness of Experimentall Naturall Philosophy. The Second Part. The First Part. Of It's Usefulness to Physick* (1663)

Usefulness, II, sect. 2   *Some Considerations touching the Usefulness of Experimentall Naturall Philosophy. The Second Tome, Containing the latter Section Of the Second Part* (1671)

'Uses of Natural Things'   'Of Men's Great Ignorance of the Uses of Natural Things', Essay X of *Usefulness, II, sect. 2* (1671)

N.B. There is no standardised way of referring to Boyle's works. I have used the short-titles as found in *Works (1999–)*, vol. 1, pp. xvi–xx. Some works, however, are cited by individual tractate title rather than the full title of the collection within which they were originally published (e.g. 'Some Specimens' is an essay in *Certain Physiological Essays, Written at Distant Times, and on Several Occasions*).

A note on citations

All citations from Boyle's published works are from *Works* unless they also appear in *S.* Citations from *S.* have been preferred to those of *Works* on the basis of readability and availability. However, it should be noted that differences between *Works* and *S.* have not been recorded in the text. References to *Works* in the footnotes are by short title, *Works*, volume number (in Roman numerals) and page number (e.g. *Forms and Qualities*, *Works*, III, p. 20). Finally, the following abbreviations have been used:

vol.	volume
fol.	folio
r	recto
v	verso (after a numeral)
v	verse (before a numeral)
A, B . . .	first, second column
w.	written

Introduction

The following study is an attempt to give a systematic treatment of the corpuscular philosophy of Robert Boyle. It focuses on the central concepts of that philosophy such as matter and the qualities of matter, causation, laws of nature, motion and the incorporeal. It seeks to give an explication of each of these concepts and, as far as is possible, provide an integrated interpretation of how they fit together to constitute his mechanism. As such this study falls within the genre of what Rupert Hall has recently called 'rational intellectual history' (A. R. Hall 1993, p. 243).

Such an approach to the thought of Robert Boyle calls for some explanation and it is the purpose of this introduction to provide this. For instance, it is not always clear just what the corpuscular philosophy is or what mechanism amounts to. Nor is it immediately obvious how the two are related. Moreover, some may regard it as a modern presumption even to entertain the possibility that Boyle's thought can be systematised, let alone to undertake the task. Such a study might be characterised as following a 'history of ideas' approach or as 'internalist' and therefore could be open to the typical problems that beset any study that over-emphasises the autonomy of the text and the logical relations between ideas expressed in the text, while at the same time being oblivious to the socio-religio-political context in which these ideas were birthed. This latter point is especially pertinent in the light of the important recent work in Boyle studies. In the last few years our understanding of many aspects of Boyle's thought and its development have been set on a new footing by research that is extremely context-sensitive. This introduction then, seeks to explain the meanings of the terms 'corpuscular philosophy' and 'mechanism' as I understand them, to establish the value of systematising Boyle's thought, to outline recent developments in Boyle studies and to delimit the scope of the project in relation to those developments.

1 The corpuscular philosophy and mechanism

Back in 1972 J. E. McGuire noted that 'no adequate analysis of the various meanings of "the mechanical philosophy" has yet been given' (McGuire 1972, p. 523). And although the contours of the mechanical philosophy in the seventeenth century are now more fully understood, there is still need for a detailed analysis of the semantic range of this term.[1] The problem is rendered the more difficult in that the mechanical philosophy differs from, but has an important connection with, the science of mechanics in the seventeenth century. Work on a taxonomy of mechanics has recently been undertaken by Alan Gabbey (1993) and, as we shall see, his preliminary soundings have some implications for our analysis of Boyle's mechanical philosophy.

What did Boyle mean by the term 'corpuscular philosophy' and in what sense is it right to speak of Boyle's 'mechanism'? It is common knowledge that Boyle coined the term 'corpuscularian' and was the first to style his type of natural philosophy as the 'corpuscular philosophy'. He was also perhaps the chief populariser of the term 'mechanical philosophy'.[2] He tells us in the *Excellency of Theology* that 'the corpuscularian or mechanical philosophy strives to deduce all the phænomena of nature from adiaphorous matter, and local motion' (*Works*, IV, p. 19).[3] So it is clear that Boyle used 'corpuscular philosophy' and 'mechanical philosophy' as virtual synonyms. I say *virtual* synonyms because there is a nuanced difference in the two titles of his philosophy: the 'corpuscular philosophy' connotes the role of particulate matter in the explanations of natural phenomena, whereas the 'mechanical philosophy' connotes the role of the twin principles of matter and motion. Again in the Preface to 'Some Specimens' he tells us that he speaks of a philosophy '[w]hich because it explicates things by corpuscles, or minute bodies, may (not very unfitly) be called corpuscular' and '[w]hich because they [the minute particles of matter] are obvious and very powerful in mechanical engines, I sometimes also term it the mechanical hypothesis or philosophy' (*Works*, I, p. 356). Boyle frequently employs the terms 'corpuscular hypothesis' and 'mechanical hypothesis' which, while used interchangeably with his other titles, serve in some contexts to connote the provisional nature of the theory.[4] Thus we find a defence of his philosophy in a work entitled 'The Excellency and Grounds of the Mechanical Hypothesis'.

Now there are two issues of importance that arise from these summary statements of the content of the corpuscular or mechanical philosophy. First, it is explanatory. It 'strives to deduce all the phænomena of nature' and it 'explicates things by corpuscles'. Thus some form of reductionism is constitutive of this philosophy.[5] Ayers is surely right when he claims that the 'intuitive basis of philosophical mechanism' is 'the thought that mechanical change is intelligible in itself as qualitative change is not' (Ayers 1993, p. 55). Second, it explicitly appeals to the notion of machines or engines. Again Ayers has articulated an important facet of the mechanical philosophy when he says, 'the perceptible functioning of machinery supplies an overt illustration of the intelligible principles which covertly govern nature as a whole' (Ayers 1991, II, p. 135). Though it must be stressed that the sorts of machines that feature in mechanical explanations for Boyle can be as simple as scales and levers as well as more sophisticated apparatus such as clocks.[6] In Boyle's most important work on the mechanical philosophy, the *Forms and Qualities*, he tells us that his aim is to make it probable to you by experiments . . . that almost all sorts of qualities . . . *may* be produced mechanically – I mean by such corporeal agents as do not appear either to work otherwise than by virtue of the motion, size, figure, and contrivance, of their own parts (which attributes I call the *mechanical affections* of matter, because to them men willingly refer the various operations of mechanical engines); or to produce the new qualities, exhibited by those bodies their action changes, by any other way than by changing the *texture*, or *motion*, or some other *mechanical affection*, of the body wrought upon.

(*Works*, III, p. 13, *S*. p. 17)

It is this connection with machines that is the link with the science of mechanics. For, Pseudo-Aristotle's *Mechanics*, which had been rediscovered in the Renaissance and was an important stimulus to the development of early modern mechanics, dealt with problems that arose from the construction and operation of machines that were designed to manipulate nature. It was only a small step from the study of such machines to the claim that many (if not all) natural objects were themselves constructed like machines and functioned in a machine-like way. In fact, Boyle commonly calls the world itself a 'great automaton'.[7] Yet in taking this step, Boyle and others were cutting themselves adrift from the conceptual foundations that gave rise to the ancient study of mechanics. For, according to Pseudo-Aristotle, mechanics is the study of nature deviating from her course through the manipulative action of machines;[8] that is, there is a dichotomy between phenomena brought about by nature, the study of which is *physics*, and phenomena induced by art or mechanical skill, the study of which is *mechanics*. Whereas for Boyle *et al.* this distinction effectively collapses. Nature herself is a machine so the mechanical philosophy is the study of nature and is equivalent to physics.[9] So Boyle's mechanical philosophy is a philosophy of all natural and non-natural material phenomena.

Yet contemporaneous with the emergence of the mechanical philosophy, the meaning of the 'science of mechanics' was undergoing an important shift. As Gabbey has shown, mathematicians like Barrow and Wallis were by the 1660s speaking of mechanics as the geometry of local motion that makes no reference to machines (Gabbey 1993, pp. 138–139). And it could well be that the emergence and long term importance of this new style of mechanics has tended to obfuscate the origins of the term 'mechanical philosophy'.

Now even though Boyle conceived of the mechanical philosophy as an overarching study of things corporeal, he was far from being committed to a Hobbesian materialism that would entail that the corpuscular philosophy is a 'theory of everything'. In fact, in the *Excellency of Theology* he tells us that 'neither the fundamental doctrine of Christianity [the gospel], nor that of the powers and effects of matter and motion [the mechanical philosophy], seems to be more than an epicycle . . . of the great and universal system of God's contrivances, and makes but a part of the more general theory of things' (*Works*, IV, p. 19).[10] Boyle was committed to a range of incorporeal entities that were beyond the explanatory resources of the mechanical philosophy. Nonetheless the mechanical philosophy promised a comprehensive heuristic for the explanation of all corporeal phenomena.[11] As such, its central concepts were a theory of matter and its qualities, a theory of motion and its laws and the basic explanatory strategy of the explication of natural phenomena in terms of a handful of fundamental properties, and this in terms analogous to those used in explaining the operations of machines. It is this 'philosophy' that will be taken as the primary referent of the terms 'mechanical philosophy' and 'corpuscular philosophy' in the chapters that follow. The term 'mechanism' will be used as a modern synonym of 'mechanical philosophy'. It is not, to my knowledge, a term used by Boyle to describe his philosophy and will be used in the chapters that follow for convenience and because of its widespread contemporary usage.

2 Systematisation

Having established the meanings of the term 'mechanical philosophy' and its synonyms as they will be used in the ensuing chapters, it is now required that I legitimate the attempt at systematisation that is undertaken below. For there are no less than four objections to such an enterprise. First, there is Boyle's own self-confessed aversion to system-building. Second, there is the danger of crediting him with the intention of making a systematic contribution to the corpuscular philosophy when in fact he did not. Third, one leaves oneself open to the charge of making connections between different parts of Boyle's thought that are not explicitly made in the texts themselves. The real danger here arises when these connections are the result of crass anachronism. And fourth, there is the presumption of ironing out inconsistencies in the corpus and excising works that are not easily accommodated into the interpretative framework of the systematiser.[12] Let us address each objection in turn.

As to the first, it is true that Boyle inherited Bacon's aversion to system-building, but it is a specific type of system that he has in mind and not systematisation *per se*. What he objects to is the erection of superstructures that either lack any observational foundation or are supposedly impervious to correction or error. Rather, Boyle says,

> That then, that I wish for, as to systems, is this, that men, in the first place, would forbear to establish any theory, till they have consulted with . . . a considerable number of experiments, in proportion to the comprehensiveness of the theory to be erected on them. And, in the next place, I would have such kind of superstructures looked upon only as temporary ones; which though they may be preferred before any others, as being the least imperfect, or, if you please, the best in their kind that we yet have, yet are they not entirely to be acquiesced in, as absolutely perfect, or uncapable of improving alterations.[13]

('Proëmial Essay', *Works*, I, p. 303)

In fact he advocated systematisation in the constructing of Baconian histories of scientific knowledge. This involved the systematic accumulation of experimental data in every domain of natural philosophy.[14] So the task of systematisation is not at odds with Boyle's own understanding of the natural philosopher's task, nor his philosophical 'value system'. But even if it were, there might still be value in attempting to draw together and organise his natural philosophy into a well-structured and, hopefully, coherent whole.

With regard to the second objection, the falsity of attributing to Boyle the intention of presenting a systematic contribution to the corpuscular philosophy, it must be conceded that Boyle himself was not a systematiser. There are a number of reasons for this. First, there is his method of work which would clearly have vitiated any tendency toward systematicity. Thanks largely to the work of Michael Hunter and Ted Davis on the Boyle archive and on the composition of Boyle's *Notion of Nature*, we now have a fairly detailed knowledge of Boyle's method of operating in recording his thoughts and in composing his published works. From the early to mid-1650s Boyle had his thoughts recorded on loose folios, and later bifoliates, and these were filed in a haphazard manner with the result that many were lost, disordered or misplaced amongst other papers. Boyle did not withdraw to his study and compose a book from start to finish with a view to publishing. It is well known that substantial parts of many of his published works were written years, in some cases decades, before they went to press. In the case of *Notion of Nature* Boyle was even making alterations as it was being printed (Hunter and Davis 1996, pp. 209–210 and p. 224). Moreover, as a result of such a disordered process of composition, we find a degree of repetition, prolixity and disorder in many of Boyle's published works that is almost unparalleled in the seventeenth century. So rather than being systematic, Boyle's method of work in composing his publications is better characterised as sporadic, disordered and unsystematic and this is reflected in the works themselves.

A second reason for Boyle's lack of systematicity is a deep strain of eclecticism in his philosophical method. Boyle's natural inquisitiveness led him into a rich and varied terrain from which he gathered everything from anecdotes, recipes and pithy sayings to complex metaphysical arguments. There was almost no aspect of the history of philosophy and contemporary thought in which he failed to dabble. As one would expect, such eclecticism militated against systematisation simply by virtue of the disparate range of phenomena and ideas that Boyle was interested in. Yet even so, everything was plied and sifted for what could be utilised for the bolstering of the corpuscular hypothesis. In fact, in the *Appendix to the First Part of the Christian Virtuoso* Boyle explicitly acknowledges the virtues of eclecticism. Using Eleutherius as his mouthpiece Boyle tells us,

> that sect seems to lay the most probable claim to the title of philosophy, that some call the *Potamonian* sect, others the *Eclectic*; since the professors

of it did not confine themselves to the notions and dictates of any one sect, but in a manner include them all, by selecting and picking out of each that which seemed most consonant to truth and reason, and leaving the rest to their particular authors and abettors.[15]

(*Works*, VI, p. 700)

Yet while Boyle was not a systematiser in the way he composed his natural philosophy, there is an important historiographic consideration that can be adduced in defence of a systematic treatment of his mechanical philosophy. By the end of the scientific revolution, science and philosophy, which in the Renaissance were still inextricably bound, had bifurcated. On this view the mid-seventeenth century was a transitional period. The Aristotelian 'system' was in its demise and, with the emergence of experimentation, scientific instrumentation and diversification of interest, there came an unprecedented degree of specialisation in natural philosophy. In fact, natural philosophy itself was undergoing a process of dissolution. And Boyle can be seen as a transitional figure here. He is still marked by the scholastic heritage in that he sought to replace that system by another. This is evidenced in the way he is at pains in the 'Excellency of the Mechanical Hypothesis', and elsewhere, to stress the comprehensiveness of his corpuscular philosophy as if it is a system adequate enough to replace the old philosophy of the schools; after all it was 'the New Philosophy'. Yet his own experimental interests were incredibly diverse and often unrelated to each other. The extent to which they were related to each other lies in the way in which they were all able to be subsumed under the rubric of the corpuscular philosophy. In short, Boyle's contribution as a natural philosopher is characterised both by system and by diversity; by an all-encompassing hypothesis in theory and by a high degree of specialisation over a range of subjects in practice. In the practice of Boyle's 'science' we see the seeds of a trend away from systematisation and in his corpuscular philosophy we see yet another 'intellectual system of the universe'.

If this brief historiographical sketch is correct, if Boyle is accurately regarded as a transitional figure in the parting of ways for philosophy and science then, by coupling this with our observations on his method of work and his eclecticism, we have an explanation for Boyle's lack of systematisation in articulating his mechanical philosophy. Yet at the same time we have an expectation that there is a system there; that Boyle's claims about the comprehensiveness of the mechanical hypothesis are not empty rhetoric.

With regard to the third objection, that there is a danger of anachronism in filling in the gaps by drawing out implications and connections from what Boyle said, I contend that the potential benefits of this approach outweigh its dangers. Consider the dual phenomena of conscious and unconscious latency. There are theses whose implications may be stated, but which themselves may never be expressed though firmly held by a philosopher. But there are also implications of ideas or hidden premises which a thinker fails ever to grasp. The problem for the historian of ideas is that he or she cannot discriminate between these two forms of latency. And so, many are sceptical that there is any value in drawing out 'latent' ideas. Yet as long as one is honest about what is and is not explicitly stated in the text, much can be gained from this drawing of connections and implications. It enables us to understand in a deeper way the concerns of the thinker involved. And there is a reflexive element in the process in that it enables the historian of ideas to reflect on why she or he saw the connection, and therefore on the ways in which our modern agendas and perspectives differ from and can be fruitfully brought to bear on the past. An example from the following study may help to bring this out. In chapter 7 I argue that, given Boyle's view on the qualities of matter and his voluntaristic conception of laws of nature (the view that laws are imposed on matter by God), it follows for Boyle that the causal interactions between corpuscles are not a species of law-like relation. That is, causes and laws come apart; they are two different things. Boyle nowhere explicitly says this. In fact, it was not until the second half of the twentieth century that the question of whether causation is a species of law-like relation was even stated clearly.

A further point should be made about the problem of anachronism that bears on this study. It has to do with the broader issues of terminology and taxonomy. It is commonplace to examine thinkers from the past using categories and particular demarcations within a field of knowledge that were not familiar to the author under scrutiny. Two instances are apposite here. First, there is the vigorous discussion in the literature on Boyle's views on the 'secondary qualities'. Yet this is a term that, to my knowledge, Boyle only used twice in his published works, and which only became a term of art after Locke. Boyle preferred to speak of sensible qualities. Moreover, underlying this discrepancy in terminology is a subtle difference in the group of qualities being referred to and this difference is normally glossed over by modern commentators. A second less conspicuous instance lies in the question: what is Boyle's theory of perception? Boyle would have stopped at this question and asked for some clarification. For he speaks not of perception but of sensation; and the term 'perception' is for him almost exclusively reserved for ideas in the rational soul. But once some clarification was given to Boyle he and the modern inquirer could proceed, for, in spite of some terminological and taxonomical disparity, many of the modern philosopher's concerns do correspond with those of Boyle. Or we should say, many of the philosophical problems Boyle addressed remain unsolved even today.

And this brings us to the fourth and final objection to the systematisation of Boyle's thought, viz. the presumption of ironing out apparent inconsistencies and excising works that are not easily accommodated into the interpretative framework of the systematiser. On this point it is important to emphasise that there is no necessary connection between systematisation and conceptual coherence. There can be, and there are, philosophical systems that contain inconsistencies. In fact apart from the crudest forms of solipsism and trivialism it is difficult to name one entirely coherent system. Alan Gabbey's salutary remarks are worth quoting here.

Every intellectual system in the history of thought has been saddled with its share of inconsistency and incoherence, of antinomies, of problematic conceptual situations, of simple contradiction. *A fortiori*, the same holds for that unmanageably complex shoal of ideas, hypotheses, procedures, theories and systems, that shelters under the umbrella of 'The Mechanical Philosophy'.

(Gabbey 1985, p. 9)

So the commentator has merely to be honest when inconsistencies occur. It is important to point them out, it may be instructive to attempt to resolve them and clear judgment is required to determine which are genuine and which are only apparent. But beyond this, the existence of inconsistencies and inchoate elements in a 'system' should arouse no concern. In fact, the point has been made elsewhere that Boyle's method of work lent itself to a degree of tolerance of cognitive dissonance (Shapin 1993, Blair 1992, Anstey 1999). As was characteristic of many seventeenth-century virtuosi, Boyle (often through his amanuenses) simply made notes literally 'as thoughts came into his head'. The *Boyle Papers* contain a number of commonplace books and are replete with miscellaneous folios on a plethora of subjects, many of which were reworked and some of which were drawn upon for works that were ultimately published. Many others remain unconnected with any work and seem to have been written for no purpose other than to record reflections on particular issues when they came to mind. Is it any wonder then that inconsistencies are to be found in Boyle's thought?

3 Recent developments in Boyle studies

It is not too much to say that the last twenty years witnessed a renaissance in Boyle studies. An important stimulus to the revival of interest in Boyle's thought has been the publication of the *Boyle Papers* on microfilm and the accompanying catalogue of these papers (Hunter 1992). This has made more widely accessible the resources from which to gain an appreciation of the complexity and richness of Boyle's thought, in turn resulting in the publication of such materials as his early ethical writings, various biographical memoirs and notes, and selected tracts and fragments of scientific, medical and philosophical importance.[16] Furthermore, the wide availability of the *Boyle Papers* has enabled scholars to study Boyle's method of work in composing some of his well-known publications such as his *Notion of Nature* (Hunter and Davis 1996). The high points of this wave of recent scholarship are, of course, the recent publication of a new edition of Boyle's *Works* edited by Michael Hunter and E. B. Davis and the forthcoming edition of Boyle's correspondence edited by Hunter and Antonio Clericuzio.

The new wave of Boyle scholarship has also furnished us with greater insight into Boyle's intellectual development and sources of influence. Boyle's career is now far better understood thanks to a host of biographical studies that have flowed from Michael Hunter and others. Hunter's astute use of archival material has furnished us with a far clearer chronology of Boyle's emergence as a natural philosopher. And his publication of biographical and autobiographical materials from the Boyle archive (Hunter 1994b) has provided us with the richest source yet of contemporary reflections on Boyle's character. One recurring theme in both the biographical studies and work on Boyle's theology and natural philosophy is his diffident nature. In fact, this is the unifying motif in Rose-Mary Sargent's study of Boyle's experimental philosophy, *The Diffident Naturalist* (1995). Jan Wojcik's recent *Robert Boyle and the Limits of Reason* (1997) has, by contrast, shed much light on the central theological controversies which provide the context for a number of Boyle's theological works.

Yet it has not only been work on the Boyle archive and *Works* that has contributed to the 'reconsidered' view of Boyle.[17] A broader movement of revisionist historiography, particularly in early modern matter theories, has deeply impacted our picture of Boyle. Antonio Clericuzio (1990a, 1990b and 1993) has shown that Boyle accepted certain chemical notions derived from van Helmont; John Henry (1986) has challenged the traditional construal of the mechanical philosophers believing in inert matter; and William Newman and Lawrence Principe have reoriented our understanding of early modern alchemy both in terms of its relation to chemistry and its points of continuity with Renaissance and medieval alchemy.[18] In his recent seminal study Principe (1998) has painstakingly documented Boyle's ongoing fascination and practice of alchemy, arguing that, contrary to the traditional picture, Boyle's interest increased throughout his natural philosophical career.

All of these developments, to a greater or lesser degree, have some bearing on how Boyle is interpreted in the ensuing study. A case in point is the hitherto problematic issue of Boyle's 'atomism', an issue that bears on the very nature of the corpuscular philosophy itself. In a number of places when Boyle describes the corpuscular philosophy he emphasises its nature as a *via media* between some of the perennial metaphysical disputes in philosophy. What emerges is that the neutrality of the corpuscular hypothesis on the issues of the divisibility of matter, the *fuga vacui*, and so on is constitutive of the corpuscular philosophy itself. This was widely appreciated by Boyle's contemporaries.[19] What matters to Boyle is not the subtle and possibly insoluble nest problems of divisibility, etc., but the efficacy of the mechanical mode of explanation in terms of the mechanical affections of bodies. Boyle believes that the theory could proceed even though 'the jury was still out' on the metaphysical issues.[20] This position of neutrality Boyle consistently maintained throughout his natural philosophical career.[21]

However, these avowals of neutrality pose a problem, for Boyle often appears to write as an atomist. He uses the term 'atom' frequently to describe the smallest particles of matter.[22] One of his earliest surviving reflections on natural philosophy is entitled 'Of the Atomicall Philosophy' (*BP* vol. 26, fols 162–75) and it is to this philosophy that he seems well disposed. Furthermore, in some manuscripts Boyle has systematically replaced the term 'atom' with that of 'corpuscle'.[23] This might suggest that Boyle writes as an atomist and subsequently 'corrects' his manuscripts to conform with his official position of nescience. It is not surprising then that a number of twentieth-century interpreters, such as R. S. Westfall (1956) and M. Mandelbaum (1964), have claimed that he was an atomist. Thus there is an apparent tension between Boyle's self-professed nescience on the issue of divisibility and his use of an atomist terminology.

Happily, our new understanding of seventeenth-century matter theories can resolve this tension. For the tension is predicated upon a very strict interpretation of the meaning of the term 'atom' and a polarisation between continuists and atomists. What the recent work on early corpuscularianism has revealed is that in the early seventeenth century, there were matter theories that posited that the basic building blocks of all material things were corpuscles that, while in principle divisible, were never in fact divided in nature. Moreover these basic corpuscles were sometimes called atoms. Some of these corpuscularians were read by Boyle in his formative stages as a natural philosopher. For example, William Newman (1996) has shown that Boyle's early reflections on matter theory owe a significant debt to the Wittenburg medical professor Daniel Sennert, who used the term 'atom' to denote minute corpuscular clusters.

If therefore we look for two senses of the term 'atom' in Boyle, a strict sense meaning uncuttable and a loose sense meaning smallest particle of matter which for all intents and purposes is indivisible, our apparent tension dissolves. Boyle uses the term 'atom' in a systematically ambiguous way. When he is speaking of the Epicureans the strict sense his always in view, as it is when he is speaking of the issue of divisibility and declaring his nescience.[24] But Boyle also uses the term 'atom' many times in passing in the loose sense. So we can confidently assert that Boyle never in fact wrote as an atomist in the strict sense. And this is entirely consonant with his preference for the term 'corpuscle'. Boyle prefers it because it is neutral on the issue of divisibility. In fact he called his philosophy corpuscular and claimed that it was not properly called the 'atomical' philosophy at all (*Christian Virtuoso*, I, *Works*, V, p. 513). Thus, it is more likely to have been the aptness of the term 'corpuscle' that led him on occasions to replace 'atom' with 'corpuscle' rather than any fears of association with Epicurean atheism, as Marie Boas Hall (1987, p. 118) has suggested. After all, Boyle continued to use the term 'atom' in his published works. So Boyle's use of the term 'atom' should not be seen as problematic. We now appreciate, thanks to recent research, that it merely reflects the broader theoretical and semantic context of the corpuscular matter theories of his day.

The cumulative effect of this wave of scholarly activity is that we now have a more well-rounded understanding of Boyle than ever before, at least since the time of the first editor of his *Works*, Thomas Birch. We are better placed to understand his intellectual development, his eclectic interests and his ethical, alchemical, theological and experimental pursuits. But surprisingly, there is still no sustained philosophical treatment of his corpuscular philosophy in the secondary literature. The time for some attempt at systematisation of Boyle's philosophical views is ripe and it is the aim of this study to provide it.

4 Scope

As for the scope of the study, it is largely metaphysical in focus. I attempt to give a systematic interpretation of Boyle's corpuscular philosophy, an interpretation of how he thought that the giant mechanism of the world fitted together in its various parts. I treat of Boyle's matter theory, his theory of qualities, his primitive 'mechanics' with its unique account of laws of nature and his account of mind/body interaction. I have purposely almost entirely ignored Boyle's epistemology (except his views on perception) and his ethics, subjects that are calling for scholarly attention and are not wholly unrelated to the metaphysical concerns addressed here. But I had to delimit the scope of the study to keep it within manageable proportions.

Likewise I have largely ignored the issue of Boyle's intellectual development except where this has an undoubted influence on my conclusions. Several points need to be made here. First, Michael Hunter has shown that there was a critical change of direction in Boyle's intellectual pursuits in the years c. 1649 to c. 1653 when he effectively became a scientist (Hunter 1995a). My interest is with Boyle's thought after this critical turning-point. Second, E. B. Davis has pointed out that Boyle's interest in Descartes was stimulated by his assistant Robert Hooke in the years 1658–1662 (Davis 1994, pp. 159–160). I believe that this was a critical juncture in Boyle's development as a natural philosopher. From this point on there is an increased interest in and assimilation of Cartesian philosophy by Boyle. In fact, from this period on Cartesian categories came to dominate his anthropology and his dovetailing of the corpuscular philosophy with his natural theology. So much so that in late 1671 Henry More could write to Boyle 'when I was with you, you seemed not to be concerned for yourself, but for *Des Cartes*' (*Works*, VI, p. 514).[25] It also roughly coincided with a period of immense experimental and philosophical activity leading to a prolific philosophical output in the 1660s, much of which was published later. The foundations of Boyle's corpuscular philosophy were laid out during this period in works such as the *Forms and Qualities* and substantial parts of his *Notion of Nature*. In all, this was the seminal and most fertile period in Boyle's (natural) philosophical development. Third, I claim that there were very few, if any, significant conceptual developments in Boyle's articulation of the corpuscular philosophy after the 1660s. If there is an exception to this it is his reflections on the doctrine of the plurality of worlds which seem to have played a crucial role in the development of his thoughts on the contingency of laws.

Finally, this study refers only tangentially to Boyle's discussions of the problem of form. Following E. McMullin (1978b), it is helpful to distinguish between three broad categories of explanation: nomological, structural and genetic. The following study is concerned with Boyle's structural and nomological explanations of nature. The third mode of explanation, genetic, really concerns the problem of form. What accounts for a body's specificity? How do bodies reproduce? And in virtue of what are natural objects able to be grouped into kinds? These questions have been dealt with in part by Norma Emerton in her very important study of the transformation that the notion of form underwent in the seventeenth century (Emerton 1984). (Though she has not treated teleological aspects such as Boyle's account of final causes.) Boyle had many fascinating things to say about these questions, but an analysis of them is beyond the scope of this study. In fact, it was Boyle's very repudiation of the Aristotelian notion of form that allows us to examine his nomological and structural explanations of natural phenomena in relative isolation of the notion of form. For Boyle the two grand principles in nature, both ontologically and explanatorily, are matter and motion. Thus, the following exposition of Boyle's corpuscular philosophy has its starting point in his theory of the qualities of matter, a subject to which he devoted a large proportion of his experimental and literary efforts. What sort of distinctions did Boyle make among the qualities? What qualities do the smallest parts of matter have and how are these related to the properties that we observe in day to day phenomena? What analysis does Boyle give of the sensible qualities such as colour and taste? These are the questions addressed in Part I of this study. Having surveyed the contours of Boyle's theory of qualities, I then progress in Part II to unpack the way in which Boyle conceived the various parts of this qualified matter to interact in motion according to the laws of nature, and how incorporeal substances might interact with the corporeal realm. It is hoped that what follows goes some way toward satisfying what Boyle would call 'the requisites of a good interpretation'.

Notes

1 The ensuing discussion is not intended to fill this lacuna but merely to provide some terminological clarity in order to assist the reader to understand the scope and nature of the study that follows.

2 See *Forms and Qualities*, *Works*, III, p. 5, *S.* p. 4 and 'Some Specimens', *Works*, I, p. 356. Boyle uses the term 'corpuscularian' as both an adjective and a noun. It is derived from the Latin diminutive for body, *corpusculum*. Henry More (1659, p. 18) appears to have been the first to use the term 'Mechanick Philosophy'. See E. A. Burtt 1932, p. 162, *pace* R. S. Westfall 1971b, p. 41 who says 'We owe the name, "mechanical philosophy" to Boyle' and A. R. Hall 1983, p. 177.

3 Note that I have corrected *Works* which has 'form' where *Works 1744* has 'from'. See also 'Chemists' Doctrine of Qualities', *Works*, IV, p. 281, *S.* p. 133, 'Excellency of the Mechanical Hypothesis', *Works*, IV, p. 68, *S.* p. 138, *Christian Virtuoso, I*, *Works*, V, p. 513 and 'Chymical Paradox', *Works*, IV, p. 501.

4 See the 'Excellency of the Mechanical Hypothesis', *Works*, IV for the use of all four designations of his philosophy.

5 For a discussion of the relation between reductionism and the mechanical philosophy see A. Pyle 1995, pp. 506–508 and Appendix 5. Pyle seeks to establish the

'essential independence' of reductionism and the mechanical philosophy. He gives a number of examples of thinkers who were committed to the former but not the latter, and so demonstrates that not all reductionists were mechanists. However, he fails to address whether there could be mechanical philosophers who denied reductionism. My claim here is that there were none just because reductionism is an essential element of mechanism.

6 See Boyle's discussion of mechanical explanations in his 'Hydrostatical Discourse', *Works*, III, p. 601.

7 See for example *Forms and Qualities*, *Works*, III, p. 48, S. p. 71. See also *ibid.*, p. 34, *S.* p. 49 and *Notion of Nature*, *Works*, V, p. 143, p. 190 and p. 217.

8 Machines included any artefact used to manipulate nature such as a lever. See *Mechanics*, 'Among questions of a mechanical kind are included those which are connected with the lever', 847^{b}10, *Barnes*, II, p. 1299.

9 The classic statement of this is found in Descartes' *Principles*, IV, 203, *CSM*, I, pp. 288–289.

10 See also 'Excellency of the Mechanical Hypothesis', *Works*, IV, p. 68, *S.* p. 139.

11 See P. Anstey forthcoming.

12 For a perceptive and well-documented discussion of the types of problems that arise in the writing of the history of ideas, see Q. Skinner 1969 and for constructive discussions see the introductions to D. Clarke 1989 and M. Ayers 1991, I.

13 For more reservations about system-building see *Excellency of Theology*, *Works*, IV, pp. 54–55 and *Boyle to Oldenburg*, 13 June 1666, *Oldenburg*, III, p. 161. For Boyle's knowledge of Bacon's aversion see *Excellency of Theology*, *Works*, IV, p. 59.

14 See 'Proëmial Essay', *Works*, I, 307.

15 Boyle goes on in this passage to liken the eclectics to 'a posey, that consists only of those several flowers gathered out of the several meadows, and united in one bundle'. Similar sentiments can be found in Charleton, *Physiologia*, pp. 4–5.

16 See for example J. Harwood 1991, M. Hunter 1994b, 1993, 1997, L. M. Principe 1998 and P. Anstey 1999.

17 See M. Hunter 1994a.

18 See for example W. R. Newman 1994a, 1994b, L. M. Principe 1998 and W. R. Newman and L. M. Principe 1998.

19 For Boyle's conception of his corpuscular philosophy as a *via media* see 'Some Specimens', *Works*, I, pp. 355–359 and *Effluviums*, *Works*, III, p. 661. This feature of Boyle's corpuscularianism was widely appreciated by his contemporaries. See for example Oldenburg's review of the *Forms and Qualities* in *Phil. Trans.*, 11, 2 April 1666, pp. 191–192 and his Epistle Dedicatory in *ibid.*, 57, 25 March 1670, p. 1145. Likewise it is what lies behind John Evelyn's comment in his letter to William Wotton that Boyle was 'a Corpuscularian without Epicurus', M. Hunter 1994b, p. 87. For further discussion see P. Anstey 1999, pp. 78–79.

20 Or as Boyle would put it, *adhuc sub judice lis est*. See *Excellency of Theology*, *Works*, IV, p. 43.

21 It has even led one commentator, P. P. Wiener (1932) to interpret Boyle as an instrumentalist with regard to the nature of matter, a view that has been decisively refuted by M. Mandelbaum 1964, pp. 89ff.

22 For a sampling see 'Requisite Digression', *Works*, II, p. 49, *S.* p. 175, 'Proëmial Essay', *Works*, I, pp. 309–310, *Fluidity and Firmness*, *Works*, I, p. 414, *Porosity*, *Works*, IV, p. 790, *Effluviums*, *Works*, III, p. 661, *Christian Virtuoso, I*, *Works*, V,

p. 513 and p. 515, *Excellency of Theology*, *Works*, IV, p. 43, 'Theological Distinction', *Works*, V, p. 547.

23 See Boyle's 'Notes upon the Sections about Occult Qualities', *BP*, vol. 22, fols 101r–122v and M. B. Hall 1987, p. 114. See also R. Kargon 1966, p. 98 for the claim that Boyle also did this while paraphrasing Gassendi or Charleton.

24 See for example *Forms and Qualities*, *Works*, III, p. 7, *S*. p. 7.

25 See P. Anstey 1999, pp. 65–69 for a discussion of Boyle's interest in Cartesianism throughout the 1660s.

Part I
The theory of qualities

1 Distinctions among the qualities

Robert Boyle is the philosopher of the qualities *par excellence*. Of all the British natural philosophers of the mid-seventeenth century, it is he who carried out the most detailed experimental work on the qualities and produced the most sustained theoretical expositions of the corporeal qualities according to the mechanical philosophy. His researches covered an extremely wide range of qualities and continued throughout his career as a natural philosopher. And it was Boyle, of all the mid-seventeenth mechanists, who was most influential in his theoretical expositions of the nature of the qualities of bodies.[1] His impact on Newton and Locke's understanding of the qualities of bodies is widely known.[2] And a measure of the impact of his work on the continent can be seen in Jean Baptiste Du Hamel's *De Corporum Affectionibus tum Manifestis tum Occultis*. Published in 1670, just four years after Boyle's *Forms and Qualities*, this book by the first secretary of the French Royal Academy of Sciences draws heavily on Boyle's work on the qualities in both its content and structure.[3] But why did Boyle place such an emphasis on corporeal qualities in his work? And why is it appropriate to begin a study of his corpuscular philosophy with an exposition of his theory of qualities? In short, what is it that accounts for the importance of the qualities in Boyle?

1 The importance of the qualities

There are at least three ways in which the subject of the qualities of bodies is of central importance in the natural philosophy of Robert Boyle. First, there is the simple fact of its significance in quantitative terms. Boyle wrote many works on the qualities of bodies. Second, there is the intimate relation between the theory of qualities and the corpuscular hypothesis itself. It is one of the central tenets of that hypothesis. Moreover, the theory of qualities was perhaps the key doctrine that featured in Boyle's polemics against rival philosophies. And third, when it comes to an assessment of the significance of Boyle's thought for the history of philosophy and for the history of science, it is the theory of qualities that motivated much of his most important experimental work and where he made his most significant contributions to human knowledge.

The quantitative significance of Boyle's theory of qualities is primarily a result of his Baconian heritage. His overall aim for his writings on this subject was to compile a history of the qualities, in the Baconian sense, that would provide a firm basis for an adequate theory of the qualities.[4] To that end he wrote extensively on the qualities and performed hundreds of experiments to determine their nature. His published works include a number of treatises or histories on particular qualities.[5] And he augmented these histories with three theoretical treatises that where intended as introductions to the theory of qualities according to the corpuscular hypothesis. These works were philosophical in style and were viewed by Boyle as integral parts of the broader project. By far the longest and most important is the *Forms and Qualities*. Boyle tells us in his 'Proëmial Discourse to the Reader' that he conceived this work as 'a general preface to the History of Qualities' (*Works*, III, p. 4, *S*. p. 2).[6] The other theoretical treatments of the qualities are the 'History of Particular Qualities' and the 'Chemists' Doctrine of Qualities', both of which were published along with various histories of particular qualities. The project was never completed, but it appears that Boyle continued to conceive of his researches into the qualities in Baconian terms, for the last work he published before his death, *Experimenta et observationes Physicae* (1691), while written many years before, was penned as a contribution to a Baconian-style natural history.[7] From the fact that he approved its publication we can infer that the overarching Baconian agenda of his researches into the qualities remained with him until the end of his life.[8]

However, it is too simplistic to see Boyle as single-mindedly following the Baconian agenda throughout this period and even in these publications. For his work on the qualities sprang from other motives as well. In addition to furnishing his readers with natural histories, Boyle used both his theoretical and experimental excursions into the doctrine of the qualities for polemical purposes in order to bolster the corpuscular hypothesis. Thus works such as the *Forms and Qualities* and the 'Chemists' Doctrine of Qualities' cannot be considered exclusively as theoretical expositions of the corpuscularian conception of the qualities, for they are also polemical works, aimed at diminishing the credibility of the peripatetic and Paracelsian views of qualities.[9] Of course this is evident from the very title 'Of the Imperfection of the Chemists' Doctrine of Qualities'. This work is a concise and more lucid treatment of the key polemical issues raised in Boyle's earlier *Sceptical Chymist* (1661).[10] But what is not often appreciated is that the *Forms and Qualities* aims to make the mechanical production of 'almost all sorts of qualities' more probable by the reporting of experiments. Thus, it contains an extended section listing experiments that allegedly render mechanical explanations of the qualities more tenable than their rivals.[11]

Another very important motivation for Boyle's experimental work on the nature of the qualities was his interest in physiology. As Robert Frank has ably documented, Boyle's experimental work on the spring and weight of the air was intimately linked with his researches into the nature of respiration (Frank 1980, chapters 5 and 6).[12] Likewise his researches into the nature of nitre were not simply motivated by its usefulness in providing empirical grounds for a belief in the corpuscular hypothesis, but also for chemical reasons – it was 'an indispensable reagent'; and even economic reasons – the need to maintain the supply of saltpetre for the production of gunpowder (Frank 1980, pp. 121–122).

Thus it can be seen that both theoretical and experimental work on the qualities of bodies are of critical importance to Boyle's natural philosophy. In quantitative terms, the doctrine of qualities is the dominant theme in both Boyle's scientific works and his expositions of the corpuscular philosophy. Of his forty-two published works, twenty-seven of them deal with the qualities of bodies, as do many of his contributions to the *Philosophical Transactions*. And there is much important material in the *Boyle Papers* that treats of the doctrine of the qualities, not least his tract on occult qualities.[13]

Yet of more importance for the ensuing study is the integral role that the theory of qualities plays in the corpuscular philosophy itself. Boyle is most explicit about this in the *Forms and Qualities*. He begins his 'Preface' to that work by saying,

> The origin . . . and nature of the qualities of bodies is a subject that I have long looked upon as one of the most important and useful that the naturalist can pitch upon for his contemplation. For the knowledge we have of the bodies without us being, for the most part, fetched from the informations the mind receives by the senses, we scarce know anything else in bodies, upon whose account they can work upon our senses, save their qualities . . . And as it is by their qualities that bodies act immediately upon our senses, so it is by virtue of those attributes likewise that they act upon other bodies, and by that action produce in them, and oftentimes in themselves, those changes that sometimes we call *alterations*, and sometimes *generation* or *corruption*.
>
> (*Works*, III, p. 11, *S.* p. 13)

According to Boyle one cannot speak of causes and effects in nature without referring to qualities of some kind, for it is by their qualities that bodies interact causally with both percipients and their environment. Thus Boyle claims that the natural philosopher's 'business is to enquire into the production and causes' of the qualities ('History of Particular Qualities', *Works*, III, p. 293, *S.* p. 99). This is especially true of the mechanical philosophy which attempts to explicate all natural phenomena by appeal only to the two grand principles of matter and motion. According to the corpuscular hypothesis, motion itself is a mode of matter even though it is also the chief among secondary causes.[14] Moreover, if an alternative account of nature is to appear credible at all, it will only be made so by its proponent giving us clear and particular explications at least of the grand phenomena of qualities: which if he shall do, he will find me very ready to acquiesce in a truth that comes ushered in and endeared by so acceptable and useful a thing as a philosophical theory of qualities.

('Chemists' Doctrine of Qualities', *Works*, IV, p. 284, *S*. p. 137)

It is the theory of qualities that is the point of departure for Boyle from the peripatetics' and chemists' accounts of nature.

A final point on the centrality of the qualities for the corpuscular hypothesis, and this is not a point that Boyle makes, is that one cannot speak of laws of nature without reference to qualities. Law statements always contain terms that refer to qualities of some sort. In fact, the qualities of bodies seem to have some sort of priority when it comes to the epistemology of laws. We gain knowledge of laws in virtue of our knowledge of the qualities of bodies. So it is essential, if we are to get clear on Boyle's views on causes and laws, to address the issue of the nature qualities about which he writes so much.

The third reason why the doctrine of the qualities in the corpuscular philosophy of Boyle is important has to do with Boyle's legacy. In any assessment of his place in the history of ideas and of his contributions to scientific knowledge, it is to his reflections and experiments on the qualities that we turn. Virtually all of Boyle's lasting contributions to science arise from his work on the qualities. One need only instance his role in the discovery of the indicator tests for acids and alkalies; his work on the qualities of air and its implications for theories of respiration; and the eventual discovery of Boyle's Law.[15] And in the history of ideas it is Boyle's transitional role in the emergence of the distinction between primary and secondary qualities that is perhaps his most significant philosophical legacy.

So an explication of Boyle's doctrine of the qualities is a fitting place to begin a systematic study of his corpuscular philosophy. To that end we need first to clarify the historical context of Boyle's discussions of the qualities. This will enable us to understand the conceptual framework from which Boyle approached the subject of the qualities and will enable us to steer our way through the various distinctions between the qualities that were important in his philosophy and the philosophical issues to which they gave rise. It is to that historical context that we now turn.

2 The historical context of Boyle's theory

The historical context of Boyle's discussions of the qualities is best understood by tracing the emergence and significance of three of the salient distinctions among the qualities of bodies. These are the Aristotelian distinction between first and second qualities, the scholastic distinction between occult and manifest qualities and the Lockean distinction between primary and secondary qualities. The first two of these distinctions were entrenched in philosophical reflection on the qualities of matter before Boyle, whereas the third, the

Lockean distinction, only emerged in the latter half of the seventeenth century and acquired its philosophical importance after Boyle. What follows in this section is not an exhaustive study of these three distinctions, but a summary treatment that aims to put Boyle's own views on the distinctions between the qualities into sharper focus. Moreover, these three distinctions are not the only ones that have a bearing on Boyle's natural philosophy. For instance, there is the distinction between modes and accidents which is taken up later in chapter 4, §6.

2.1 Aristotle's first and second qualities

The first distinction among the qualities that is relevant to understanding Boyle's theory of qualities has its roots in Aristotle's theory of matter. The Stagirite adopted a modified version of Empedocles' four element theory of matter, claiming that matter consists of earth, air, water and fire.[16] This was supplemented with a theory that construed qualities as pairs of opposites (this had Ionic origins), the most important of which were the two pairs of tangible qualities; hot and cold and wet and dry. Among scholastics these two pairs of opposites were commonly called the first qualities or even primary qualities (*primae qualitates*). They were differentiated from the 'second qualities' such as the opposites heavy and light, dense and rare. (It is important not to confuse them with Lockean secondary qualities.[17])

In Aristotle's philosophy the theory of qualities as opposites, along with the matter/form distinction, the doctrine of privation and a substance/attribute ontology is used to augment the four element theory of matter (in part) to solve the problem of change.[18] How can something change and yet remain the same thing, and what brings change about? According to Aristotle, each element possesses some combination of the first qualities, though never a pair of opposites at the same time. These qualities are subject to change: hot becomes cold, dry moist etc. As a result of this qualitative change, the element in question is transformed.[19] So water when heated can become air, and so on. And while the first qualities were used to explain changes in the elements, the elements in turn were the major explanatory tool in accounting for the other qualities of bodies. This explains why in the *Sceptical Chymist* Boyle argues against the four element theory as an inadequate explanation of the origin of the qualities and not against the role of the first qualities.[20] A full explication of the explanatory role of the first qualities and their relation to the elements need not detain us here; suffice to say that Aristotle's appeal to the opposites of hot/cold and wet/dry to explain other qualities is tied to a rather subtle epistemological thesis about the primacy of the sense of touch. (This will become relevant when we examine the Lockean distinction below.) What is important for us to glean however, is first, that for Aristotle the first qualities are the *explanans* in the theory of the qualities (via the theory of elements) and second, that his method of explaining the qualities of matter can be broadly described as reductive.[21]

Now by the early seventeenth century there were, in addition to Aristotle's theory, a variety of theories of matter, such as the natural minima theories and Paracelsus' *tria prima*. These new theories quite naturally appropriated the Aristotelian construal of qualities as pairs of opposites in order to explain change. So while the theory of matter that originally underlay this division of the qualities of matter was replaced, there remained a residual Aristotelian pairing and partitioning of the qualities among non-Aristotelian natural philosophers.[22] Even amongst those who rejected Aristotelianism outright there was a tendency to think and speak of the qualities in terms of the original Aristotelian distinctions. So for example, in Charleton's *Physiologia*, the most important discussion of the qualities in English before Boyle, we find that the basic Aristotelian framework for the qualities is integral to the structure of his discussion.[23]

It is not surprising then to find Boyle adverting to the scholastic categorisation of the qualities when he is speaking of such qualities as hot and cold. There are numerous passing references in Boyle to the first qualities and to the distinction between the first and second qualities. For instance, Boyle opens his *Hidden Qualities* by saying, 'Besides the four first qualities of the air, (heat, cold, dryness and moisture) . . . I have often suspected, that there may be in the air some yet more latent qualities or powers . . .' (*Hidden Qualities*, *Works*, IV, p. 85).[24] This reference, as in most places, is entirely unselfconscious; talk of the four first qualities was part of natural philosophical parlance. So while Boyle explicitly rejects many of the features of the views of matter that are associated with the scholastic distinction between first and second qualities in works such as the *Sceptical Chymist*, his unpublished *Reflexions*,[25] the 'Chemists' Doctrine of Qualities' and the *Forms and Qualities*,[26] he is quite prepared to categorise the qualities in Aristotelian terms. But it is important to realise is that by Boyle's day, following the work of Bacon and Sennert, the Aristotelian first qualities had become the *explananda* and not the *explanans*. It was the nature of heat and cold that called out for explanation and provided the rationale for a work like Boyle's *Cold* (1665).[27] Just how this inversion of the explanatory role of the Aristotelian primaries came about is part of the story that will unfold as we explore Boyle's theory of qualities.

2.2 Occult versus manifest qualities

A second distinction that features prominently in the historical context of Boyle's theory of qualities is that between occult and manifest qualities. That the occult/manifest distinction was an important part of the polemical context within which Boyle worked, can be seen in the writings of major mechanical philosophers on either side of Boyle. Charleton includes a chapter entitled 'Occult Qualities made Manifest' in his *Physiologia* and the remarks of Newton that 'occult qualities put a stop to the Improvement of natural Philosophy' are notorious.[28] There is now an extensive literature on occult qualities in the seventeenth century.[29] This has been significant, not only in shedding light on the status of the theory of qualities in the seventeenth century and its relation to Aristotelianism, but also as a central plank in revisionist historiography of the role of mechanism in the scientific revolution. It is therefore of crucial importance that we get clear on Boyle's understanding of the occult/manifest distinction and ascertain what role occult qualities had in his theory of qualities.

Like the first/second distinction, this distinction was widely discussed by the scholastics and predates Boyle. However it does not originate with Aristotle.[30] By the early seventeenth century four ideas are tied up with the notion of an occult quality. First, occult qualities are *insensible* or 'hidden'. That is, 'they are the unknown Causes of manifest Effects'.[31] Second, they are *unintelligible*. This is because they cannot be explicated by the first four qualities or by the four elements. Now the insensibility and unintelligibility of occult qualities are crucially linked in the scholastic theory of scientific knowledge (*scientia*). Most qualities are considered to be insensible. But they are intelligible just because they can be explicated in terms of the first four qualities. Those insensibles that are unintelligible are those recalcitrant qualities that resist reductive explanations in terms of hot, cold, wet and dry. These are the occult qualities.[32] Third, some occult qualities are considered to be *real qualities* where 'real' has a specialised meaning arising from the fairly elaborate ontologies of such late scholastics as Suárez.[33] Very roughly 'real' can be taken to mean ontologically distinct: qualities that can exist apart from the substance in which they inhere. Fourth, occult qualities are thought to be *powers*. So for example, the effects of the lodestone are said to arise from an insensible cause, a cause that has the power to bring about observable effects.

What then is Boyle's opinion of occult qualities and of the occult/manifest distinction? Fortunately a tract about occult qualities, mentioned above, has survived in the *Boyle Papers* and this affords a very clear account of his views. With regard to their being insensible, Boyle takes it as virtually definitional that occult qualities are hidden.[34] It is the 'hiddenness' of the occult qualities that poses the greatest challenge to the corpuscular philosophy. Boyle has two strategies to allow himself epistemic access to the occult. First he posits the Baconian notion of a scale of causes. Since qualities are causes and the purpose of natural philosophy is to traverse the scale of causes, the challenge for Boyle is to uncover those causes of such phenomena as magnetic or electrical effects. That is, certain intermediate causes on the scale are known, and every scale of causes has its origin in the first cause, God. However, the problem lies in elucidating those causes that are hidden. To that end, Boyle and other mechanists apply an inductive procedure, an extrapolation from causes on the scale that are known to unknown ones. There are notorious problems in justifying these inferences and this has come to be known as the problem of transdiction, but Boyle's procedure is roughly as follows: all intermediate causes to which we have epistemic access at various levels on the causal scale are mechanical in nature, therefore we can inductively infer that all causes will be mechanical in nature.

Boyle's response to the *unintelligibility* of occult qualities is tied to the scholastic claim that they are either forms or real qualities. He regards the notions of forms and real qualities as totally unintelligible. So if an Aristotelian were to claim that a particular occult quality is a real quality, Boyle would object in the strongest terms.[35] This is because the transdictive inference at the heart of his theory of qualities renders occult qualities intelligible – all occult qualities on his view are explicable in mechanical terms. This is not to say that everything is intelligible. One of the central tenets of Boyle's epistemology is that there are many things above reason. But it is one of the key points in Boyle's polemics against the Aristotelians, and in Boyle's view, one of the virtues of the corpuscular hypothesis.

Finally, with regard to occult qualities being powers to bring about certain perceptible effects, this too conflicted with the corpuscular hypothesis. The conflict was not, as is popularly believed, because Boyle holds to a doctrine of inert matter.[36] For, Boyle admits certain powers to matter (see chapter 7, §2). Rather, it is because the qualities that feature in ultimate mechanical explanations are not power-like qualities, or in modern parlance, they are not dispositional properties. However, having said this, it must be stressed that Boyle accepts the occult/manifest distinction and even includes notes about the occult qualities magnetism and electricity in his *Mechanical Qualities*.[37] He frequently speaks of occult qualities without any critical or polemical intent, as if they are a natural phenomenon that must be addressed by the corpuscular hypothesis.[38] In fact, Boyle thinks that he most likely has the explanatory resources to give mechanical explanations of many occult qualities. He tells us that he considers 'these three doctrines of effluvia, of pores and figures, and of unheeded motions, as the three principal keys to the philosophy of occult qualities' (*Effluviums*, *Works*, III, p. 660).[39] Therefore, Boyle's doctrine of the qualities is not an all-out assault on the occult qualities, as Keith Hutchison (1982) has shown.[40] Boyle accepts occult qualities,[41] but he rejects the Aristotelian account of them.

2.3 Locke's primary and secondary quality distinction

The third salient distinction that makes up the historical context of Boyle's theory of qualities is that between primary and secondary qualities. By the early eighteenth century this had emerged as the most philosophically important distinction among the qualities of bodies. The first philosophical deployment of the distinction using the terms 'primary' and 'secondary' is rightly attributed to Locke, but it has historical antecedents at least as far back as Galileo and, some would say, Democritus.[42] Galileo foreshadowed the distinction in *The Assayer*,[43] but there is no evidence that his brief discussion there had any impact on Boyle or his contemporaries. The distinction is certainly present in Descartes and Hobbes, although they did not use the terminology of primary and secondary qualities.[44] But they provide us with strong evidence that a conceptual shift in the salient distinctions among the qualities was taking place in the early seventeenth century. The Aristotelian first qualities were losing ground to the 'primaries' of the mechanical philosophy and Boyle made an important contribution to this reorientation. I will attempt here to sketch the bundle of philosophical issues that were involved in the eventual deposing of the Aristotelian first/second distinction and the instalment of the Lockean primary/secondary distinction. This has no pretension of being a definitive analysis, but merely the broad brushstrokes of a philosophical development that cries out for more detailed research.

Aristotle, as we have seen, sought to reduce all qualities to his first four qualities; hot, cold, wet and dry. Thus for the Stagirite the first four qualities have not just an epistemic priority over the others in that they are the *explanans*, but also an ontological priority. The first qualities are so named because in the order of being all other qualities of matter are derived from them. Now what is important to notice here is the role of ontological reduction and its concomitant, explanatory reduction. The same place for reduction is found in Boyle's theory, only on his view the *explanans* is different. For Boyle, all qualities, including the first qualities of Aristotle, are to be reduced to shape, size, motion and texture. The key parallel between the two views is reduction, the key difference lies in what needs to be reduced and to what it is reduced.

Ironically enough, the very qualities that played the central role in Boyle's reduction programme were the least likely candidates for Aristotle. This is because Aristotle distinguished between what became known as the common and proper sensible qualities.[45] The division has to do with qualities that can be perceived by only one sense (proper) and those that can be perceived by more than one (common). The proper sensibles were such qualities as colour, flavour and sound whereas the common sensibles were movement, rest, number, figure and size. What is interesting about the common sensibles is that they, of all the sensible qualities, have the lowest 'epistemic credit-rating'. Our senses, according to Aristotle, are least reliable when it comes to perceiving the common qualities of shape, size and motion, the very qualities to which Boyle gives priority.[46]

For Aristotle, the first four qualities also have pride of place because of their connection with nourishment and perception and therefore life. Working within his biological model, Aristotle argues that the qualities of hot, cold, wet and dry are necessary for nourishment.[47] Without nourishment there is no life. So the existence of animate substances depends crucially upon the presence of the first qualities. In fact, their bodies are made up of these qualities.[48] And this brings us to the special connection between the first four qualities and the sense of touch. For, the first qualities according to Aristotle are perceived through the sense of touch;

> the food of all living things consists of what is dry, moist, hot, cold, and these are the qualities apprehended by touch . . .[49]
>
> (*On the Soul*, 414^b6ff, *Barnes*, I, p. 660)

Thus, they came to be called the tangible (from *tangere*) or haptic (from ἅπτω) qualities of matter.[50] The sense of touch, in virtue of its connection with these qualities, is integral to nourishment and therefore life. Without touch there is no nourishment. In fact, the sense that is most closely connected with nourishment, taste, is actually an example of the sense of touch.[51] Hunger is analysed as the desire for dryness and heat, whereas thirst is the desire for the moist and cold.[52] This special connection between the first qualities and the sense of touch in turn gives epistemic priority to the sense of touch over the other senses. So much so that without touch animals cannot have any other sense perception, and even though the other senses are not essential for life, they are essential for an animal's well-being.[53]

By contrast, for Boyle and other mechanical philosophers and sympathisers such as John Beale, the sense of touch has a rather low status. Boyle calls it 'the most dull of the five senses' (*Effluviums, Works*, III, p. 694).[54] This is rather puzzling because the mechanical philosophy is sometimes characterised as a philosophy of nature that uses the sense of touch as a paradigm for all sensation.[55] How could Boyle have such a low view of the sense of touch when, on this construal, it is so fundamental to the mechanical philosophy?

The answer seems to lie in the fact that while touch was the paradigm case of the contact criterion, it was really the latter that was the explanatory model for all sense perception. Physical contact was seen to be necessary for all sense perception and the analysis of each sense was to be modelled in a way that was analogous to that of touch, (rather than, say, the late scholastic theory of vision which appealed to the transmission of forms).[56] Touch however, remained distinct from the other senses in that its *locus* was the whole body and not some specialised sense organ. So, while the objects of the sense of touch still continued to be characterised as the tangible qualities, this was on the basis of the *locus* of the sense rather than any appeal to the contact criterion. Therefore, while some mechanists like Charleton believed that 'all Sensation is a kind of Touching' (*Physiologia*, p. 248),[57] the mechanists did not uniformly reduce sense perception to various forms of the sense of touch. For, some of the leading mechanists, like Boyle, still accepted Aristotle's common and proper sensible distinction and they thought that there was some neurophysiological basis for this (see chapter 2, §5). It is possible that this distinction provided a ground for prioritorising the efficacy of the senses, however, Boyle, to my knowledge, is nowhere explicit about this. Finally, it should be emphasised that since dualism was widely accepted by mechanists, all sense perception, at least in humans, had to be analysed in terms that contained a non-mechanical component.

To return to Aristotle, it is clear that, together with the doctrine of the four elements, the distinction between matter and form and the doctrine of opposites, the first four qualities furnish him with a comprehensive theory of change. Whereas for Boyle, as we shall see in chapter 2, the qualities of shape, size, motion (and rest) and texture have ontological priority for both conceptual and explanatory reasons. He cannot conceive of matter without them. Moreover there is only a minimal role for contrariety in Boyle's theory. It is restricted to a simple doctrine of privation that pertains to certain qualities, such as cold, which is explained as being a privation of heat rather than being a positive quality.[58] Furthermore, since the doctrine of the elements is denied, touch, for Boyle, has no priority over the other senses in gaining epistemic access to the 'primary' qualities and all activity is accounted for in terms of motion and efficient (and final) causation. Moreover, Boyle is working with a radically different matter/form distinction. For Aristotle and his followers, form is (roughly) that which when combined with matter makes it a specific substance; it imparts specificity.[59] Substances must have both matter and form. Whereas for Boyle, form is merely the arrangement of parts or figure of an object. He calls it an object's stamp.[60] It is merely a structural property of the concretion of corpuscles that make up the body.

Finally, on the scholastic view, occult qualities are those qualities of bodies that are inexplicable in terms of the first four qualities. Their effects are perceptible, but the qualities as causes are not. Therefore, for the scholastics, the occult/manifest distinction is not co-extensive with the insensible/sensible distinction. And neither is it for Boyle. His occult qualities are not those that cannot be reduced to the first qualities, but those for which there is no adequate mechanical explanation. Thus, while his theory shares with the scholastics the fundamental need for ontological reduction in order to explain the occult qualities, the metaphysical underpinning of Aristotle's theory of matter is almost entirely absent from his view.

Now continuous with the emergence of these fundamental differences between Boyle and the Aristotelians there emerged another use of the term 'sensible quality'. 'Sensible qualities' came to designate those qualities that are in some sense dependent upon the senses either for their existence or at least for their correct explication. So another sensible/insensible distinction emerged, but it was not orthogonal to the Aristotelian distinction. Rather it was a close relative. Since shape, size, motion and texture now had pride of place in the reductive explanations of all material qualities, their objective existence was unquestioned. But this was not the case for the sensible qualities. This is for two reasons. First, there were no compelling conceptual grounds nor any ontological grounds giving assurance of their independent existence. This was because the phenomenology of these qualities appeared to tie them intimately with percipients. Second, the emergence of Cartesian dualism led to the immaterial soul playing a central role in the theory of perception amongst the mechanists. Thus, these seemingly percipient dependent qualities emerged as a separate category of qualities. They were those qualities which it was thought would require a *unique* reductive analysis; a *reductive analysis that included sense organs and the soul*. These 'new' sensible qualities were also, by definition, sensible qualities in the Aristotelian sense. But 'sensible quality' had now acquired a new connotation. And it was 'sensible qualities' in this new sense that Boyle appears to have been the first to dub 'secondary qualities' (*Forms and Qualities*, *Works*, III, p. 24, *S.* p. 32). What is interesting here is that we have another instance of an inversion of the Aristotelian direction of explanation. In *On the Soul* Aristotle sought to demarcate the five senses by reference to their objects such as colours, sounds etc.[61] By contrast, Boyle sought to explicate colours and sounds by reference to the senses.

I conclude then, that the demise of the cluster of interrelated Aristotelian doctrines of opposites, forms, elements and activity, built as it was around an epistemology that gave priority to the sense of touch, when combined with the (re)emergence of the ontological priority of shape, size, motion and texture, led to a recasting of the philosophically important distinctions among the qualities. The distinction between the first four qualities and the others simply receded once they became an *explanandum* of the mechanical philosophy and the distinction between the 'new' sensible qualities (or secondary qualities) and shape, size, motion and texture grew in philosophical importance. It was Boyle, above all others, who effected this transition from scholasticism to the new philosophy. It was Locke who reaped its fruit.

3   Boyle's distinctions among the qualities

The replacement by the mechanical philosophers of Aristotle's first qualities by the qualities shape, size, motion and texture was, as has already been mentioned, motivated both by conceptual considerations (one cannot conceive of matter without them), and by explanatory considerations. (A detailed treatment of these considerations is given in the next chapter.) And, of course, it was far from an original development in the theory of qualities. It was in fact a revival of the ideas of Democritus and Epicurus, whose theory of qualities was popularised and legitimated by the *nouveaux atomistes* Gassendi and Charleton and even by Descartes who was opposed to atomism.

The salient distinction among the qualities of bodies for a mechanical philosopher like Boyle, was that between shape, size, motion and texture and all the other qualities. This over-arching division is consistently maintained throughout his writings and is absolutely central to his corpuscular hypothesis. So central that in the 'History of Particular Qualities' Boyle, when discussing the meaning of the word 'quality' tells us that

> there are some other attributes, namely *size, shape, motion*, and *rest*, that are wont to be reckoned among qualities, which may more conveniently be esteemed the *primary modes* of the parts of matter, since from these simple attributes or primordial affections all the qualities are derived. But this consideration relating to words and names, I shall not insist upon it.
>
> (*Works*, III, p. 292, *S*. p. 97)

Boyle subsumed all the commonly accepted divisions among the qualities under this fundamental dichotomy. He called shape, size, motion and texture the 'mechanical qualities'. And by parity of reasoning we can dub the other qualities of bodies as 'non-mechanical' qualities. Boyle acknowledges that there are numerous ways of dividing up the non-mechanical qualities and that none of them is entirely satisfactory.[62] However, in the 'History of Particular Qualities' he is content to work within the one outlined below and he seems to hold fairly consistently to this division throughout his other discussions of the qualities.

Amongst the non-mechanical affections of matter Boyle maintains further distinctions. First there is the familiar division between *manifest* and *occult* qualities. As we have seen, manifest qualities are those derivative qualities of bodies that are perceptible and are amenable to mechanical explanations. The manifest qualities are of three types. The first type are the (Aristotelian) *first qualities*: hot, cold, moist and dry. Then there are *second qualities* or what he sometimes dubbed 'chemical qualities' or 'chemical operations'. These include such qualities as precipitation, solubility and corrosiveness. Next there are *third qualities* or medical qualities such as qualities of thickening the blood or appeasing pain. Occult qualities are those qualities whose effects are evident but which are insensible and not amenable to mechanical explanations. The most important ones being those that 'appear' to be cases of action at a distance such as magnetism and electricity. In addition to all the aforementioned qualities there are the *sensible qualities*: colour, taste, odour, sound and perhaps heat. The difference between the manifest and occult qualities on the one hand and the sensible qualities on the other is that a full explanation of the sensible qualities requires some reference to percipients.

We can represent Boyle's divisions among the qualities diagrammatically as follows:

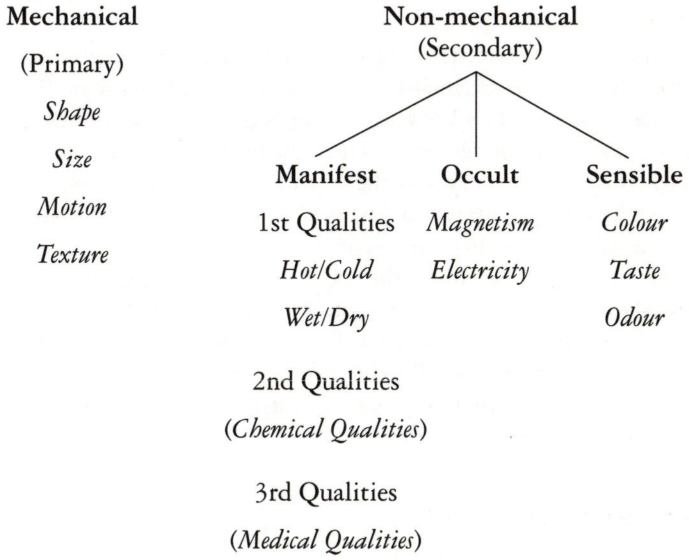

Mechanical **Non-mechanical**

(Primary) (Secondary)

Shape

Size

Motion **Manifest**   **Occult**   **Sensible**

Texture 1st Qualities   *Magnetism*   *Colour*

Hot/Cold   *Electricity*   *Taste*

Wet/Dry   *Odour*

2nd Qualities

(*Chemical Qualities*)

3rd Qualities

(*Medical Qualities*)

Figure 1

The relation between the occult and manifest (insensible and sensible) qualities in the above table highlights the element of relativity in its divisions. At first sight it would appear that the mechanical and sensible qualities should be grouped under the manifest qualities and Boyle sometimes says as much.[63] However, it is often the case that the shape, size and motion of certain corpuscles are not manifest and the new connotation of 'sensible qualities' might imply that what are perceived as colours etc. are merely the effects of imperceptible but objectively existing qualities of corpuscles and therefore that the sensible qualities are also occult. Likewise, Boyle acknowledges that many of the medical qualities are considered to be occult.[64] The point is that when 'occult' is taken to mean merely insensible, every quality will have determinate instances that render it occult. So, as we have seen, occult qualities were not just those qualities that could not be perceived. They were also those qualities which seemed to violate the basic axioms of mechanical interactions amongst corpuscles and therefore for which mechanical explanations were difficult to find. Magnetism and electricity were classed by Boyle as occult qualities, but just what other qualities were occult was not as clearcut.

A second source of relativity in the above division has to do with the nature of heat. Boyle, following the Aristotelian division, groups it with the first manifest qualities. However, in the *Forms and Qualities* and elsewhere he occasionally uses it as an instance of a sensible quality like sound or colour, a quality that is related to the sense of touch.[65] But regardless of these sources of relativity in the divisions he adopts, the key distinction remains that between the mechanical and non-mechanical qualities. It is the former which have ontological and explanatory priority.

One final distinction between the qualities should be mentioned in order to complete this basic outline of Boyle's categorisation of the qualities. Boyle in at least one place, the *Christian Virtuoso, II*, adopts the Aristotelian distinction between proper and common sensibles, where the proper sensibles, like colour, are perceived by one sense only and the common sensibles, shape, size and motion, are perceived by a number of senses. The adoption of this distinction renders what he calls the mechanical qualities a species of sensible quality. But Boyle was not alone in this among the mechanists, for this distinction was widely adopted in the mid-seventeenth century even among anti-Aristotelians. For example, Charleton says 'no scholar can be ignorant of that division of sensibles into *Common* and *Proper*' (*Physiologia*, p. 249). Needless to say that all this confirms why Boyle himself says that the distinctions among the qualities is to a large extent an arbitrary matter.

4 Two philosophical issues

Having outlined the reasons why the theory of qualities is of the utmost importance for Boyle's corpuscular hypothesis and having sketched the historical background to the various distinctions among the qualities that are found in Boyle's works, it remains now to place the ensuing chapters on Boyle's theory of qualities into the context of the overall aim of this study, viz. a systematic presentation of his mechanical philosophy. The following three chapters each deal with a philosophical problem that must be resolved if we are to explicate the remainder of Boyle's mechanism. Chapter 2 addresses the issue of the distinguishing criteria for the mechanical or primary qualities of bodies. The fundamental shift from the ontological and epistemological primacy of the Aristotelian first qualities to the primacy of the qualities of shape, size, motion and texture cries out for explanation. In virtue of what are shape, size, motion and texture more important than, and to be demarcated from, the other qualities of bodies? Having discussed Boyle's answer to this question, I turn in chapters 3 and 4 to address the question of the ontological status and location of the sensible qualities. Are the sensible qualities merely ideas in the incorporeal mind? Or are they identical to insensible structural arrangements of corpuscles? Only when we have answers to these questions that address the corpuscular philosophy at the micro-level will we be able to proceed to the analysis of Boyle's mechanism at the macro-level. That is, once we have elaborated Boyle's theory of qualities we will be able to spell out his understanding of the motion of corpuscles, the laws of nature and the relation between matter and incorporeal beings.

The structure of the ensuing discussion is as follows. First, I attempt to identify the criteria by which Boyle discriminated between (what have come to be known as) the primary and all the other qualities of bodies. The discussion of these criteria is itself instructive as to the nature of Boyle's scientific method. I also discuss potential problems with the criteria that Boyle employs and interpretations of Boyle's distinguishing criteria with which I disagree. Finally, having outlined Boyle's views on perception (Chapter 3), in Chapter 4 I turn to the sensible qualities themselves and attempt collect the various theses that Boyle entertained in addressing the crucial issues of the ontological status and spatial (or non-spatial) location of the sensible qualities. I argue for the thesis that Boyle had no systematic doctrine of the sensible qualities. Boyle was very insistent on what he did *not* believe about the sensible qualities. In particular he was quite unambiguous in his rejection of the peripatetic and spagyrists' doctrines. But in the final analysis there is no systematic doctrine of the sensible qualities to be found in his writings. This is a controversial thesis because many scholars have held the opposite view. However, as I hope will become apparent in the ensuing discussion, the diversity in their interpretations bears witness at least to the fact that if Boyle held an unambiguous position on the sensibles, then it is extremely difficult to recover. It takes some degree of exegetical wizardry to extract from Boyle some of the positions ascribed to him in the literature. But to claim that Boyle posited no systematic doctrine is not to say that he made no philosophical contribution to the problem of primary and secondary qualities. Far from it. Even a cursory survey of the range of Boyle's writings on the qualities reveals an acute awareness of the philosophical issues involved. In fact, Boyle was the first natural philosopher to sketch the logical geography of the subject and in all likelihood he set up the issues in a way that enabled Locke to formulate his view.

Notes

1   For early important treatments of qualities in Britain see Bacon's *Natural and Experimental History for the Foundation of Philosophy: Or Phenomena of the Universe* first published in 1622 and republished in Bacon 1857–74, V, Digby's *Two Treatises* (1644), Charleton's *Physiologia* (1654) and Hobbes' *Concerning Body* (1655), Part IV, *English Works*, I. For an early appreciation of Boyle's leading contribution to the doctrine of qualities see William Wotton's *Reflections upon Ancient and Modern Learning* (2nd edn, 1697), pp. 261–262.

2   For Boyle's influence on Locke compare the Theoretical Part of the *Forms and Qualities* with Locke's *Essay*, II, viii. For treatments in the secondary literature see M. Mandelbaum 1964, chapter 1, R. S. Woolhouse 1983, pp. 104ff (a more cautious view), P. Alexander 1985 and M. Ayers 1991, II, pp. 139–153. For Boyle's impact on Newton see for example J. E. McGuire and M. Tamny 1983, pp. 262ff and R. S. Westfall 1971a, pp. 369–377.

3   See Du Hamel 1670, especially book I, chapter 2. For a review of this work see *Phil. Trans.*, 65, Nov 14 1670, pp. 2105–2107. One contemporary who amply demonstrates the impact of Boyle's work on the qualities is Dr John Beale, who in 1666 was so impressed with Boyle's works on the qualities, that he urged Boyle to have them all republished in a form suitable for use in libraries. For Beale's proposal see his letters to Boyle dated 13 July and 30 July 1666 in *Works*, VI, pp. 404–410.

4   Bacon explicitly tells us in the *Great Instauration* that the natural and experimental histories for the foundation of philosophy are to include 'a separate history of such virtues as may be considered cardinal in nature. I mean those original passions or desires of matter which constitute the primary elements of nature; such as dense and rare, hot and cold, solid and fluid, heavy and light, and several others' (Bacon 1857–74, I, p. 142). On the Aristotelian echoes of this quote see §2, this chapter.

5   During the period from 1661 to 1675 Boyle published six major contributions to the project. The first, *Certain Physiological Essays* (1661) was written in the 1650s. In the 'Proëmial Essay' he informs us that the many experiments and observations in these essays were 'collected in order to a continuation of the Lord Verulam's *Sylva Sylvarum*, or natural history', *Works*, I, p. 305. See also *ibid.*, p. 306. The project continued with *Colours* (1663), *Cold* (1665), *Forms and Qualities* (1666–7), *Cosmical Qualities* (1670) and ended with *Mechanical Qualities* (1675). A number of other works published within this period are also loosely related to the project. For example, the *Sceptical Chymist* (1661) attacks the theory of the elements because 'there are a thousand phænomena in nature, besides a multitude of accidents relating to the human body, which will scarcely be clearly and satisfactorily made out by them [proponents of the elements]', *Works*, I, p. 459. That is, the theory of elements is an obstacle to a correct account of the qualities. Finally, Boyle's *Spring of the Air* (1660) and *Gems* (1672) were also conceived in part as natural histories. See *Gems*, *Works*, III, p. 515 and n. 12 below. For Boyle's important reflections on his contributions to the project see his 'Advertisements' to his *Mechanical Qualities*, *Works*, IV, pp. 231–236. The date of these comments is significant because the

bulk of Boyle's experimental work and theoretical reflections on the nature of the qualities had been completed by this time.

6 The opening sentence of 'History of Particular Qualities', a work which was prefixed to the collection of tracts concerning the cosmical qualities, reveals that Boyle sees this work as being continuous with the *Forms and Qualities*, *Works*, III, p. 292, *S*. p. 97. See also p. 294, *S*. p. 99, where he alludes to his treatment of substantial and subordinate forms in the *Forms and Qualities*. Likewise the 'Chemists' Doctrine of Qualities' was inserted as a theoretical digression into the collection that makes up the *Mechanical Qualities*, which otherwise consists of histories of particular qualities.

7 See *Experimenta et Observationes Physicae*, *Works*, V, p. 567.

8 Ralph Cudworth's comments in a letter to Boyle of 16 October 1684 are testimony to the fact that Boyle's contemporaries saw the continuity between Boyle and Bacon. He says, 'The writers of hypotheses in natural philosophy will be confuting one another for a long time, before the world will ever agree, if ever it do. But your pieces of natural history are unconfutable, and will afford the best grounds to build hypotheses upon. You have much outdone Sir *Francis Bacon* in your natural experiments', *Works*, I, p. cxxii.

9 However, much of Boyle's early polemics may also be seen as a Baconian legacy.

10 For the polemical content of the *Sceptical Chymist* see L. M. Principe 1998, chapter 2.

11 See *Forms and Qualities*, *Works*, III, p. 13, *S*. p. 17 and the sub-section entitled 'Considerations and Experiments touching the origin of Qualities and Forms. The Historical Part', *ibid.*, pp. 66–112, omitted from Stewart 1991.

12 M. B. Hall (1987, p. 112) claims that Boyle was working to a 'master plan' conceived in the 1650s to establish the mechanical philosophy on a solid empirical footing and to replace the peripatetic doctrine of qualities. Thus she considers Boyle's *Spring of the Air* as a peripheral work prompted by his learning of von Guericke's air-pump. But this seems wrong on two counts. First, as Frank (1980) has documented, many of the experiments of *Spring of the Air* and its theoretical digressions resulted from Boyle's active engagement in the vigorous research programme into physiology that was being pursued at Oxford in the late 1650s. And second, Hall's thesis appears to emphasise Boyle's polemical and philosophical agenda to the exclusion of his other interests and aspirations. *Spring of the Air* reveals that Boyle's interests were interwoven, that he could work on a number of fronts simultaneously: developing the theory of qualities and exploring physiology. In the 'Preface' to his *Defence*, appended to the second edition of *Spring of the Air*, Boyle tells us of *Spring of the Air* that 'it was not my chief aim to establish theories and principles, but to devise experiments, and to enrich the history of nature . . .', *Works*, I, p. 121. Thus he saw the work as part of the Baconian programme.

13 See for example 'A new Frigorifick Experiment', *Phil. Trans.*, 15, 8 July 1666, pp. 255–261 and 'An Historical Account of a Strangely self-moving Liquor', *Phil. Trans.*, 176, 1685, p. 1188, *Works*, V, pp. 71–73. For Boyle's tract on occult qualities see his 'Notes upon the Sections about Occult Qualities', *BP*, vol. 22, fols 101r–122v, published in M. B. Hall 1987, pp. 124–141.

14 See *Forms and Qualities*, *Works*, III, p. 47, *S*. p. 69.

15 For Henry Power's anticipation of Boyle's observations on the indicator tests see Webster 1967, p. 166 and for the discovery of Boyle's Law see Webster 1965.

16 See *Metaphysics* A, 985ª31–3 and *Generation and Corruption*, 330ª30–331ª5, in *Barnes*, II, p. 1558 and I, pp. 540–541 respectively.

17 As M. B. Hall does, see her 1987, p. 142, n. 6. In fact, regrettably this is a common conflation in the literature. For instance, Ian Hacking in *The Emergence of Probability* (1975) tells us that the primary and secondary quality distinction 'was hardly new with Bacon or Boyle. As Fracastoro put it, the qualities "that are called primary generate and alter everything, but those that are called secondary, namely light, taste, and sound, do not act on one another but merely serve to arouse the senses"', p. 29. M. A. Stewart in turn has taken Hacking's word for it (personal communication, see Stewart 1987, p. 108). However, the translation that Hacking quotes fails to capture Fracastoro's meaning. The latter wrote, 'Quod igitur materiales qualitates multa possint efficere, manifestum est, nam primae quidem vocatae omnia generant, & alterant: secundae vero appellatae lux, odor, sapor, & sonus nihil quidem inter se agunt, quoniam contrariae non sunt, sensus tamen mouent, sed & hoc iis medicantibus quae spirituales vocantur', *De sympathia et antipathia* (1546) in *Operum pars prior*, 1591, pp. 111–112. The obvious omission in Hacking's quote, 'quoniam contrariae non sunt', gives the reason why the 'second qualities' cannot generate and alter all things. It is because they lack contrariety. Clearly Fracastoro is a long way from the Lockean distinction. (I am grateful to M. A. Stewart for the reference in I. Hacking.)

18 See *Physics*, I for arguments that contraries are needed for change, in *Barnes*, I, pp. 512ff.

19 See *Generation and Corruption*, 329ᵇ–330ª, in *Barnes*, I, pp. 539–540.

20 See *Sceptical Chymist*, *Works*, I, Part V, pp. 543–561. Boyle does believe that in Aristotle's system the four elements and the first four qualities are mutually dependent. See *ibid.*, p. 469.

21 'It is clear, then, that all the other differences reduce to the first four [qualities], but that these admit of no further reduction', *Generation and Corruption*, 330ª25–26, *Barnes*, I, p. 540. The first four qualities appear to be the only qualities of bodies that Aristotle calls ἀρχαί, see *Generation and Corruption*, 329b6ff, in *Barnes*, I, p. 539.

22 Needless to say there were also upholders of the four element theory who adopted a different theory of the qualities. Boyle discusses an interesting variety of Aristotelianism which conflated the first four qualities with the forms of the elements. See *Forms and Qualities*, *Works*, III, p. 43, *S.* pp. 62–63.

23 Witness for example, chapter XI of Book III entitled 'Heat and Cold', *Physiologia*, pp. 293–315. For Bacon see his *Great Instauration*, Bacon 1857–74, I, p. 142 and *New Organon*, Bk I, LXVI, *ibid.*, I, pp. 176–178.

24 See also *Specific Medicines*, *Works*, V, p. 79, *Mechanical Qualities*, IV, p. 235, *Cold*, II, p. 468, *Nature of Cold*, *Works*, III, p. 748, *BP*, vol. 22 fols 103 and 104. In fact, Boyle's student notebook from his second stay in Geneva contains a 'Figure que exprime les Qualites et Combinations &c des Quatre Elements', *Royal Society MS 44*. This is reproduced in L. M. Principe 1995, p. 60.

25 See his 'Reflexions on the Experiments vulgarly alleged to evince the 4 Peripatetique Elements, or ye 3 Chymicall Principles of Mixt Bodies', published in M. B. Hall 1954.

26 In the *Forms and Qualities* Boyle tells us that the new philosophers reject

   those grand disputes whether the four elements are endowed with distinct substantial forms or have only their proper qualities instead of them, and whether they remain in mixed bodies according to their forms or according to their qualities, and whether the former or the latter of those be or be not refracted. These, I say, and divers other controversies about the four elements and their manner of mixtion, are quite out of doors in their philosophy that acknowledge neither that there are four elements, nor that cold, heat, dryness, and moisture are, in the Peripatetic sense, first qualities . . .

(*Works*, III, p. 6, *S*. pp. 5–6)

27 See *Cold*, *Works*, II, pp. 462ff. For an explicit statement of this inversion see Charleton's *Physiologia*, p. 250. See also Descartes' *The World*, chapter 5, *CSM*, I, p. 89, quoted in chapter 2, n. 52 below.

28 See *Physiologia* chapter XV, pp. 341–382 and Query 31 of the *Opticks* (Newton 1730, p. 401). Of course Newton has a particular gloss on 'occult' in mind here.

29 See the seminal paper by K. Hutchison in 1982. See also R. Millen 1985 and J. Henry 1986. For the Renaissance background to occult qualities see B. Copenhaver 1988.

30 Boyle says '[t]he Peripateticks are said to have been the first Builders of this Sanctuary of Occult Qualities', *BP*, vol. 22, fol. 103r, M. B. Hall 1987, p. 126. Elsewhere he rather carelessly speaks as if the doctrine originated with the Stagirite for he speaks of '*Aristotle*, having attempted to deduce the phænomena from the four first qualities, the four elements, and some few other barren hypotheses, ascribing what could not be explicated by them . . . to substantial forms and occult qualities', *Excellency of Theology*, *Works*, IV, p. 57.

31 As Newton put it in Query 31 of his *Opticks*, *op. cit.*, p. 401, first published in 1717.

32

'But others who seeme to speake more accurately, by Occult Qualityes, meane those, which are not to be deduced either from Heat, Cold, dryness or moisture which they will call the First Qualityes; Nor from such second & manifest Qualityes as Gravity, Levity and the like, which they suppose to result from certain combinations of the first.

(*BP*, vol. 22, fol. 103r, M. B. Hall 1987, p. 126)

See also *Forms and Qualities*, *Works*, III, p. 134. For instances of this theory in the Renaissance see Agrippa's *De occulta philosophia libri tres*. For further references see K. Hutchison 1982, p. 240, n. 20 and n. 21.

33 There is a tendency in the secondary literature on Boyle's theory of qualities to identify all occult qualities with real qualities. See for example M. B. Hall 1952, p. 422 and P. Alexander 1985, p. 18. However, this is to conflate two important distinctions among the qualities and contradicts explicit statements in Boyle's *Works*. It is best to regard the occult/manifest distinction as founded on epistemic criteria and the real/accidental distinction as metaphysical. Qualities can be classed according to each distinction and there is some overlap between the various classes. But none of the classes is identical. For instance, Boyle tells us quite casually in *The Christian Virtuoso*, that many real qualities are occult (*Works*, V, p. 516) and later that real qualities may be either occult or manifest (p. 523). For further discussion of real qualities see chapter 4, §6.

34 See *BP*, vol. 22, fol. 103r, M. B. Hall 1987, p. 126 and *Specific Medicines*, *Works*, V, p. 77.

35 Here Boyle was following a common view expressed for example in Descartes'
    Principles, IV, §187, *CSM*, I, pp. 278–279, Hobbes' *Leviathan*, p. 696 and
    Concerning Body, IV, 39, §15, *English Works*, I, p. 531 and Charleton's *Physiologia*,
    Bk III, chapter XV. For complaints about forms see *BP*, vol. 22, fol. 105r, M. B.
    Hall 1987, p. 127. Boyle was acutely aware of recent criticisms of occult qualities.
    See for example his comments on Sennert in the *Sceptical Chymist*, *Works*, I, p. 550.

36 *Pace* G. Deason 1986.

37 See *Mechanical Qualities*, *Works*, IV, pp. 340–354. For a very natural discussion
    of occult and manifest qualities in peach blossoms see *Forms and Qualities*, *Works*,
    III, p. 72.

38 *Contra* P. Alexander (1985, p. 17) who claims that 'throughout his works, Boyle
    inveighs against occultness in natural philosophy'.

39 *Languid Motion* was actually written 'to facilitate the explicating of occult qualities'
    by an examination of unheeded motions, *Works*, V, p. 2.

40 I do not concur, however, with Hutchison's claim that 'Boyle took a philosophical
    stance that assumes no ultimate distinction between the occult and seemingly
    manifest', p. 246. For further discussion see chapter 3, §3.

41 Boyle tells us 'there is scarce any man that will more readily confesse a long
    Catalogue of Occult Qualities then myselfe', *BP*, vol. 22, fol. 101. See also
    'History of Particular Qualities', *Works*, III, p. 293, *S*. p. 98 and *Hidden Qualities*,
    Works, IV, p. 79. It is important to emphasise that Boyle's response to occult
    qualities was commonplace amongst mechanical philosophers in both Britain
    and on the continent. See for instance part II of Antoine Le Grand's *Historia
    Naturæ*, London 1673 (a work dedicated to Boyle). Oldenburg tells us in his
    review that 'he [Le Grand] undertaketh to explain the true Nature of the
    Qualities of Bodies by Experiments, and to make it out, that even those, that are
    commonly called Occult, may be explicated by Motion, Figure, Pores and
    Texture', *Phil. Trans.*, 19 May 1673, 94, pp. 6046–6047.

42 Democritus frag. 9. See Kirk, Raven and Schofield 1987, p. 410.

43 *The Assayer*, in S. Drake 1957, p. 274.

44 For Hobbes see his letters to Mersenne of 20/30 March 1641 and to William
    Cavendish of 16/26 October 1636 in Hobbes 1994, I, p. 108 and p. 38 and
    Concerning Body, *English Works*, I, pp. 104–105. For Descartes see *Sixth
    Meditation*, *CSM*, II, pp. 56–57 and *Replies to the Sixth Objections*, *CSM*, II, p. 297.
    The earliest use of the term in English that I have found is in Charleton's
    Physiologia (1654), p. 325 and p. 337. But a close reading reveals that Charleton
    is still thinking in Aristotelian categories. The publisher's note to the *Forms and
    Qualities* tells us that Boyle had some notes on the 'Production of second
    Qualities', (*Works*, III, p. 2) but from the fact that these notes were differenti-
    ated from the notes on the sensible qualities it seems reasonable to conclude that
    they relate to non-mechanical qualities other than the sensible qualities. The
    term is used a number of times by John Beale in his correspondence with Boyle,
    but all the relevant letters post-date the publication of the *Forms and Qualities*.
    See *Works*, VI, pp. 404ff. For the term 'secondary affections' see Glanvill's *Plus
    Ultra*, 1668, p. 95.

45 See *On the Soul*, II, 6, 418ª6ff, in *Barnes*, I, pp. 665ff.

46 See *ibid.*, 428ᵇ18–25, *Barnes*, I, p. 681. On Boyle's adoption of the proper/
    common sensible distinction see chapter 2, §5 below. For further discussion of
    the distinction in Aristotle see R. Turnball 1978 and D. Modrak 1987, chapter

3, especially p. 79. Apparently the epistemology of the common sensibles 'obsessed Renaissance writers and provoked much of the sixteenth- and early seventeenth-century reflection on primary and secondary qualities', K. Park, 1988, p. 474. Park tells us that as far as she knows 'the history of this central question is unexplored', *ibid.*, n. 22.

47 See *On the Soul*, 414b6ff, *Barnes*, I, p. 660.

48 '[T]he material constituting the bodies of all animals consists of the following – the hot and the cold, the dry and the moist', *On Length and Shortness of Life*, 466^a20–21, *Barnes*, I, p. 742.

49 See also 423^b27–29, *Barnes*, I, p. 674 and *Generation and Corruption*, 329^b6ff, especially, 'Since, then, we are looking for principles of perceptible body; and since perceptible body is equivalent to tangible, and tangible is that of which the perception is touch, it is clear that not all the contrarieties constitute forms and principles of body, but only those which correspond to touch', 7–10, *Barnes*, I, p. 539.

50 So John Beale writes to Boyle 'you have provided us a liquid and ample account of the four chief tangibles, heat, cold, fluidity, firmness', 13 July 1666, *Works*, VI, p. 406.

51 See *On the Soul*, 434^b18ff, *Barnes*, I, p. 691. See also R. Sorabji 1971, pp. 85ff.

52 See *ibid.*, 414^b11–14, *Barnes*, I, p. 660.

53 See *ibid.*, 435^a11ff, *Barnes*, I, p. 691. For a discussion of the connections between the sense of touch and the proper sensibles see C. Freeland 1992, pp. 243–248. For a general discussion of Aristotle's theory of perception see S. Gaukroger 1981.

54 See also *Beale to Boyle*, *Works*, VI, p. 406. Contrast Boyle here with Descartes in *The World*, 'Of all our senses, touch is the one considered the least deceptive and most certain', *CSM*, I, p. 82.

55 S. Gaukroger sees Descartes' attempt 'to model all perceptions on contact senses such as touch' as 'a crucial part of the mechanist programme', in Introductory essay, in 1990, p. 17. For Descartes' view see *Replies to the Fourth Set of Objections*, *CSM*, II, p. 175 and Rule 12 of the *Rules*, *CSM*, I, p. 40.

56 A clear illustration of the onset of the demise of the contact criterion is found in the change that Locke made to II, viii, §11 of the *Essay*. In the first three editions, beginning in 1690, he wrote,

> The next thing to be considered, is how bodies operate on one another; and that is manifestly by impulse, and nothing else. It being impossible to conceive that body should operate on *what it does not touch* . . . or when it does touch operate any other way than by motion.

However, the fourth edition, 1700, has 'The next thing to be consider'd, is how *bodies* produce *Ideas* in us, and that is manifestly by impulse, the only way which we can conceive Bodies operate in.' Locke, having come under the influence of Newton, was now prepared to countenance that God could superadd certain powers to matter. See A. Koyré 1965, p. 155.

57 Another to hold this view was Ralph Bathurst, see his 'Quæstio Secunda – An omnis sensus sit tactus?' (1651), in T. Warton 1761, pp. 222–228, (for the date of Bathurst's proposition, which is wrongly given in Warton see R. Frank 1980, p. 319, n. 131). For Aristotle's acceptance of the contact criterion for the sense of touch see R. Sorabji 1971, pp. 86ff. For the contact criterion in Locke see *Essay*, IV, ii, §11.

58 See 'Nature of Cold', *Works*, III, pp. 733–754.

59 For more detailed discussion see N. Emerton 1984, chapter 2. On the reinter-pretation of the notion of form see *ibid.* chapters 4 and 5. For Boyle's most important critique of the Aristotelian notion of form see *Forms and Qualities*, *Works*, III, pp. 37ff, *S*. pp. 53ff. For an example of a minor critical treatment see *Christian Virtuoso, I, Appendix, Works*, VI, pp. 689–690.

60 See *Forms and Qualities*,

> though I shall for brevity's sake retain the word form, yet I would be understood to mean by it not a real substance distinct from matter but only the matter itself of a natural body, considered with its peculiar matter of existence, which I think may not inconveniently be called either its specifical or its denominating state, or its essential modification – or, if you would have me express it in a word, its stamp.
>
> (*Works*, III, p. 28, *S*. p. 40, see also p. 47, *S*. p. 69)

61 See R. Sorabji 1971.

62 See 'History of Particular Qualities', *Works*, III, pp. 292–293, *S*. pp. 97–98. For another important passage relating to distinctions among the qualities see *Mechanical Qualities, Works*, IV, p. 235.

63 For the mechanical affections as manifest see for example *BP* vol. 22, fols 107r and 117r, in M. B. Hall 1987, p. 128 and p. 138. For the sensible qualities as manifest see for example *Forms and Qualities, Works*, III, p. 53, *S*. p. 77.

64 See 'History of Particular Qualities', *Works*, III, p. 293, *S*. p. 98.

65 See *Forms and Qualities, Works*, III, p. 23, *S*. p. 32. See also 'Nature of Cold', *Works*, III, p. 738.

2 Distinguishing criteria for the primary qualities

We have seen that Boyle maintained a number of distinctions between different types of qualities, the most important one being that between the *mechanical affections* of matter and all of matter's other qualities. It is this division that is the focus of this chapter. It will be convenient to call this the primary and secondary quality distinction for two reasons. First, because there is no doubt in Boyle that the mechanical affections were considered primary and all others secondary or derivative. That is, the mechanical affections of matter had both an ontological and an epistemological priority over all the other qualities. And second, because that is how it is spoken of in almost all of the secondary literature on Boyle's theory of qualities, even if at times commentators have the more specific category of sensible qualities in mind when they speak of secondary qualities. However, at the same time one must be aware that Boyle never (to my knowledge) used the term 'primary quality' for the mechanical affections of matter. In fact, it would have been somewhat inconsistent for him to use this term because it is the primary *affections*, or *modes*, of matter that he uses to explain the origin of the qualities. Boyle says on a number of occasions that he does not count the mechanical affections of matter among the qualities.[1] Moreover, Boyle (to my knowledge) only uses the term 'secondary quality' twice in his published works; once in the *Forms and Qualities* where it refers to the sensible qualities and once in *Certain Physiological Essays* where it refers to medicinal qualities such as the laxative virtue of rhubarb.[2] Bearing all this in mind, let us now turn to Boyle's crucial distinction among the qualities.

1 The general characterisation of Boyle's 'primary and secondary quality' distinction

Boyle's primary and secondary quality distinction is normally characterised in the following way: the primary qualities of material bodies are the determinables size, shape, motion or rest and texture.[3] And each part of matter has a determinate size, shape, motion and for aggregates, texture. The primaries are the mechanical attributes of bodies in virtue of which bodies interact causally with each other and bring about the changes that we see around us. All the remaining qualities of bodies are secondary to these primaries because they are in some sense reducible to them. The secondary qualities are 'derived from', or are 'deduced from' the primary qualities. They include such qualities as colour, solubility and magnetism.

There is a number of qualifications one could add to this characterisation. For instance, Boyle sometimes adds the relational properties of posture, order and position to this list of primaries.[4] But overall this characterisation is true to the spirit of Boyle's distinction. For when he mentions the primaries in passing, or in a context in which he is not explicating their nature, it is almost always this list of primaries that is given. A typical example is in his 'Chymical Paradox', where, in the context of discussing an experiment done with oil of aniseed, he says,

> ... our experiment affords us a considerable argument in favour of that part of the corpuscular or mechanical hypothesis, that teaches inanimate bodies to differ from one another, but in the bigness, shape, motion, contexture, and, in a word, the mechanical affections of the minute parts they consist of.
>
> (*Works*, IV, p. 501)[5]

However when one turns to Boyle's more detailed discussions of the qualities this simple characterisation is clearly not the whole story. We have already seen that Boyle maintains a number of distinctions among the secondaries and it is evident from the *Forms and Qualities* that, for Boyle, there is actually a degree of structure or ordering among the primaries as well. This structure is in part determined by Boyle's application of the criteria by which he distinguishes the primaries from the secondaries and in part determined by certain reductive principles which lie at the heart of the corpuscular hypothesis. It is in unpacking this structure that we are able to determine what Boyle's distinguishing criteria actually are.

Boyle continually and consistently distinguishes between primary and secondary qualities (though of course these are not his preferred terms) and this distinction plays an integral role in his corpuscular hypothesis. Hence, it is safe to assume that he does have a criterion or perhaps a number of criteria by which he distinguishes them. He does not divide the qualities arbitrarily. However, one looks in vain in his works for an explicit discussion of criteria as such. It is only by carefully unpacking his more systematic discussions of qualities that we can unearth them. And to this end it is best to follow Boyle's train of thought on the structure of the primaries as revealed in the theoretical part of the *Forms and Qualities*, making occasional references to other works where required.

When turning to the *Forms and Qualities* one finds two interlocking strands in his reasoning, strands that proceed in opposite directions. There is what might be called the 'bottom-up' approach whereby Boyle works from the qualities of the smallest parts of matter and proceeds to the properties of molecular corpuscles. And there is the 'top-down' approach where he applies certain reductive theses, proceeding from the properties of bodies at the macro-level to those at the micro-level. Let us examine each in turn, keeping in mind that Boyle is thinking of matter at three different levels: there are the smallest insensible corpuscles, then there are the insensible compound corpuscles and thirdly the bodies of the manifest world.

2 The 'bottom-up' approach to matter

2.1 *Matter in its original state*

Boyle begins the bottom-up part of his analysis of the qualities by claiming that in its original state matter was undifferentiated and without motion.[6] It was most likely a motionless block of extended substance. But why should matter have originally been undivided? Boyle does not tell us. Perhaps it is because this is most consistent with the account of the creation of the world in the first two chapters of *Genesis*.[7] However, he does tell us that motion is required to break it up into its various parts. The numerous parts of matter are the 'genuine effect of variously determined motion'. This view is intentionally at odds with Epicurean atomism which postulates a rain of atoms perpetually moving downwards in the void and which assumes that motion is an essential attribute of matter. By contrast Boyle was at pains to stress that motion, in the Epicurean sense of an innate propensity to move, was not essential to matter, and that all the parts of undivided matter were 'perpetually at rest' (*Forms and Qualities*, *Works*, III, p. 15, *S*. p. 18).[8] Thus, by positing undivided original matter, Boyle was consciously distancing himself from the atheistic overtones of Epicurean atomism.[9] The notion of undivided original matter provides him an *a priori* reason to include God in his cosmogony.

Moreover, at the outset Boyle attributes a number of properties to matter that do not feature in the list of primaries. All matter is homogeneous, extended, divisible, impenetrable and indestructible. He says, 'there is one catholic or universal matter common to all bodies, by which I mean a substance extended, divisible, and impenetrable' (*Forms and Qualities*, *Works*, III, p. 15, *S*. p. 18).[10] The doctrine of the homogeneity of matter, the view that all matter is the same substance, was possibly derived from Aristotle, for Boyle draws an explicit parallel between his view and Aristotle's prime matter (*materia prima*) in the *Sceptical Chymist* (*Works*, I, p. 504 and p. 506).[11] But the view is also to be found in the Stoics, Gassendi, Charleton and Descartes. It commits Boyle to a form of *monism* about the corporeal, a view that is markedly different from the pluralism of Greek atomists.[12] Moreover, it entails the possibility of universal transmutation which is a thesis at the heart of his critique of the peripatetic and spagyrist theories of elements.[13]

As for 'a substance extended, divisible, and impenetrable', the details of Boyle's view and their philosophical interconnections are rather murky. That he considers matter a substance is entirely consonant with his substance/attribute ontology and is uncontroversial (see chapter 4, §6). But the other three notions are more difficult. Certainly when Boyle speaks of extension he has in mind the Cartesian definition of matter. Yet he has serious reservations about claiming that extension is *the* defining characteristic of matter and this is an issue he takes up in a number of places. In short, his view appears to be that, while extension is a necessary characteristic of matter, it is not sufficient to capture its essence. Impenetrability, at least, appears to be another necessary characteristic of matter. But Boyle is unsure and regards the issue as unresolved, claiming that Descartes' definition of matter 'is more easy to find fault with, than to substitute a better' (*Excellency of Theology, Works*, IV, p. 43).[14] The real problem with extension is its conceptual connections with the notions of the void, place and divisibility. Witness for example the definition of extension that Boyle gives in a comment on divisibility in his notes on Epicurean atheism,

> the very Nature of Corporeal Extension requires, that there be Pars *extra partem*, one Part, whether actual or designable, that is placed without another, and not precisely coextended with it.
>
> (*BP*, vol. 2, fol. 22)

Should this incline one to accept infinite divisibility? Moreover, if one accepts the Cartesian definition of matter, then a void becomes impossible. But this is another issue on which Boyle, notoriously, declared his nescience.

Turning to impenetrability, we find a paucity of references to this quality in Boyle's writings. So it is difficult to elaborate any clear doctrine of impenetrability and its philosophical implications for the doctrine of place. In his notes on occult qualities in the *Boyle Papers*, Boyle gives us what appears to be a definition of impenetrability. He says, 'one parcell of matter can toutch another but by it's surface (there being noe penetration of dimensions) . . .' (*BP*, vol. 22, fol. 115r, in M. B. Hall 1987, p. 136).[15] This is a standard definition.[16] But the salient issue regarding impenetrability is its place in the definition of matter. We know that Boyle considered matter to be impenetrable, but did he follow More and consider it to be an essential quality of matter having the same status as extension?[17] Or did he, along with the Cartesians, consider it to be essential to matter only in a secondary sense? In his 'Possibility of the Resurrection' Boyle seems undecided. He speaks of the 'true notion of body' consisting 'alone in its extension, or in that and impenetrability together' (*Works*, IV, pp. 198–199, *S*. pp. 202–203). But in the posthumous *Appendix to the First Part of the Christian Virtuoso*, Boyle speaks more confidently about looking 'upon matter, as being only as a substance extended and impenetrable' (*Works*, VI, p. 689).[18] One positive conclusion we can make is that Boyle reveals that he was sensitive to what was a live issue in the mid-seventeenth century. The young Newton was, by the early 1670s, already siding with More against Descartes on impenetrability.[19] Perhaps Boyle was moving in the same direction. However, More's definition of matter allowed for extended spiritual substances. God and angels were extended, but penetrable beings. But in *Final Causes* (1688, w.1677), Boyle tells us that souls lack extension, therefore, presumably, siding with Descartes.[20] In the final analysis, given the lack of a sustained discussion of this quality, it appears that we cannot attribute to Boyle a consistent view of impenetrability and its relation to matter. Matter is impenetrable, but whether it is essentially so is unclear.[21]

With regard to the infinite divisibility of matter, Boyle again expressed nescience, only on this issue he was far more explicit than on the issue of extension. From what he tells us of the general programme of the corpuscular hypothesis it appears that this nescience on divisibility (and the void and other issues) was actually constitutive of the corpuscular hypothesis itself. In 'Some Specimens' he tells us that

> both the Cartesians and the Atomists explicate the same phænomena by little bodies variously figured and moved. I know, that these two sects of modern naturalists disagree about the notion of body in general, and consequently about the possibility of a true vacuum; as also about the origin of motion, *the indefinite divisibleness of matter* . . . but in regard that some of them seem to be rather metaphysical than physiological notions, . . . I esteemed that, notwithstanding these things, wherein the Atomists and Cartesians differed, they might be thought to agree in the main, and . . . be looked on as, upon the matter, one philosophy. Which because it explicates things by corpuscles, or minute bodies, may (not very unfitly) be called corpuscular . . .
>
> ('Some Specimens', *Works*, I, pp. 355–356, italics added)

This sort of comment is reiterated a number of times in prefatory remarks about the corpuscular hypothesis and it is clear that Boyle believes that the issue of the divisibility of matter need not be resolved for the corpuscular hypothesis to retain its explanatory power. For instance, in the 'Proëmial Discourse to the Reader' in the *Forms and Qualities*, Boyle tells us that 'I have forborne to employ arguments that are either grounded on, or suppose, indivisible corpuscles called *atoms*' (*Works*, III, p. 7, *S.* p. 7).[22] It is clear therefore that Boyle considers divisibility to be a metaphysical issue that is orthogonal to the efficacy of mechanical explanations. To be sure, if the issue were to be resolved in favour of infinite divisibility, then divisibility would have to be included as one of the essential characteristics of matter, or at least as one of its 'primary affections'.[23] But Boyle thinks such a resolution highly unlikely. In fact, the issue of the divisibility of matter, (and the more abstract problem of the divisibility of the continuum, *compositio continui*), is one of Boyle's favourite and most frequently cited examples of the limits of our powers of reason. In *Things Above Reason* he mobilises the example over and again as something beyond our rational powers.[24]

Given this nescience and the insolubility of the problem of divisibility, it is only to be expected that Boyle's expositions of the corpuscular philosophy are consistently neutral on the issue. Indeed, what we find in his expositions and even in some of his experimental treatises, is that Boyle distinguishes between what we can dub conceptual (or theoretical) and practical (or contingent) atomism.[25] The point is that it may be that there are physical constraints in the divisibility of very small particles such that they cannot be divided beyond a certain limit. This is practical atomism: there is a contingent limit to the smallness of corpuscles. Yet this is neither to say that these corpuscles cannot be divided in imagination nor that God cannot divide them. Boyle puts it like this in the *Forms and Qualities*:

> though it [a particle of matter] be *mentally*, and by divine omnipotence, divisible, yet by reason of its smallness and solidity nature doth scarce ever actually divide it; and these may in this sense be called *minima* or *prima naturalia*.
>
> (*Works*, III, p. 29, *S.* p. 41)[26]

Again, at the beginning of his history of firmness he says,

> when I speak of the grossness of corpuscles, I pretend not to determine, whether or no body or matter be so perpetually divisible, that there is no assignable portion of matter so minute, that it may not at least mentally (to borrow a school-term) be further divided into still lesser and lesser parts . . .
>
> ('Fluidity and Firmness', *Works*, I, p. 401)[27]

By adopting this distinction, Boyle can work with natural minima which are the building blocks for the corporeal world, and yet does not foreclose on the possibility of infinite divisibility. Thus it is not incorrect to call his smallest corpuscles *atomic corpuscles* as distinct from *molecular corpuscles* as I shall do, as long as it is borne in mind that 'atomic' here implies neither conceptual atomism nor its denial.[28] Second, it enables us to account more easily for Boyle's occasional (usually guarded) comments that divisibility is an essential property of matter, such as in his *Notion of Nature* where he says that 'motion does not essentially belong to matter, as divisibility and impenetrableness are believed to do' (*Works*, V, p. 210).[29]

So matter is a homogeneous, extended substance that is impenetrable and divisible (up to a point!). It seems natural then to ask why these properties were not included in the list of primaries. M. A. Stewart (1987, p. 111) rightly observes that there is an 'interesting theoretical distinction' here. But what is its basis and what makes it interesting? Part of the answer seems to be that Boyle was simply undecided on the essentiality of impenetrability and divisibility. But perhaps there is more to it. This is an issue to which we will return in §3.3 below.

2.2 Matter divided

Boyle continues the bottom-up part of his reasoning by claiming that matter is in actual fact divided. This is the direct result of motion imposed on matter by God, a doctrine he explicitly attributes to Descartes.[30] The fact that motion was 'instituted' by God means that it is not essential to matter.[31] Boyle says, 'local motion, or an endeavour at it, is not included in the nature of matter, which is as much matter when it rests as when it moves . . .' (*Forms and Qualities*, *Works*, III, p. 15, S. p. 19).[32] Once he has established how it is that matter is actually divided, Boyle goes on in the *Forms and Qualities* to discuss the nature of the parts of this matter. First he claims that it follows from the fact that matter is divided,

> that each of the primitive fragments, or other distinct and entire masses of matter, must have two attributes – its own magnitude, or rather *size*, and its own *figure* or *shape*.
>
> (*Works*, III, p. 16, S. p. 20)

Boyle believes that the attributes of size and shape are possessed by the parts of matter in virtue of the motion that was imparted to it at the beginning. He spells this out in the 'History of Particular Qualities' where he tells us that matter 'being all of one uniform nature, is according to us diversified only by the effects of local motion'. Local motion breaks up the universal matter into its distinct parts and each part necessarily has its own determinate shape and size. So size and shape presuppose or, as Boyle puts it, are 'deduced' from motion and matter ('History of Particular Qualities', *Works*, III, p. 297, S. p. 105). And it is because of this that motion, and not shape and size, is the 'grand principle' of all that happens in nature. As Boyle says, 'motion, not belonging to the essence of matter . . . , and not being originally producible by other accidents as they are from it, may be looked upon as the first and chief mood or affection of matter' (*Forms and Qualities*, *Works*, III, p. 35, S. p. 50). Thus motion has a chronological priority over shape and size.[33]

2.3 The essentiality criterion

Boyle then goes on in the *Forms and Qualities* to furnish us with an inductive argument. He claims that experience shows us that all observable parts of matter have these two qualities, shape and size, therefore it is reasonable to conclude that the insensible parts do too. Then he quickly proceeds beyond this inductive consideration to a conceptual one. Given the fact that matter is divided, Boyle says that size, shape and motion are essential properties of its parts.

> For, being a finite body, its dimensions must be terminated and measurable; and though it may change its figure, yet for the same reason it must necessarily have *some figure* or other. So that now we have found out and must admit three essential properties of each entire or undivided,

> though insensible, part of matter: namely, *magnitude* . . .shape, and either
> *motion* or *rest* (for betwixt them two there is no mean) . . .
> *(Works*, III, p. 16, *S.* p. 20)[34]

In effect he has introduced a criterion of essentiality; every part of matter so
divided *must* have a determinate shape, size and motion (or rest). Here is an
unambiguous *a priori* criterion for distinguishing the determinables size, shape
and motion (or rest) from all the other qualities of matter. It follows that it is
a necessary condition of something being matter that it have shape, size and
motion (or rest). But Boyle then wavers. Conscious, I suggest, of his 'official'
view that motion is non-essential he attempts to draw a further distinction.
Size and shape, but not motion, are not only essential attributes they are also

> *inseparable accidents* of each distinct part of matter – *inseparable* because,
> being extended yet finite, it is <u>physically impossible</u> that it should be
> devoid of some bulk or other and some determinate shape or other . . .
> *(Works*, III, p. 16, *S.* p. 20, underlining added)[35]

Motion does not qualify as an inseparable accident because it is physically
possible that a portion of matter have no motion. However, Boyle's appeal to
'physical impossibility' here does not add anything to the essentiality criterion
already adduced. For if a property is essential then it is, by definition, physically
impossible that a particular should lack it and retain its identity. The distinction then between essential accidents and inseparable ones appears to be
explanatorily redundant. And it is little wonder that later on in the *Forms and
Qualities* we find Boyle calling motion an inseparable quality.[36] So Boyle's initial
attempt to introduce some structure into his account of the primaries fails and
is not consistently maintained by him.

However, there is a difference between both shape and size on the one hand
and motion on the other in Boyle's account of matter, but the distinction
between inseparable accidents and essential properties does not bring it out.
It is easier to uncover this distinction if we introduce some terminology from
contemporary discussions of properties. According to Boyle, size, shape and
motion (or rest) are essential qualities *qua* determinables. Something cannot
be matter if it does not have some shape, size and motion or rest. By contrast,
the determinates of size, shape and motion are non-essential and non-relational.
Any corpuscle must have some determinate shape, size or motion, but which
size, shape or motion it has is accidental. It is a purely contingent matter. Boyle
says of shape that,

> *figure*, for instance, comprehends not only triangles, squares, rhombuses,
> rhomboids, trapezions, and a multitude of polygons whether ordinate
> or irregular, but, besides cubes, prisms, cones, spheres, cylinders, pyramids,
> and other solids of known denominations, a scarce numerable multitude
> of hooked, branched, eel-like, screw-like, and other irregular bodies . . .
> ('Chemists' Doctrine of Qualities', *Works*, IV, p. 281, *S.* p. 133)[37]

If the determinate properties happen to change, the corpuscle would still be matter. Presumably this is the point that Boyle is making when he says, 'whether or no the shape can by physical agents be altered, or the body subdivided, yet mentally both the one and the other may be done, the whole essence of matter remaining undestroyed' (*Forms and Qualities*, *Works*, III, p. 16, *S*. p. 20).

So shape, size and motion *qua* determinates are accidental intrinsics. However, it is not clear that on Boyle's view the shape and size of atomic corpuscles in the real world can change in the way their motion does. In the quote above he speaks of it as being conceivable that they might vary, but seems hesitant actually to claim that they do vary. So while it is physically possible that they change their shape and size (for shape and size are accidental intrinsics) in actual fact this never, or hardly ever, happens. In fact, Boyle's mechanism seems to require that they remain invariant in spite of change of motion and arrangement. His is not a plasticine world of ever-changing atoms, but one containing atoms of fixed shapes and sizes. This then is a contingent difference between the property of motion and the properties of both shape and size.[38] It is a consequence of Boyle's adoption of practical atomism.

In the *Forms and Qualities*, Boyle certainly says that size is an accident. The reason he gives is that it can at least be subdivided mentally without destroying its essence. Yet, notoriously if something is conceivable it is not entailed that it is possible. And the relevant question here is: can atomic corpuscles have different sizes? When we turn to the 'Excellency of the Mechanical Hypothesis', Boyle again evades the issue. He mentions the primary qualities of matter in the following order: motion, figure, size, posture, rest, order or texture. And he goes on to say that 'the first two of these, for instance, are each of them capable of numerous varieties' (*Works*, IV, p. 70, *S*. p. 141).[39] The omission of the third quality as having 'numerous varieties' is rather conspicuous. It seems then that Boyle believed that size was an accident of atomic corpuscles, but that he never spelt out just how this was so.

Boyle's silence here leaves unanswered a number of philosophical questions. First, if atomic corpuscles can have a variety of sizes, just how big can they get? Why are there not observable atomic corpuscles? Is it just a contingent fact that they are all insensible?[40] If so what explains this? Second, if it is maintained that atomic corpuscles are partless, and that they can vary in size, then their size must be an irreducibly intensive quality. To be sure their size will be a determinate property, but problems arise when one attempts to give an account of what it is in virtue of which two atomic corpuscles differ in size. Needless to say, Boyle did not consider these issues.

2.4 *Texture*

The next stage in the 'bottom-up' approach to matter comes with the introduction of texture. Boyle defines texture in this way:

> when many corpuscles do so convene together as to compose any distinct
> body, . . . then from their other accidents (or modes) . . . there doth emerge
> a certain disposition or contrivance of parts in the whole, which we may
> call the *texture* of it.
>
> (*Forms and Qualities*, *Works*, III, p. 22, *S.* p. 30)[41]

Texture is a structural property of particle aggregates and, like the determinates
size, shape and motion, it is an accidental property. It is derived from the shape,
size, motion and posture of the atomic corpuscles, where posture is defined as
the position of a corpuscle relative to other corpuscles.[42] As the motion and
especially the posture of the atomic corpuscles change, so too does the texture
of the cluster of particles. But more importantly, texture is an essential property
of molecular corpuscles. So here again we have the application of the essentiality
criterion, only this time it applies to corpuscles at the molecular level. Texture
is not essential at the atomic level because, by definition, no atomic corpuscles
have it.[43] But at the molecular level it is 'physically impossible' for a corpuscle
to lack it.

Now one very important feature of Boyle's corpuscular philosophy is the
role of certain insensible molecular corpuscles that he calls *primary concretions*.
These corpuscles are extremely small but at the same time they have a major
role in Boyle's accounts of form and generation. They include such corpuscles
as the seminal principles that are responsible for the reproduction of animate
substances and perhaps even minerals. The efficacy of these primary concretions, according to Boyle, arises from two factors. First, they are extremely
resistant to division or modification, thus they persist in chemical reactions
and can be recovered in their original form.[44] Second, they are qualified with
just the requisite textures to enable the reproduction of the diverse range of
forms we observe throughout the natural realm. The notion of primary
concretions and the role that Boyle assigns them can easily be traced through
Lucretius to Epicurus. In fact, its origins lie in the Anaxagorean notion of
seeds.[45] However, it must be stressed that in modern terms they are effectively
'theoretical entities' for which the only evidence is the recurrence of the form
within nature that they are called upon to explain.[46]

So shape, size and motion (or rest) are primaries in virtue of the essentiality
criterion applied at the level of atomic corpuscles. Texture is a primary in virtue
of the essentiality criterion applied at the level of molecular corpuscles. This
then is genuine structure among the primaries. It rules out simplicity as being
a further criterion by which to distinguish the primaries and secondaries. For
while shape and motion are all simple, irreducible properties that cannot be
analysed in terms of any others, texture is a structural property. It can be
analysed in terms of the other primaries. It is natural then to inquire as to why
Boyle should include a derivative property among his primaries. After all some
commentators are adamant that texture is not a primary quality.[47]

I have five reasons for including texture among the primaries. First, the
primary objective of this chapter is to explain why Boyle distinguished between

the *mechanical affections* of matter and all the others. There is no doubt that texture is a mechanical affection on Boyle's view and I have followed the trend in the secondary literature by calling the mechanical affections primary qualities even though Boyle seems not to have used the latter term. Second, I concede that many of the instances in Boyle's writings of appellations referring to a list of qualities that include the term 'primary' have as their referent only shape, size and motion. However, at times Boyle does call texture a primary affection or at least imply that it is. For instance in his 'Essay on Nitre' he speaks of 'motion, figure, and disposition of parts, and such like primary and mechanical affections . . . of matter' (*Works*, I, p. 364).[48] So given the fact that Boyle did not use the term 'primary quality' and that he does not restrict the use of 'primary' to shape, size and motion, there seems to be some degree of arbitrariness as to which qualities an interpreter might subsume under the term. Third, since texture as both a *mechanical affection* and a *catholic affection* of matter[49] plays such a central role in the application of his reductive principles (along with size, shape and motion), and these reductive principles are used to differentiate the primary qualities from the secondaries, it seems only natural to call it a primary quality.

Fourth, since, according to Boyle, it is the very small molecular corpuscles or primary concretions that do all the work in our causal and qualitative explanations of the phenomena we see about us, it seems natural to focus on their essential attributes and texture is one of them. Of course, if texture is a primary, so too is posture, or the relative position of corpuscles. Yet this presents no problems of interpretation and is consistent with many of Boyle's lists of mechanical affections. That he often omits it in his lists is due to the fact that it is assumed in virtue of the very existence of texture. And fifth, Boyle's contemporaries normally included texture in the list of primaries and understood him to have included texture. The most important one being Locke, who is supposed to have taken over elements of Boyle's doctrine of qualities as the basis of his primary and secondary quality distinction. Even a cursory glance at his *Essay* reveals that he often included texture in his list of primaries.[50]

However, in the final analysis, it is clear that this is no more than an issue about the use of one term and at that a term that is not Boyle's. Whether or not texture is dubbed 'primary' makes no difference to the analysis of Boyle's theory of matter as outlined above. Let us return then to Boyle's distinguishing criteria. The essentiality criterion is a purely ontological criterion. There is no epistemological consideration that is relevant to its application. Boyle is not tacitly employing a distinction between appearance and reality by which he distinguishes primaries from secondaries, nor is he claiming that non-primary qualities are somehow percipient-dependent. His employment of this *a priori* criterion to matter is independent of the existence of percipients. And of course the criterion entails the universality of the primary properties; these properties are instantiated wherever there is matter. Hence Boyle often calls them the 'catholic affections' of matter.[51] Thus there is no need for him to employ a weaker universality criterion in order to distinguish the primaries from the secondaries.

Finally, the essentiality criterion rules out the possibility that matter may come in various kinds. For it is constitutive of Boyle's mechanical hypothesis that matter is of just one kind. It is not as if there could be one kind of matter which is essentially magnetic, and another kind that has gravitational attraction as an essential property. This is precluded *a priori* by the corpuscular hypothesis. According to it, there is just one kind of matter, so if a quality fails to be universal then one must be able to give a reductive account of it in terms of the primaries. Of course it is possible on Boyle's view that there be a contingent universal property of all matter (perhaps magnetism is a good candidate here), but because it is non-essential it would not count as a primary. But is essentiality a *sufficient* condition of primacy for Boyle? We have already seen that he considers certain properties to be essential to matter which are not listed among the primaries: such properties as extension, divisibility etc. This would indicate that essentiality is not sufficient and, in order to determine why, we need to turn to Boyle's 'top-down' account of the properties.

3 The 'top-down' approach to matter

One of the most distinctive features of Boyle's corpuscular hypothesis is its reduction programme.[52] Boyle aims to identify all the properties of the basic particulars of his theory of matter and he achieves this by applying a range of different reductive principles. The general nature of the reduction is that the qualities of observable molecular corpuscles are reduced to the qualities of unobservable molecular ones and they in turn are further reduced to atomic corpuscles. It is the qualities of the atomic corpuscles that are basic for Boyle, but following Epicurus and Lucretius, it is the insensible *molecular* corpuscles that are the building blocks of the manifest world. It is not surprising then to find that not all the reductive principles force a reduction down to the level of atomic corpuscles. And this is consonant with Boyle's inclusion of texture as a primary quality, for texture is not a quality of atomic corpuscles.

What then are Boyle's reductive principles? First, as in almost all reduction programmes, there is the general principle of *parsimony* (or Ockham's Razor). Boyle is particularly concerned with economy and regards the economy of the corpuscular hypothesis as one of its main advantages over its rivals. He says when criticising the Aristotelian view that,

> unless we admit the doctrine I have been proposing, we must admit that a body may have an almost infinite number of new real entities accruing to it without the intervention of any physical change in the body itself . . .
>
> (*Forms and Qualities, Works*, III, pp. 18–19, S. p. 24)[53]

Of course, he is prepared to admit an infinity of shapes (and sizes?) of corpuscles, but unlike real qualities, they are not akin to substances but merely modes of matter. Second, there are what can be called *inductive principles* in Boyle's reduction programme. They are inferences from the observed to the unobserved that serve to delimit the range of possible properties at the basic level. Third, there is what I have called a *polemical principle*. The application of this principle seems largely motivated by Boyle's reaction to the doctrines of the chemists and peripatetics. Fourth, there is an *explanatory principle* in Boyle's reduction programme and finally Boyle uses Aristotle's common/proper sensible distinction to distinguish between the qualities. We need not dwell on the principle of parsimony here, so let us turn to the others.

3.1 *Inductive principles in Boyle's reduction programme*

Boyle nowhere explicitly says that he is employing inductive principles in his reduction programme, however it is very clear that they are operating implicitly in his reasoning. They serve to set parameters for what qualities can exist at the micro-level and which ones can count as primary. The first principle is that *there are no fundamental qualities of insensible corpuscles that are not qualities of corpuscles in the manifest world.*[54] Boyle has three strong reasons for holding this. First, this principle is the conclusion of a well-supported inductive inference from observations of the properties of bodies of ever-decreasing magnitude. For Boyle, all the new objects revealed by the microscope exhibit the very same properties as those objects of the manifest world, so why should the as yet unobservable corpuscles not have the very same properties? As he penetrated further into the micro-level no new properties of objects were discovered. It therefore seemed reasonable to him that this would be the case all the way down. Second, this principle is in accord with his desire for parsimony. Third, it is consonant with his view that explanation essentially involves an *explanans* that is already clearly understood (see §4 below). If completely unknown properties were to appear at the microscopic level they would be inexplicable.

It might even be claimed that this inductive principle is the centre-piece of his whole reduction programme. For it appears that nowhere in his extant writings does Boyle positively attribute to insensible corpuscles a property that is not attributable to observable bodies (with the possible exception of indivisibility). Furthermore, it is not just the properties of bodies that are the same at the fundamental level, but also the laws that govern their behaviour. He claims that

> both the mechanical affections of matter are to be found, and the laws of
> motion take place, not only in the great masses and the middle-sized
> lumps, but in the smallest fragments of matter . . .
>
> ('Excellency of the Mechanical Hypothesis',
> *Works*, IV, p. 71, *S.* p. 143)[55]

A second inductive principle implicit in Boyle's reasoning is this: *if it is not a universal quality at the macro-level, then it is not a universal quality at the micro-level*. This principle is narrower in scope than the first. Boyle seems to use it to delimit the number of candidates for primacy at the micro-level.[56] According to the mechanical hypothesis, not only are there no qualities of insensible corpuscles that are not qualities of observable corpuscles, but only those qualities that are universal at the macro-level qualify as candidates for primaries at the micro-level. Hence, qualities such as magnetism cannot be primaries, they must be explained mechanically in terms of the primaries. The qualities that this principle admits include shape, size, texture, impenetrability, solidity and possibly colour.

3.2 *A polemical principle in Boyle's reduction programme*

A further principle in Boyle's reduction programme arises out of his rejection of the Aristotelian doctrine of the qualities. One of Boyle's points of departure from Aristotelianism is the familiar one about explanatory circularity, the point of Molière's famous ridicule that opium puts one to sleep because it has a dormitive virtue.[57] Boyle's response is to seek an account of the powers of bodies that offers more explanatory power and more parsimony than the Aristotelian theory. There are a number of strands to his attempts to furnish his readers with a more adequate theory of power-like qualities. But the one that he seems to adhere to most consistently is the principle that *all power-like qualities are reducible to, or in some sense dependent on, the mechanical affections of matter*. Again Boyle was nowhere explicit that this was a reductive principle as such. But most of his treatments of powers are attempts at a reduction of powers to either the primary qualities or relations between corpuscles which themselves are only characterised by the primaries. Now we might be tempted to gloss this reductive principle, albeit anachronistically, as an attempt to reduce all dispositional properties to categorical properties. But this is a little too clearcut for Boyle. For first, as we have seen, Boyle believes that matter is impenetrable and impenetrability is definitely a power and second, as will become clear below (chapter 7, §2), Boyle did allow certain minimal causal powers to matter. The emphasis in Boyle on the question of powers is to provide mechanical explanations of what in the Aristotelian view were explanatorily redundant and ontologically superfluous entities, that is faculties and real qualities. Boyle's aim is not to achieve a completely inert matter, but to give a parsimonious and intelligible explication of the behaviour of bodies.

It would normally be expected at this point that we turn to Boyle's celebrated lock and key analogy in the *Forms and Qualities* as evidence of his reductive claims about powers. But since the interpretation of this passage is a vexed issue to which we will turn later (chapter 4, §6) and since the immediate context of that passage is on the relative nature of the qualities of bodies rather than on the subject of powers, we will turn instead to an important passage in *Notion of Nature*. There, in a discussion that is explicitly about powers and directed against the schoolmen (and others), Boyle tells us that, the term faculty may, indeed, be allowed of, if it be applied as a compendious form of speech, but not as denoting a real and distinct agent; since in reality the power or faculty of a thing is (at least) oftentimes but the matter of it, made operative by some of its mechanical modifications; [I say some, because the complex of all makes up its particular nature]. . . . sometimes, if not frequently, the effect of what is reputed a natural power or faculty, is produced by the texture, figure, and, in a word, mechanical disposition of the agent, whereby it determines the action of a remoter agent to the produced effect. . . . And so a key may either acquire or lose its power of opening a door, (which, perhaps, some schoolmen would call its aperitive faculty) by a change, not made in itself, but in the locks it is applied to, or in the motion of the hand, that manages it.

(*Notion of Nature*, *Works*, V, p. 247)

It is by employing this reductive principle that Boyle hopes to account for those qualities that seem to call for a dispositional analysis. However, as we shall see (chapter 4), not all that Boyle says about the non-mechanical qualities is compatible with a strict reduction to the mechanical affections. The point that is relevant here is that the general assumption of this reductive principle is that the mechanical affections are not faculties or powers and that those qualities that are powers can be explained in terms of those qualities that are not power-like. This seems to be true, but how rigorously this division can be applied to the affections of matter remains questionable, particularly in the light of the nature of impenetrability. Furthermore, it is not clear whether, in Boyle's mind, the 'mechanical affection'/power dichotomy is a criterion for distinguishing the mechanicals from other qualities or whether it is a happy consequence of the already established distinction between mechanical and non-mechanical qualities.

Finally it should be noted that this reductive principle is not an inductive one, for many of the manifest qualities are dispositional and at least one of them, colour, is a candidate for the status of primary quality. It seems therefore, that Boyle is motivated by polemical reasons in his exclusion of dispositional qualities from the primaries. Thus he is able to preclude a property like gravity from being a primary even though it might not be precluded by the application of the inductive reductive principles.

3.3 *An explanatory principle in Boyle's reduction programme*

Boyle also appears tacitly to employ a broad *explanatory* principle in his reduction programme, one that is intimately linked to his mechanism. The principle is that the most fundamental properties of bodies, to which all others can be reduced, are those that are involved in mechanical explanations of phenomena. Thus the 'centre of gravity' for all of Boyle's explanations of the multifarious qualities of bodies is the small group of mechanical affections (shape, size, motion and texture) which he believes are the minimum set of qualities required to give comprehensive mechanical explanations.

Over and over again his accounts of such phenomena as magnetism, chemical reactions, gravity, sensible qualities, etc. are in terms of these 'mechanical affections' of corpuscles. They are the fundamental resources of the mechanical hypothesis. And this furnishes us with at least part of an answer to the question as to why not all the qualities of universal matter are included in Boyle's list of primaries. Why are such qualities as divisibility, impenetrability and extension not primaries? At least part of Boyle's answer is that they are not 'mechanical' affections of matter. In Boyle's view they make little or no contribution to the explanatory power of the theory.[58]

So there is implicit in Boyle a set of reductive principles that work together in the 'top-down' approach to matter to demarcate those properties of bodies that are primary from those that are not. The principle of parsimony provides the rationale for the whole reductive programme. The inductive principles lend an air of empirical respectability to what seems such an overtly *a priori* theory. The non-dispositional requirement provides a point of departure from the main rival to the theory and the explanatory principle, the requirement that the primaries feature in mechanical explanations of phenomena, furnishes the theory with just that explanatory power that the Aristotelian view lacked. Together these principles reveal the obvious utility of those properties that qualify as primaries in Boyle's corpuscular hypothesis. And in combination with the essentiality criterion they yield what is, in seventeenth-century terms, a coherent theory of matter that seems to promise an exciting new research programme.

4 Boyle on scientific explanation

It is worth digressing at this point to draw some threads together about Boyle's general programme for the corpuscular hypothesis and in particular his understanding of explanation. We have seen that Boyle is committed to ontological reduction and that he employs a set of (mostly implicit) reductive principles by which he reduces all corporeal phenomena to the primary affections of matter, that is its shape, size, motion (or rest) and texture. But he also believes that his corpuscular hypothesis is superior to its rivals because of its explanatory powers.[59] What then does Boyle understand explanation to be? What is it about these reductions that qualify them as explanatory? Here the work of Michael Friedman and Ernan McMullin is particularly helpful in enabling us to shed some light on Boyle's view.[60]

It appears that there are two strands, or more accurately, two necessary conditions for a mechanical (and therefore reductive) explanation for Boyle. First, there is the condition that it involves *structural explanation*. McMullin defines structural explanations in the following way:

> When the properties or behavior of a complex entity are explained by alluding to the structure of that entity, the resultant explanation may be

called a *structural* one. The term 'structure' here refers to a set of constituent entities or processes and the relationships between them. Such explanations are causal, since the structure invoked to explain can also be called the *cause* of the feature being explained.

(McMullin 1978b, p. 139)[61]

Clearly Boyle's emphasis on the role of the texture of corpuscles enables us to classify many of his explanations of the qualities of bodies as structural, such as his explanation of salts as being composed of stiff and sharp particles.[62] To be sure, sometimes he goes beyond textural considerations and appeals to the shape and motion of atomic corpuscles. But in most, if not all, of these cases it is not incorrect to claim that it is the *structure* of the individual atomic corpuscles that is the *explanans*. Likewise when we turn to Boyle's use of the clock metaphor and allied mechanical metaphors, it is invariably the structure of the components of the machine that are referred to as analogous to the kinds of explanations that the corpuscular hypothesis gives. Witness for example how Boyle, in *Notion of Nature*, likens mechanical explanations to 'one who knows the structure and other mechanical affections of a watch' (*Works*, V, p. 245). It might be objected that Boyle complements these structural explanations with nomic explanations. However, while Boyle often mentions *nomic explanations* in the same breath as his structural ones, he is rarely specific and never gives us any determinable laws that might serve as actual nomic explanations. Throughout the emphasis is always upon corpuscular structure, though he recognises that laws do have some role too.

The second necessary condition of a reductive explanation for Boyle is that it reduces unfamiliar phenomena, or phenomena that are difficult to understand, to ones that are familiar and are easily understood.[63] This *familiarity condition* of explanation has not been evident in our foregoing exposition of Boyle's reduction principles. So in order to assess the correctness of our attribution of it to Boyle we must turn to his explicit statements about the nature of explanation or, in his terms, explication. Here is a sample of references. To start with, Boyle, in *Notion of Nature*, considers the general purpose of an explanation to be thus:

> to explicate a phænomenon, it is not enough to ascribe it to one general efficient, but we must intelligibly shew the particular manner, how that general cause produces the proposed effect.
>
> (*Works*, V, p. 245)

But what qualifies as 'intelligibly shewing' here? He goes on to elaborate his claim by the familiar watch analogy. But he is more specific in the 'Excellency of the Mechanical Hypothesis'. Having discussed the 'superficial' nature of the peripatetic explanations, Boyle turns to the corpuscular hypothesis.

> But to come now to the *Corpuscular* philosophy, men do so easily understand one another's meaning, when they talk of *local motion, rest,*

bigness, *shape*, *order*, *situation*, and *contexture* of material substances, and these principles do afford such clear accounts of those things that are rightly deduced from them only . . .

(*Works*, IV, p. 69, *S*. p. 140)[64]

It is the explanation that enables one to 'easily understand one another's meaning' which counts as an adequate one. As Boyle says in the *Forms and Qualities*, 'to explicate a phenomenon being to deduce it from something else in nature more known to us than the thing to be explained by' (*Works*, III, p. 46, *S*. p. 67).[65] He also accepts the contrapositive that phenomena that are inexplicable are those that cannot be understood by things that are familiar to us. Boyle says,

> we sometimes find that a thing hath some property belonging to it, or doth perform somewhat, which, by reflecting on the beings and ways of working that we know already, we cannot discern to be reducible to them or derivable from them, we then conclude this property or this operation to be inexplicable . . .
>
> (*Things Above Reason*, *Works*, IV, p. 422, *S*. pp. 234–235)[66]

Thus it is clear that Boyle accepted the familiarity condition. But as Friedman points out, such a condition on explanation leads to some unwelcome consequences. The problem is that on this view 'most of the explanations in contemporary physics, which postulate phenomena stranger and less familiar than any that they explain, could not possibly explain' (Friedman 1974, p. 10). One need only instance a property like 'charm' that is attributed to quarks to illustrate the inadequacy of the familiarity condition. Friedman certainly has spotted a serious weakness of this view. However, a more serious problem, one that Friedman does not discuss, is that this view of explanation, when used exclusively, leads us into a version of the Learner's Paradox found in Plato's *Meno*.[67] The privileged epistemic status of the *explanans* in the familiarity view is that it must already be known. But if scientific knowledge is only acquired through scientific explanation, and the only phenomena that can explain are familiar, then one can never know anything unfamiliar. If one knows nothing, then one can never learn anything, for there is nothing familiar to function as the *explanans*! Certainly Boyle would have shied away from these paradoxical consequences of his view of explanation. But the fact remains that the familiarity criterion put constraints on the sorts of explanations that were possible not just for Boyle, but also for his corpuscularian descendants, in particular Newton. It is perhaps worth speculating then, that Newton's equivocation on the ontological status of gravitational attraction has its roots as much in the familiarity condition of explanation as it does in polemical reductive principle that sought to expunge matter of powers.

Now given that Boyle also admits nomic explanations, though he nowhere emphasises them nor gives any examples of such explanations, it is pertinent to ask what relation these explanations have to the familiarity condition. What we find on examining Boyle's references to laws of nature as an *explanans* of phenomena is that in his account of laws, far from appealing to the familiar and what is already understood, Boyle adopts what has come to be called the inference to best explanation. In the case of laws the familiarity condition is not appealed to at all. In fact, the explanation of the regularities we observe in nature is God, an incorporeal being who is a paradigm of things above reason, that is of the inexplicable. So it appears that it is only in the domain of structural explanation that Boyle uses the familiarity condition. Nomic explanations are another species of explanation altogether.

It has recently been argued by Alan Chalmers (1993a, pp. 552–556) that Boyle's corpuscular hypothesis fails the very conditions that Boyle specifies for an excellent hypothesis. Boyle's failure to deal with impenetrability as a mechanical quality in this regard has already been noted. Chalmers points out a number of other deficiencies in Boyle's theory. These include Boyle's failure to specify the determinable mechanical laws that help explain natural phenomena, his failure to specify determinate corpuscular structures because he was restricted to specifying only intermediate causes on the scale of causes and the failure of the mechanical analogies that he appealed to as paradigms of mechanical explanations. I suggest that a large part of the responsibility for these failures can be attributed to the familiarity condition of explanation that Boyle adopts. Should he not have held this condition there would be no reason why the end point on the scale of causes should not include non-mechanical affections of atomic corpuscles, and no reason why he could not introduce the notion of force to explain impenetrability, gravitational attraction, cohesion, etc.

Finally, it is important to stress that there is one way that Boyle's approach to scientific explanation has been construed that is of little interpretative utility. It is the claim that Boyle sought to reduce the qualitative to the quantitative, that is, to explain qualities in terms of more fundamental properties that can be quantified. This interpretation of Boyle was popularised by R. Harré. He claims that 'Boyle's method is to try to prove the general principle that qualitative changes in perceptual objects are generated by quantitative, motion and arrangement changes, in the corpuscles of the physical world' (Harré 1964, p. 81).[68] At first sight this may seem correct. It is true that Boyle appealed to changes in motion and texture to explain natural phenomena. The problem however, lies in the presumed qualitative/quantitative dichotomy. First, it is somewhat anachronistic. Boyle's understanding of the quality/quantity distinction is normally (and often disapprovingly) set in Aristotelian terms. For instance, in *Forms and Qualities* he refers to Suárez' opinion that quantity can be separated from substance (*Works*, III, p. 7, *S*. p. 8, n. *a*). But, for Boyle, 'quantity' in the mechanical hypothesis refers to determinate size.[69] Second, when pressed the distinction does not map neatly onto the mechanical affection/non-mechanical quality distinction. To be sure, qualities were definitely the *explananda* of the mechanical hypothesis, but they were not distinct from quantities, except in so far as 'quantity' referred to size. In fact, many qualities such as the spring of the air could be and actually were quantified. Moreover shape, one of the mechanical affections, is not a quantifiable property of bodies.

5   An Aristotelian criterion for distinguishing the primaries

Finally, to return to Boyle's distinguishing criteria for the primary and secondary qualities, there is an Aristotelian criterion that Boyle uses to demarcate these qualities. It is included here not because of its importance – it is singularly unimportant in Boyle's theory of qualities – but for its intrinsic interest as an example of Boyle's Aristotelian heritage. In fact, I know of only one place where Boyle actually discusses this criterion, the *Christian Virtuoso, II*.

As mentioned in chapter 1, §2.3, Aristotle distinguished between the common and proper sensibles. Boyle, possibly following medieval and Renaissance faculty psychology,[70] believed that there is a neurophysiological basis for this distinction. A particular region of the brain is the location of the 'common sense'. This is where the nerves attached to the various organs of sense terminate and 'as it were lose themselves in the brain'. This rendezvous point performs the function that

> *both* discerns those objects of sense that are called common, because they are discoverable by several sensories, as magnitude, figure, motion, &c. *and* distinguishes the proper objects of one particular sense from that of another, as light from sound, and heat from taste.
>
> (*Christian Virtuoso, II, Works*, VI, p. 741)

A consequence of this is that it furnishes Boyle with an epistemological criterion for sorting out the mechanical affections from the (proper) sensibles. Put simply, the sensibles are discerned through only one sense whereas the primaries are discerned by more than one sense.[71] The restricted focus of the qualities under discussion should be noted here. Normally when Boyle is contrasting the mechanical affections of matter with other qualities, all the non-mechanical qualities are in view and not just the sensible ones.[72] However here we find, in a passage not particularly concerned with the qualities, that the mechanical and sensible qualities are clearly contrasted. The explanation for this seems to be that when epistemological issues are to the fore, like the nature of perception, the distinction among the qualities that most naturally presents itself to Boyle is that between the mechanical affections and the sensibles. The fact that Boyle's main concerns are ontological in nature perhaps accounts for why there are so few occasions in Boyle's works where these two sets of properties are brought together and explicitly contrasted to the exclusion of the other non-mechanical properties. This is all the more noteworthy when one considers that the contrast between the primary qualities and the sensibles is such a recurring theme in Descartes.[73]

Now what is important about this conspicuously unimportant criterion for distinguishing the qualities is the mere fact of its presence in Boyle. For this is a further indication of the way in which the doctrine of the qualities is in transition during the mid-seventeenth century. Boyle's distinction between common and proper senses is not a mere quirk of a 'primitive' grasp of neurology. Rather it is symptomatic of the fact that Aristotelian epistemology still had a grip in neuroscience in the mid-seventeenth century and that the new theory of qualities had not fully untangled itself from the complex set of interrelated philosophical theses that constituted the scholastic world-view. While on the ontological front, considerations of parsimony and intelligibility had led to a deposing of the primacy of Aristotle's first qualities, certain residual features of the Aristotelian theory of qualities remained, the distinction between common and proper sensibles and its relation to his account of the senses being a good example. In fact, the legacy of Aristotle's theory of the qualities, tied as it is to his epistemology of the senses, is felt through the rest of the century by such philosophers as Leibniz down (at least) to Berkeley. Thus it will not do, as some contemporary treatments of the primary and secondary quality distinction have done, to treat this distinguishing criterion (primaries are perceptible by more than one sense) in an historical vacuum divorced from the complex epistemology and theory of qualities that originally motivated it.[74]

6 Summary

Here then is a summary of Boyle's account of the distinction between the primary and secondary qualities of matter. Matter is created undifferentiated, motionless and homogeneous in all its (potential) parts. It has the attributes of extension, divisibility and impenetrability, and is indestructible. Boyle prefers to remain agnostic on the questions of infinite divisibility and the essentiality of impenetrability to matter. Once God sets original matter in motion each of its various parts acquires a determinate size and shape. Thus motion is chronologically prior to shape and size, but together these three are the essential attributes of matter at the level of atomic corpuscles and texture is essential to molecular corpuscles. They are essential because matter cannot be conceived without them. Thus fundamental to Boyle's distinction is an *a priori* essentiality criterion. Texture is included because the basic building blocks of all observable natural phenomena are not the atomic corpuscles but primary concretions of these particles.

When Boyle approaches the nature of the qualities of matter from the macroscopic level and tries to reduce its multifarious qualities to qualities possessed by matter at the microscopic level, he employs a number of inductive principles, each of them guided by the desire for parsimony. First, he posits (implicitly) that there are no primary qualities of insensible corpuscles that are not qualities of observable corpuscles. This inductive principle is motivated by the desire for parsimony and intelligibility. Second, he requires that if a particular quality is not universal at the macro-level, then it is not one of the primary qualities. This criterion cuts out the vast majority of qualities apart from the ones included by the essentiality criterion. Another principle, one that is motivated by his anti-Aristotelian polemics, is that all faculties of bodies are reducible to mechanical affections or relations between corpuscles. (Though as we shall see in chapter 4, he is not entirely consistent in his analysis of power-like qualities.) A final important principle in Boyle's reduction programme, by which he demarcates the primary and secondary qualities, is that the primary qualities of corpuscles at the fundamental level must be of the kind that feature in mechanical explanations such as those appealed to in explaining the workings of a clock.

There is a further, though comparatively unimportant, criterion by which Boyle distinguishes the primaries and secondaries. This is the Aristotelian legacy found in his distinction between common and proper sensibles, a distinction for which there is a neurophysiological basis. Together all the reductive principles enable Boyle to isolate just those mechanical affections of matter, shape, size, motion (or rest) and texture, that are the basis of all the other secondary or non-mechanical qualities of matter. Thus it can be seen that the primary and secondary quality distinction in Boyle's corpuscular hypothesis is not part of an argument for the corpuscular hypothesis, but rather it is an essential feature of that hypothesis itself. It is not that, for example, the secondary qualities are in some sense percipient-dependent and therefore do not qualify as being fundamental explanatory features of matter according to the corpuscular philosophy. Rather, the distinction between the primary and secondary, or better the mechanical and non-mechanical qualities, is constitutive of the corpuscular philosophy itself.

Notes

1   *Pace* R. Jackson 1968, p. 55 and J. Mackie 1976, p. 15 probably following Jackson and more recently R.-M. Sargent 1995, p. 105. See for instance *Cosmical Qualities*, *Works*, III, 'I consider that the qualities of particular bodies (for I speak not here of magnitude, shape, and motion, which are the primitive modes and catholick affections of matter itself). . . .', p. 306. See also, 'History of Particular Qualities', *Works*, III, p. 292, *S*. p. 97. For Boyle's discussion about the difficulty of giving a precise meaning to the term 'quality' see *ibid.* and *Forms and Qualities*, *Works*, III, pp. 21–22, *S*. pp. 28–30. The misconception that Boyle introduced the term 'primary quality' seems quite widespread from the 1960s on (see for example J. Mackie 1976, p. 15). I suggest that Jackson's influential article, first published in 1929, is to blame. Jackson is also wrong in claiming that for Boyle the sensible qualities are not really qualities (Jackson 1968, p. 55, p. 57 and p. 58).

2   See *Forms and Qualities*, *Works*, III, p. 24, *S*. p. 32 and *Certain Physiological Essays*, *Works*, I, p. 309. For the term 'secondary affections' see 'Essay on Nitre', *Works*, I, p. 364.

3 See for instance J. Passmore 1967, p. 359, F. J. O'Toole 1974, pp. 299–300, R. Harré 1964, p. 37. Of course Boyle does not have the labels 'determinable' and 'determinate' which we owe to W. E. Johnson (1921). Some scholars object to the inclusion of texture here. See §2.4 below.

4 See *Forms and Qualities*, *Works*, III, p. 26, *S*. pp. 36–37, 'Excellency of the Mechanical Hypothesis', *Works*, IV, p. 69, *S*. p. 140 and p. 153 and 'Possibility of the Resurrection', *ibid.*, p. 199, *S*. p. 203.

5 See also 'Essay on Nitre', *Works*, I, p. 364.

6 See *Forms and Qualities*, *Works*, III, p. 15, *S*. pp. 18–19. See also *Notion of Nature*, *Works*, V, p. 179, *S*. pp. 189–190, and *Works*, V, p. 189 where Boyle supposes 'the common matter of all bodies to have been at first divided into innumerable minute parts'. See also *Sceptical Chymist*, *Works*, I, p. 474, *Proposition I* and 'Requisite Digression', *Works*, II, p. 42 and p. 38, *S*. p. 164 and p. 159 where Boyle says, 'God . . . having resolved before the Creation to make such a world as this of ours, did divide (at least if he did not create it incoherent) that matter which he had provided into an innumerable multitude of very variously figured corpuscles . . .'. The view is to be found in Gassendi *Syntagma philosophicum*, Physics, 3, 1, *Brush*, p. 400 and in Charleton's *Physiologia*, p. 109, but denied by Descartes, see *The World*, *CSM*, I, p. 91 and *Principles*, II, §36, *ibid.*, p. 240. Charleton could well be Boyle's source for the idea as he was for the young Newton, see J. E. McGuire and M. Tamny 1983, p. 32 and p. 337.

7 From the early 1650s through to the 1670s there was a spate of works attempting to present a corpuscularian account of the generation of the universe in a way that was consistent with the *Genesis* narrative. See for example More's *Conjectura cabbalistica* (1653), de Beaufort's *Cosmopoeia Divina* (1656), Amerpoel's *Cartesius Mosaizans* (1669) and Cordemoy's *Copie d'une lettre écrite à sçavant Religieux* (1668).

8 Boyle wrongly attributed the Epicurean view of the essentiality of motion to matter to Gassendi (see *Examen*, *Works*, I, p. 194). For Gassendi's view of the origin of motion, which was the same as Boyle's, see *Syntagma philosophicum*, *Physics*, p. 335B, *Brush*, p. 417. For the claim that motion is not essential to matter in Boyle see for example, *Forms and Qualities*, *Works*, III, p. 15, *S*. p. 19, and *ibid.*, p. 35, *S*. p. 50. In both the 'Requisite Digression', *Works*, II, p. 42, *S*. p. 165 and the *Forms and Qualities*, *Works*, III, p. 48, *S*. p. 69 he claims that the idea can be traced as far back as Anaxagoras. For the idea in Anaxagoras Boyle quotes Aristotle's *Physics*, VIII, I, 250^{b}24–26, see *Barnes*, I, p. 418. See also fragment 13 in Kirk, Raven and Schofield 1983, p. 363. For the importance of Anaxagoras in Boyle's understanding of the history of atomism see M. Hunter and E. B. Davis 1996.

9 See especially *BP*, vol. 2, fols 5–7.

10 Boyle is undecided as to whether the undivided original matter was finite or infinite, see *High Veneration*, *Works*, V, p. 138. However he often speaks of the 'innumerable corpuscles' and 'numberless atoms' that make up the corporeal world. See *Forms and Qualities*, *Works*, III, p. 48, *S*. p. 69, *Notion of Nature*, *Works*, V, p. 179, *S*. p. 190, 'Requisite Digression', *Works*, II, p. 48, *S*. p. 173. Gassendi denied that there is an infinite number of atoms, see *Syntagma philosophicum*, *Physics*, 3, 1, 8, in *Brush*, p. 399.

11 See also 'Possibility of the Resurrection', *Works*, IV, p. 198, *S*. p. 202. For a sampling of references to universal matter see *Forms and Qualities*, *Works*, III, p. 15, p. 16, p. 35, *S*. p. 18, p. 20 and p. 50, *Notion of Nature*, *Works*, V, p. 179, *S*. p. 190, 'History of Particular Qualities', *Works*, III, p. 297, *S*. p. 105 and *Sceptical*

Chymist, *Works*, I, p. 474. For the homogeneity of matter in Descartes see *Principles*, II, §22, *CSM*, I, p. 232. For Gassendi see *Syntagma philosophicum*, *Physics*, 1, 3, *Brush*, p. 400. For Charleton this was a general property of matter which he styled its 'Consimilarity of Substance', *Physiologia*, p. 111. The subject of Boyle's monism has received scant treatment on the secondary literature on Boyle's corpuscular hypothesis, the exception being B. J. T. Dobbs' treatment of Boyle's matter theory in its relation to Newton, see Dobbs 1975, p. 46 and pp. 199–204 and 1985.

12 The Greek atomists were at least metaphysical dualists in that they posited both matter and the void. But were they extreme pluralists, accepting an infinite number of little 'Parmenidean worlds'? Perhaps the question is a little anachronistic. Yet it is clear that they formed their atomism, at least in part, as a defence of pluralism in response to the Zenonian defence of Parmenides' monism. It is surprising that in the surviving fragments of Leucippus and Democritus there are no explicit references to the homogeneity of matter. See *Generation and Corruption*, 325ª, *Barnes*, I, p. 530 and *Physics* 187ª, 1–3, *ibid.*, p. 319.

13 See for example, *Forms and Qualities*, *Works*, III, pp. 93–94. See Oldenburg's review of the *Forms and Qualities* for the claim of a contemporary that Boyle believed in transmutation, *Phil. Trans.*, 11, 2 April 1666, p. 193. For secondary literature see T. Kuhn 1952 and especially B. J. T. Dobbs 1975, chapter 6.

14 See also *Spring of the Air*, *Works*, I, p. 38 for a very similar expression. It appears that early on Boyle acquiesced in Descartes' definition of matter. See 'Requisite Digression', *Works*, II, p. 42, *S*. p. 165 probably written in 1659 when Boyle first paid serious attention to Descartes' philosophy.

15 See also *Notion of Nature*, *Works*, V, p. 190, where Boyle says in passing 'among bodies, there can be no penetration of dimensions'.

16 Boyle's definition is similar to that of Descartes. See Descartes' *Letter to More*, 15 April, 1649, *CSMK*, p. 372. For discussions of Descartes' view see Gabbey 1980, pp. 299–300, n27, 1985, pp. 29ff and D. Garber 1992, pp. 144–148.

17 See *More to Descartes*, 11 December 1648, *AT*, V, pp. 239–240. For Cudworth see *True Intellectual System*, I, p. 157.

18 For a more guarded comment see *Notion of Nature*, *Works*, V, p. 210.

19 See *De Gravitatione*, in A. R. Hall and M. B. Hall 1962, p. 91. Most scholars believe that this was written before 1672.

20 See *Final Causes*, *Works*, V, p. 416.

21 Thus, while the point of A. Gabbey and A. Chalmers still carries, viz. that there is a failure among the mechanists to bring together the notions of force and impenetrability, they both overstate the importance of impenetrability for Boyle. See A. Gabbey 1985, pp. 31–32 and A. Chalmers 1993a, p. 545. More serious is the misreading of R. Jackson who misconstrues the polemical context of the *Forms and Qualities* as being written against the Cartesians. He claims

[t]he objection against the Cartesians is that their refusal to recognise impenetrability as a quality, common to all bodies and distinguishing them from the space they occupy, makes it impossible to talk in any straightforward sense of bodies at all.

(1968, p. 56)

22 See also *Mechanical Qualities*, *Works*, IV, 236, 'Proëmial Essay', *Works*, I, p. 311, 'Fluidity and Firmness', *Works*, I, p. 377 and *Effluviums*, *Works*, III, p. 661. Boyle

had a dispute with Hobbes over the role of divisibility in the explication of fluidity and firmness, see *Examen*, *Works*, I, pp. 234–236.

23 See 'Fluidity and Firmness', *Works*, I, p. 430.

24 See *Things Above Reason*, *Works*, IV, p. 408, p. 411, p. 423 and p. 446, *S*. pp. 211–212, p. 217, p. 235 and p. 240. See also 'Theological Distinction', *Works*, V, p. 547 and *Excellency of Theology*, *Works*, IV, p. 43.

25 E. J. Dijksterhuis was perhaps the first to call Boyle a 'practical atomist' (1961, p. 436).

26 See also *ibid.*, p. 16, *S*. p. 20. The parallel with the scholastic natural minima theory is clearly what motivates Boyle's choice of terms here.

27 See also *BP*, vol. 2, fols 21–22.

28 The terms 'atomic corpuscle' and 'molecular corpuscle' are my own. As we have seen, Boyle sometimes speaks of the smallest parts of matter as *minima naturalia* or *prima naturalia* following a scholastic tradition. However, he also calls them corpuscles. This can lead to confusion for the reader, since for Boyle 'corpuscle' more commonly denotes molecular concretions of these atoms. Hence I have adopted the terms 'atomic corpuscle' and 'molecular corpuscle'. Boyle also uses the terms 'elementary corpuscle' and 'compound corpuscle', see *Sceptical Chymist*, *Works*, I, p. 515 and p. 579. For more on this see P. Alexander 1985, pp. 66–67. A. Clericuzio wrongly claims that Boyle never uses the term 'moleculæ', 1990a, p. 580. Boyle employs the term in the *Forms and Qualities*, *Works*, III, p. 105.

29 See also 'Excellency of the Mechanical Hypothesis', *Works*, IV, p. 73, *S*. p. 145.

30 See *Forms and Qualities*, *Works*, III, p. 15, *S*. p. 19. For Descartes' view see *Principles*, II, §36, *CSM*, I, p. 240.

31 See *Forms and Qualities*, *Works*, III, p. 15 and p. 47, *S*. p. 19 and p. 69. See also 'Requisite Digression', *Works*, II, p. 42, *S*. p. 165. At one point in the *Forms and Qualities* Boyle does call motion (or rest) an essential quality, but this is because he has just introduced motion as one of the 'grand and most catholic principles' of bodies, having argued that motion is essential for change.

32 See also p. 35, *S*. p. 50.

33 In his notes on Epicurean atheism in the *Boyle Papers* Boyle argues that his view of the origin of shape and size gives his account of the origins of matter a distinct advantage over that of the Epicureans. The Epicurean 'can only say, that 'tis its nature to have them: which is indeed to give no reason at all how it comes by them [shape and size]; since this Atome may be figured, without being Round, or Conical, or being endowed with whatever other peculiar figure belongs to it', *BP*, vol. 2, fol. 4. See also fol. 7 and 'Requisite Digression', *Works*, II, p. 42, *S*. p. 165.

34 For the Charletonian precedent here see *Physiologia*, book II, chapter IV which is entitled 'The Essential Properties of Atoms', pp. 111ff. It should be noted that Charleton, following Epicurus, included weight among the essential properties of atoms (*ibid.*, p. 112).

35 Compare Locke's *Essay* II, viii, §9. For Charleton's use of 'inseparable quality' see *Physiologia*, p. 129 and p. 130. The notion of inseparable attributes is found in the Epicureans. Lucretius speaks of it as a *coniunctum* that can never be separated, *De Rerum Natura*, I, vv451–2 and Sextus Empiricus reports that Demetrius of Laconia spoke of attributes that are inseparable (ἀχώριστα), *Adversus Mathematicos*, 10, A. A. Long and D. N. Sedley 1987, II, 7C, *l*.16, p. 28.

36 See *Forms and Qualities*, *Works*, III, p. 32, *S*. p. 46. Boyle tacitly acknowledges this

redundancy elsewhere when he says of extension that it is 'the property most essential to, because inseparable from a body', see *Spring of the Air*, *Works*, I, p. 38.

37 See also 'Excellency of the Mechanical Hypothesis', *Works*, IV, p. 70, *S*. p. 141.

38 It is also an important difference between Boyle's theory of matter and that version of the natural minima theory which maintained that the essential properties of atoms could change in combination. See E. J. Dijksterhuis 1961, p. 205.

39 See also 'Chemists' Doctrine of Qualities', *Works*, IV, p. 281, *S*. p. 133.

40 Boyle would almost certainly have been aware of the reaction of Epicurus and Lucretius to the view, attributed to Democritus, that there may be extremely large atoms. See Epicurus' *Letter to Herodotus*, §42 and §56 and Lucretius *De Rerum Natura*, II, vv478–521.

41 See also *Forms and Qualities*, *Works*, III, p. 31 and pp. 35–36, *S*. p. 44 and p. 51 and 'History of Particular Qualities', *Works*, III, p. 298, *S*. p. 106.

42 While Boyle never discusses the issue, it is most likely that posture is not a primary property because being a relative property it fails the essentiality criterion; one singly existing atomic corpuscle could not have posture. Even if Boyle accepts absolute space (see chapter 6), it seems a little strange to speak of a single corpuscle's posture.

43 *Pace* M. A. Stewart, who says that 'in principle even a corpuscle has a texture and even Boyle sometimes speaks in these terms (in his account of *Generation and Corruption* he ascribes texture to corpuscles at all levels) . . .', 1987, p. 112. I believe that Stewart is right in emphasising that Boyle's atomic corpuscles are theoretically divisible, but wrong to see this as entailing that they have texture. See P. Alexander 1985, pp. 78–79 and *Forms and Qualities*, *Works*, III, p. 34 and p. 36, *S*. p. 49 and p. 51 and Boyle's 'Excellency of the Mechanical Hypothesis' where he speaks of 'the texture resulting from their [single particles'] convention into a body', *Works*, IV, p. 70, *S*. p. 142. I cannot find the reference to textured atomic corpuscles in the section on generation and corruption in the *Forms and Qualities* to which Stewart refers.

44 See *Sceptical Chymist*, *Works*, I, pp. 475–476, *Forms and Qualities*, *Works*, III, p. 30, *S*. p. 42 and *Works*, III, p. 99, 'Excellency of the Mechanical Hypothesis', *Works*, IV, pp. 75–76, *S*. p. 150 and 'History of Particular Qualities', *Works*, III, p. 298, *S*. p. 106. See T. Kuhn 1952 for further references. A. Clericuzio claims that Boyle's attempt 'to found a classification of chemical substances on the basis of the notion of compound corpuscles has generally been ignored or underestimated by most scholars, who in fact have followed Kuhn's statement that Boyle's mechanical chemistry "is incompatible with belief in the existence of enduring elements"', 1990a, p. 581. But Kuhn himself was one of the first to point out the role of primary concretions in Boyle. He says that they 'play the role of the elementary atoms or molecules of various naturally occurring bodies (gold, silver, mercury, sulphur etc.)', 1952, p. 25. Moreover, there are in addition to Kuhn a number of important treatments of Boyle's primary concretions. See for instance M. B. Hall 1952, p. 466 and p. 468. Kuhn's claim about the compatibility of Boyle's chemical theory with belief in the existence of enduring elements comes immediately after his discussion of primary concretions which explicitly acknowledges the very stable compounds Boyle equated with certain chemical principles and Kuhn's claim remains true.

45 For Epicurus see *Letter to Herodotus*, §38, 10, §74, 10 and §89, 6. For Lucretius see

De Rerum Natura, I, vv58–61, vv159–214, vv501–2, vv894–6 and II, vv707–9. For the notion of seeds in Anaxagoras see G. Vlastos 1950.

46 See E. McMullin 1978b, p. 139.

47 See P. Alexander, 1985, p. 78: 'Textures are intrinsic to complex bodies but they are not primary qualities because they are not intrinsic to the simplest bodies, individual corpuscles.' See A. D. Smith 1990, p. 234 for the same claim applied to Locke. As will become clear below (chapter 4, §3), Alexander believes that for Boyle all the secondary qualities are textures. He argues for an identity thesis about the secondary qualities. He would resist the claim that texture is a primary for if, as he claims, secondaries are textures, and textures are primaries, then by transitivity, secondaries are primaries, which seems absurd. However, it will be argued below (chapter 4) that Alexander's identity thesis is wrong, and therefore it does not furnish us with a reason for *not* including textures among the primaries. For another (I believe unsuccessful) critique of Alexander's view see L. Keating 1993, pp. 315ff.

48 See also 'Requisite Digression', *Works*, II, p. 37, *S.* p. 157.

49 For example, in the *Forms and Qualities*, *Works*, III, p. 25, *S.* p. 34 Boyle speaks of bodies being endowed 'with those more catholic affections of bodies – figure, motion, texture, &c', and of 'motion, figure, and contrivance, of their own parts (which attributes I call the mechanical affections of matter)', *ibid.*, p. 13, *S.* p. 17. On the very same page Boyle again speaks of 'changing the *texture*, or *motion* or some other *mechanical affection* . . .'.

50 See *Essay*, II, viii, §9, §10, §14, §18 and §23. See also Oldenburg's review of the *Forms and Qualities* in *Phil. Trans.*, 11, 2 April 1666, pp. 192–193. For the Cartesian precedent see *The World*, chapter 5, *CSM*, I, p. 89.

51 See for example *Certain Physiological Essays*, *Works*, I, p. 308, *Forms and Qualities*, *Works*, III, p. 25, *S.* p. 34 and *Cosmical Qualities*, *Works*, III, p. 306.

52 Reduction programmes are characteristic of all of the mechanists of the seventeenth century. And Boyle's reduction programme is in the spirit of those of Descartes and Charleton before him. A nice statement of Descartes' reductionism is found in *The World*, chapter 5, 'not only these four qualities (heat, cold, moisture and dryness) but all the others as well, including even the forms of inanimate bodies, can be explained without the need to suppose anything in their matter other than the motion, size, shape and arrangement of its parts', *CSM*, I, p. 89.

53 See also 'Excellency of the Mechanical Hypothesis', *Works*, IV, pp. 70–71, *S.* pp. 141–143.

54 See P. Alexander who claims that for Boyle 'it makes sense to postulate unobservables with specific properties as long as we are careful to attribute to them the only kinds of properties with which we are familiar from everyday observation' (1985, p. 63). See also the French version of Descartes' *Principles*, IV, §201, where he says,

> it is better philosophy to judge what happens among these little bodies, which only their minuteness prevents us from perceiving, by the example of that which we see happen among bodies which we do perceive, and to account by these means for all that is in nature . . . than to explain the same things by inventing I don't know what others which bear no relation to what we perceive . . .
>
> (*AT*, IX, p. 319)

For Newton's more explicit statement of a similar inductive principle see his 'Third Rule of Reasoning' in *Principia* (1730), 1966, p. 398. This rule was first published in 1713. For discussions of philosophical problems with these inferences in Boyle and Newton see M. Mandelbaum 1964, chapter 2 and J. E. McGuire 1970.

55 See also *Forms and Qualities*, *Works*, III, p. 16, *S*. p. 20.

56 One must be careful not to read too much into Boyle here. It may be that the corpuscular hypothesis entailed this reductive principle, but that Boyle was unaware of it. However, this does not preclude its usefulness in explicating his theory.

57 See for instance *Forms and Qualities*, *Works*, III, pp. 12–13, *S*. pp. 15–16 and *Sceptical Chymist* (1661), *Works*, I, p. 557, 'what is it to me to know, that such a quality resides in such a principle of element, whilst I remain altogether ignorant of the cause of that quality, and the manner of its production and operation?' which predates Molière's *Le Malade imaginaire*, 1673. For an interesting discussion of the 'dormitive virtue' problem see K. Hutchison 1991.

58 For reasons why Boyle should have considered impenetrability to be a mechanical quality see chapter 7, §2.

59 This is the theme of the 'Excellency of the Mechanical Hypothesis', *Works*, IV, pp. 67ff.

60 See M. Friedman 1974 and E. McMullin 1978b. For a very useful taxonomy of reduction programmes see S. Sarkar 1992.

61 See also R. Harré 1985, pp. 140ff.

62 See 'Excellency of the Mechanical Hypothesis', *Works*, IV, p. 75, *S*. p. 149. See also the discussion of tastes in *Mechanical Qualities*, *Works*, IV, pp. 259ff, especially pp. 260–261.

63 M. Friedman discusses this view of explanation (1974, pp. 9–11).

64 See also the discussion of explanation in *Certain Physiological Essays*, *Works*, I, p. 308.

65 See also *Spring of the Air*, *Works*, I, p. 145: 'to explain a thing is to deduce it from something or other in nature more known than itself' and *BP*, vol. 6, fol. 70.

66 See also *Christian Virtuoso*, I, *Appendix*, *Works*, VI, p. 693.

67 See *Meno* 80^{d}ff in Plato 1989, pp. 363ff.

68 See Harré 1964, pp. 79–85 for his discussion of Boyle. K. K. Campbell 1976, pp. 55–56 seems to follow Harré.

69 See the very early use of 'quantity' to refer to size in Boyle's notes 'Of the Atomicall Philosophy', *BP*, vol. 26, fol. 163, published in R. S. Westfall, 1956, p. 112.

70 For Descartes on the common sense see *Rules*, *CSM*, I, p. 41, *Treatise on Man*, *CSM*, I, pp. 105–106, *Opticks*, *CSM*, I, p. 164 and *Letter to Mersenne* of 24 December 1640 and 21 April 1641, *CSMK*, p. 162 and p. 180.

71 For a relatively recent expression of hope that one can distinguish between primary and secondary qualities by correlating them with sense organs see J. Bennett 1971, p. 102:

[i]f one could explain the differences between primary and secondary qualities by adducing facts about their respective sensory bases or correlates, I suspect that the crux of the explanation would turn out to be the fact that the sense of touch – or rather touch-and-movement – is involved in all the primary qualities in a way in which it isn't with any of the secondary. But that is only a suspicion. Someone should write a book on the epistemology of the sense of touch.

72 See for example *Certain Physiological Essays, Works*, I, p. 308.

73 In fact in the *Forms and Qualities, Works*, III, p. 11, *S*. p. 14, Boyle explicitly criticises Descartes for not treating the other non-mechanical properties and for not giving a well-rounded account of the sensible qualities themselves. He says,

> The most ingenious Descartes has something concerning some qualities: . . . yet I find by turning over the leaves that he has left most of the other qualities untreated of; and of those that are more properly called sensible, he speaks but very briefly and generally, rather considering what they do upon the organs of sense, than what changes happen in the objects themselves to make them cause in us a perception sometimes of one quality and sometimes of another.

74 A. D. Smith is particularly insensitive to this. For instance, he claims that '[p]erceptible primary qualities must be Aristotelian common sensibles' and that 'the seventeenth century did not fully appreciate the significance of the distinction between proper and common sensibles, nor fully integrate it into the doctrine of primary and secondary qualities', and he goes on to claim that this distinction 'is indeed a priori related to the primary-secondary quality distinction' (1990, p. 242 and n. 30). But on the historiography offered here the proper/common sensible distinction lost its explanatory efficacy for the new philosophers just because the primary qualities for Aristotle were *not* the common sensibles but the proper sensibles. See also J. J. MacIntosh 1976, especially p. 93.

3 The perception of the sensible qualities

As we have seen, there is a small number of qualities that Boyle calls the sensible qualities. They include colour, taste, sound and odour. From his casual remarks about them it seems fair initially to characterise them as being those qualities that are to be explained in terms of their relation to the sense organs.[1] According to Boyle, the sensible qualities are a mere subset of what we have called the non-mechanical or secondary affections. The mechanical qualities are shape, size, motion and texture. All the others are non-mechanical. We also saw that he admits that there are numerous ways of classifying the various non-mechanical qualities; for instance one way to divide them up is to distinguish between the occult and the manifest non-mechanical qualities. But regardless of how one classifies them there is always one natural group that calls for special attention. These qualities, following Locke, have come to be known as the 'secondary qualities' and one must be cautious when adopting the Lockean terminology (for Boyle) to avoid anachronism and confusion with the other non-mechanical qualities.

The aim of both this chapter and the next is to get clear on just what, according to Boyle, is the ontological status of these qualities. Are they monadic or relational properties? Are they dispositional properties or categorical? What relation do they have to the mechanical properties of matter? Now, one might think that an understanding of the ontological status of the sensibles can be gleaned from the secondary literature on Boyle. After all, the nature of the sensible qualities has been the main focus of philosophical interest in Boyle scholarship. But alas, the terrain here is not entirely satisfactory. There is little or no agreement as to what Boyle's views actually were. The interpretations of Boyle's views on the sensibles can be grouped into three camps. There are those following Reginald Jackson (John Mackie, Edwin Curley and others), who claim that the sensible qualities, for Boyle, are powers or dispositions in objects which are a category of being over and above the primary qualities and in virtue of which objects affect our senses.[2] Thus Boyle is seen as an immediate precursor of Locke and his theory of sensible qualities is simply one more way in which Boyle's corpuscularianism influenced Locke. Then there is the texture view of Peter Alexander. He claims that for Boyle all 'non-primary qualities' of bodies are textures and that both the textures and 'primary qualities' are powers in some very deflationary sense.[3] But Alexander also draws a distinction between Boyle's 'secondary qualities' and his sensible qualities. While the former are textures the latter, according to Alexander, are ideas that are caused in the mind by textures. This brings us to a third view which is that of Maurice Mandelbaum and (more recently) Laura Keating who argue that, for Boyle, the sensible qualities are *merely* ideas in the mind.[4] It is my hope that there is an interpretation of Boyle on the sensibles that not only does justice to the relevant texts, but also enables us to account for such a diversity of opinion in the secondary literature.

A comprehensive approach to these questions requires that we go beyond merely metaphysical considerations in Boyle's natural philosophy. In particular we must turn to Boyle's views on perception. For it is not immediately clear whether they impose constraints on his theory of the sensible qualities or whether, in the conceptual development of his views, he set in place the ontology of the sensibles before venturing to explain the epistemology of these qualities. Perhaps the two developed in tandem? Whatever the case, in order to get a comprehensive understanding of Boyle's theory of the sensible qualities, one must cast one's net rather wide instead of basing one's interpretation on a few 'select texts'. Thus we turn first to Boyle's views on perception.

Boyle's published works, to my knowledge, contain only two sustained discussions of the nature of perception. These occur in the *Excellency of Theology* published in 1674, but written in 1665 and in his 'Nature of Cold' published in 1673.[5] However, there are enough scattered references to perception and the nature of the senses in works such as *The Christian Virtuoso*, *Things Above Reason*, *Forms and Qualities* and certain fragments among the *Boyle Papers* such that, when taken together, these passages furnish us with a fairly coherent account of perception and one that is substantial enough to have a bearing on his account of the nature of the sensible qualities. The paucity of material reflects Boyle's philosophical preoccupations, and it warns us not to have too high expectations of the quality of Boyle's discussions on this issue.

I will present Boyle's views on perception in four steps. First, his psycho-physiology will be discussed drawing on the posthumous *Christian Virtuoso, II*. Second, I will discuss the Cartesian account of perception as outlined in his *Excellency of Theology*, the account that Boyle thought was the most intelligible one on offer. Third, I will discuss the representational nature of Boyle's account of sensation. This will lead us into the fourth section where I list Boyle's comments in *Forms and Qualities* on the perception of the sensible qualities. It is the last two sections that have immediate ramifications for our quest to understand Boyle's position on the ontological status of the sensible qualities and will set up the discussion for the ensuing chapter.

1 Boyle's psychophysiology

In his *Christian Virtuoso, II* Boyle gives us a detailed discussion of the brain. Not surprisingly he begins by claiming that in the brain there is 'far more *mechanism* than is obvious to a vulgar eye, or even to that of a dissector' (*Works*,

VI, p. 741, italics added). He goes on to list a number of the parts of the brain and their function in receiving 'information' from the senses.[6] First there is the 'common sense'. This is where the nerves attached to the various organs of sense terminate and 'as it were lose themselves in the brain'. This rendezvous point performs the function that, '*both* discerns those objects of sense that are called common . . . as magnitude, figure, motion, &c. *and* distinguishes the proper objects of one particular sense from that of another, as light from sound, and heat from taste' (*Works*, VI, p. 741).[7] This dual function of the common sense renders it more akin to Aristotle's conception than that of Descartes. Descartes' common sense seems to have a synthesising role in sense perception, unifying the different kinds of sense perception so as to give a composite idea of the object perceived,[8] whereas Aristotle's common sense shares with Boyle's the functions of discerning proper objects and distinguishing them from each other. Interestingly however, at the end of his discussion Boyle mentions another faculty located in the pineal gland that seems to perform a similar function to Descartes' common sense. He says

> In the sixth place, it is in the brain, that the organs of the particular external senses of seeing, hearing, &c. have their general rendezvous, and if Mr *Des Cartes* and those physicians and anatomists that follow him be not mistaken (for I speak but conditionally) the reports, that all the differing sensories bring to the mind, are made in a part of the brain, viz. the conarium, or glandula pinealis . . .
>
> (*Works*, VI, p. 742)

It is this 'making of reports' from the sensories that parallels Descartes' 'fashioning (*formandas*) . . . figures or ideas which come . . . from the external senses' (*CSM*, I, pp. 40–42, *AT*, X, p. 414). The attribution of this notion to Descartes is curious in the light of the fact that Boyle does not identify it with the common sense.

The second faculty is the 'imagination', 'because it exhibits the images as it were of sensible things, which are variously contracted, enlarged, divided, compounded, or otherwise notably altered by this faculty . . .' (*Works*, VI, p. 741). All the various images that are concocted in the imagination are corporeal ideas. It is not surprising then that Boyle speaks of the 'corporeal soul' when referring to the brain and its different faculties. The third part of the brain that Boyle mentions is that in which resides the mind or rational soul, perhaps the pineal gland. Then there is a fourth faculty of the brain that is the 'workhouse wherein and whereby the animal spirits, that serve for sense and motion are . . . elaborated or produced'.[9] And finally, the brain has a special part reserved for the memory. This, like the imagination, is a corporeal faculty.[10] And memory and imagination can perform functions that are independent of the pure 'intellectual operations' of the rational soul.[11]

So far this is very similar to Descartes' psychophysiology.[12] For Descartes posited three faculties of the brain, viz. common sense, imagination and memory, each of which contain corporeal ideas. Likewise, it was from him that Boyle took a thorough-going mind/body dualism. Another crucial idea that is borrowed from Descartes is the role of the rational soul in the perception of qualities. Just as Descartes says, '[w]e know for certain that it is the soul which has sensory perceptions, and not the body' (*CSM*, I, p. 164), so Boyle claims, early in the *Forms and Qualities*, that the '*operations* of objects on the sensories', are 'perceived' by the mind 'upon the account of its union with the body'. The soul is the 'perceptive faculty' that 'observes' the goings on in the brain (*Forms and Qualities*, *Works*, III, p. 23, italics added, and p. 25, *S*. p. 31 and p. 34).[13] Yet, unlike Descartes, Boyle does not speculate on the relations between the various faculties of the brain[14] and in contrast to Descartes' distributed model of memory, Boyle has a storehouse model. According to Boyle, it is a marvel that 'there should be so many thousand distinct cells, or impressions' that are 'lodged so exactly in the order, . . . that upon a sudden command of the will, or a slight casual hint' the memories present themselves ('Advices', *Works*, IV, p. 454).[15] However, in spite of these minor differences, both Descartes and Boyle (though he is spare on details) give an exclusively mechanical account of how the qualities of bodies affect the brain.

2 Boyle on perception

Given this psychophysiology, what is Boyle's account of perception? When we turn to the *Excellency of Theology* we find that 'we know very little of the manner, by which our senses inform us'. However, 'the ingenious *Des Cartes* and his followers have given the fairest account of sensation, that is yet extant' (*Works*, IV, p. 43).[16] Here is Boyle's summary of the Cartesian view. He says, 'that which is truly called sensation, is not performed by the organ, but by the mind, which perceives the motion produced in the organ . . .'. External bodies

> by their impressions on the sensories . . . variously move the fibres or threads of the nerves, wherewith those parts are endowed, and by which the motion is propagated to that little kernel in the brain, called by many writers the Conarion, where these differing motions being perceived by the there residing soul, become sensations, because of the intimate union, and, as it were, permistion . . . of the soul with the body.
>
> (*Works*, IV, p. 44)[17]

A similar view is expressed in 'Nature of Cold':

> sensation is properly and ultimately made in, or by the mind, or discerning faculty; which, from the differing motions of the internal parts of the brain, is excited and determined to differing perceptions; to some of which men have given the names heat, cold or other qualities.
>
> (*Works*, III, p. 738)[18]

There is some lack of clarity in the two main discussions of the nature of sensation as to what exactly is the immediate object of perception. The emphasis in the extended treatment in *Excellency of Theology* is on the mind perceiving the motions in the brain,[19] whereas in the 'Nature of Cold' it appears that the immediate objects of perception are the impressions that these motions make on the mind. Boyle says that motion in the brain 'produces in the mind those perceptions which we call sensations of outward objects' (*Works*, III, p. 737). This latter view seems more consistent with Boyle's dualism, with Descartes' discussions of sensation and also with Boyle's discussions of the way different motions produce different types of sense impression in the mind. But it would be wrong to say that there is any inconsistency here in Boyle. The problem, if there is one, really arises from the fact that he employed a very fluid terminology to describe sensory perception.

It is important to emphasise that for Boyle the different motions in the brain go some way in accounting for the differences between the sensations; 'the diversity of sensations may be referred to the differing modifications of those internal motions of the brain' ('Nature of Cold', *Works*, III, pp. 737–738). But they do not give us satisfactory reasons for the discrimination of particular sensations, nor the ability of the mind to discriminate between the multifarious types and intensities of sensations. In virtue of what does one motion cause a colour sensation in the mind and another a sensation of sound? Part of the problem lies in the inscrutability of the incorporeal mind. This is indicative of the crucial role that the rational soul plays in each of Boyle's discussions of perception. Thus J. J. MacIntosh is wrong to claim that Boyle in his account of perception is 'strangely uninterested in dualism' (1983, p. 328 and p. 343). MacIntosh seems to have come to this view because he treats memory and imagination as components of Boyle's (and Descartes') theory of perception, whereas it seems more accurate to say that they constitute the elements of the theory of cognition. What Boyle calls an account of sensation is equivalent to what in modern parlance we call an account of perception and while imagination and memory are faculties of the corporeal soul for Boyle, sensation is inextricably linked to the incorporeal soul.

How do we account then for MacIntosh's further claim (1983, p. 343) that for Boyle the perceptual function of sensation is seated in the brain? It appears that virtually every reference to perception in Boyle's writings up to the end of the 1660s considers it only in relation to the rational soul. Thus, in the *Forms and Qualities*, the soul is the 'perceptive faculty' and in the important early passage from the *Excellency of Theology* written in 1665, Boyle raises a serious problem for his version of the Cartesian account of sensation.

But that, which I would on this occasion invite you to consider, is, that supposing the soul does in the brain perceive the differing motions communicated to the outward senses; yet this, however it may give some account of sensation in general, will not at all shew us a satisfactory reason of particular and distinct sensations. For if I demand, why, for instance, when I look upon a bell, that is ringing, such a motion or impression in the Conarion produces in the mind that peculiar sort of perception, seeing, and not hearing; and another motion, though coming from the same bell, at the same time, produces that quite differing sort of perception, that we call sound, but not vision; what can be answered, but that it was the good pleasure of the author of human nature to have it so?

(*Works*, IV, p. 44)[20]

What must be stressed here is that Boyle sees the problem as being one of accounting for the *soul*'s discriminating between the different types of sensations. There is no mention of the common sense, nor is there any detail about the neurophysiology involved in the reception of sense impressions. Yet, as we have seen, one of the functions of the common sense in the posthumous *Christian Virtuoso, II* is that it 'distinguishes the proper objects of one particular sense from that of another'. I suggest that this reveals that by the mid-1660s Boyle had not adopted the Cartesian emphasis on the role of corporeal faculties in sense perception.[21] Therefore, what was a problem seen solely in terms of mind/body interaction in 1665 was, by the 1680s, partly resolved by the attribution of the function of sensory discrimination to the common sense rather than the soul. Ironically, this was understood by Boyle in Aristotelian rather than Cartesian terms. So, if this thesis is correct, it follows that MacIntosh's claim is accurate for the mature Boyle, but jars with the Boyle of the *Excellency of Theology* and the *Forms and Qualities*. There are actually two sensory faculties in the mature Boyle. The first is the discerning or discriminating role of the common sense in sorting out the various deliverances of the sense organs. The second is the perception by the rational soul of the impressions made on the mind by particular motions in the brain. But the common sense and the sense organs remain subservient to the soul. Thus in his *Christian Virtuoso, I* (1690–1) he says,

[t]he outward senses are but the instruments of the soul, which hears by the intervention of the ear, and in respect of which the eye itself is but a more immediate optical tube; and the sense does but perceive objects, not judge of them. Nor do the more wary among the philosophers, trust their eye to teach them the nature of the visible object; but only employ it to perceive the phenomena it exhibits, and the changes that happen to itself by the action of it.

(*Works*, V, p. 539)

We are now in a position to discuss the meanings of the rather fluid vocabulary that Boyle employs in his discussions of perception. The nouns he uses are 'sensations', 'ideas', 'perceptions' and 'impressions'. First, on Boyle's view the sensations of sensible qualities are in the soul and not in the brain. He is quite unambiguous on this point. In 'Nature of Cold' he says 'sensation is properly and ultimately made in, or by the mind, or discerning faculty'

(*Works*, III, p. 738). Sensations are in the incorporeal mind. They are modifications of the mind that is 'excited' by the differing motions in the brain. Second, sensations are equivalent to ideas and to perceptions. For instance, in the *Forms and Qualities* Boyle speaks of the *ideas* that the external objects excite in the mind and of the 'perception of pain' (*Forms and Qualities*, *Works*, III, p. 36 and p. 24, *S.* p. 51 and p. 33).[22] Likewise, in the 'Nature of Cold' he speaks of 'those perceptions which we call sensations' which are produced in the mind (*Works*, III, p. 737).[23] However, he sometimes speaks of perceptions, not as sensations in the mind, but as acts of perceiving; that is, the having of sensations. For instance, in the *Excellency of Theology* he speaks of perception as seeing and hearing (*Works*, IV, p. 44). However, once we are aware of this ambiguity it can be seen to be relatively harmless. Third, in the same passage Boyle uses the verb 'to perceive' to refer to the mind's perception of motions in the brain, as if these are the immediate objects of perception, when it is more likely that these are the cause of the immediate objects of perception in the mind. Elsewhere he develops the analogy between perception as a function of the sense organs and perception as a function of the intellect. This latter type of perception is entirely independent of sensory perception.[24] Finally, Boyle uses the term 'impression' in three ways. It can refer first, to the alterations that external objects make on the sense organs; second, to the motions of the brain that result from its interaction with the organs of sense; and third, to the alterations that the animal spirits make on the rational soul.[25]

We can now construe Boyle's account of perception in terms of a causal chain containing five or six elements. First there is the external object, then there is the medium between that object and the percipient, light in the case of sight and air in the case of hearing (though this may be lacking as in the case of heat). Next there is the organ of sense, say the eye, followed by the neural pathway connecting the sense organ to the brain, say the optic nerve. Then there is the brain tissue itself, perhaps the pineal gland, and finally the mind or rational soul that is the 'perceptive faculty'. The two questions that remain to be answered now are these. What is the relation between the sensations or perceptions in the mind and the sensible qualities? And where on this causal chain are the sensible qualities located?

3 Boyle on representation

Given that Boyle believes that the sensations of qualities are in the incorporeal mind, what is the relation between these sensations and the qualities themselves? Ostensibly it is the relation of effect to cause. We can say, provisionally at least, that sensations are caused by the qualities of the external object. Yet it is natural to ask if Boyle thought that there was any representational character to these sensations. Surely there must be something, over and above the causal relation, in virtue of which the ideas of qualities represent (or misrepresent) the actual qualities of objects. However, Boyle's discussions of perception are rarely concerned with issues relating to the representational character of ideas. What little he does say on the matter is at times inconsistent and appears to be determined by broader contextual issues than to be parts of a well-worked-out theory. In particular Boyle does not commit himself to the elements of the peculiarly scholastic account of the representational character of thought discussed by Descartes in the *Third Meditation*. This is the notion that the intentional object of thought somehow derives its ontological status from its formal cause.[26] However, what can be gleaned from Boyle's occasional references to the representational character of thought is that, like Descartes before him and Locke after,[27] Boyle was committed to the veil of perception. A rather unsubtle expression of this view is found in his use of the pin illustration. Boyle sometimes focuses on the causal process linking the object with the sense organ and the phenomenal nature of the final effect. Sensations are conceived as the end of a causal chain, the final effect of some exterior cause. The classic illustration used to elucidate this approach to perception is that of the pin and the pain it causes. Similar illustrations were used by both Descartes and Locke.[28] Boyle's point is,

> when a pin being run into my finger causeth pain, there is no distinct quality in the pin answerable to what I am apt to fancy pain to be; but the pin in itself is only slender, stiff, and sharp, and by those qualities happens to make a solution of continuity in my organ of touching, upon which, by reason of the fabric of the body and the intimate union of the soul with it, there ariseth that troublesome kind of perception we call *pain* . . .
>
> *(Forms and Qualities, Works,* III, p. 23, *S.* p. 31)

A more interesting passage that reveals that there is a least a latent representationalism in Boyle is also found in the *Forms and Qualities*. When speaking of the actions of bodies on the sensories Boyle says,

> the perceptions of these impressions are by men called by several names, as *heat, colour, sound, odour*, and are commonly imagined to proceed from certain distinct and peculiar qualities in the external object which have <u>some resemblance to the ideas</u> their action upon the senses excites in the mind . . .
>
> *(Forms and Qualities, Works,* III, p. 36, *S.* p. 51,
> underlining added)[29]

Boyle is here characterising a view with which he disagrees, the view that our ideas of the sensible qualities of bodies resemble 'real' qualities in the bodies themselves. It is set within a representative theory of perception. Boyle says that some claim that the ideas of sensible qualities *resemble* real qualities in the objects, but it is clear that the soul perceives, not the external object, but the impressions made on the mind.[30] When we add to this the following from the 'Nature of Cold', the organs of sense, . . . do only receive impressions from outward objects, but not perceive what is the cause and manner of these impressions, the perception, properly so called, of causes belonging to a superior faculty, whose property it is to judge, whence the alterations made in the sensories do proceed . . .

('Nature of Cold', *Works*, III, p. 740, italics added)

the picture is complete. The soul perceives the impressions and, on the basis of their qualities, judges what is their cause.[31] There is no direct perception of external objects by the mind. This is confirmed by the representational terms in which Boyle describes how the mind corrects the deliverances of the senses, as 'when the eye *represents* a straight stick, that has part of it under water, as if it were crooked' ('Nature of Cold', *Works*, III, p. 740, italics added).

This brings us to the perception of the mechanical qualities. What of the sensations of the qualities of shape, motion, size and texture? Surely they in some way represent the qualities in objects.[32] And yet Boyle has given us no principled way to discriminate between the perception of sensible qualities and the mechanical affections. For instance, his discussion is not set within a Cartesian theory of clear and distinct ideas. What is it about the phenomenology of shape, size and motion that allows us to conclude that our sensations of them correspond to actual qualities in the objects? Ostensibly, the problem with Boyle's pin illustration is that he is conflating a bodily sensation, pain, with sensory impressions of qualities such as colour. No one attributes pain to pins, but as Boyle elsewhere acknowledges, we quite naturally attribute colours, smells and sounds to objects. So on the final analysis the pin illustration is an unhelpful disanalogy when it comes to explaining the representational character of sensations of the sensible qualities.[33] It seems then that Boyle is left with the problem of accounting for a difference between the perception of the sensible and the mechanical qualities in the manifest world.

The problem becomes more acute when we consider Boyle's comments on sensations produced in the absence of external objects. In volume 10, folio 29 of the *Boyle Papers* he tells us that

Whereas these Philosophers are wont to teach us that those Qualitys we call sensible are certain reall Entitys residing in the objects & producing by their proper & peculiar Actions upon the outward Organs, it will appear by severall Examples that I am about to alledge, that the same sensations as are thought necessarily to depend upon such determinate Qualitys in sensible objects may be produc'd not only without the agency of those Qualitys, but even in the absence of the Objects by a bare locall motion of some internall parts of the sentient Body itselfe.[34]

Boyle goes on to relate Descartes' story of the phantom pains of the amputee described in the *Principles*. The point is importantly different from that of the pin illustration. For there it was the pin causing the pain, whereas here there is no external agent causing the relevant motions in the brain that produce sensations of sensible qualities. The obvious question then is: why cannot we also have sensations of mechanical qualities in the absence of an external agent? Boyle's reasoning here does not entail a denial of the objective existence of sensible qualities, but only commits him to a sceptical thesis about the possibility of epistemic access to any qualities whatsoever.

However, more than one commentator disagrees that this is a problem for Boyle. Maurice Mandelbaum's interpretation of Boyle maintains that there is no distinction between the sensible qualities and primary affections of matter in this regard. He claims,

> It must not, however, be believed that Boyle assumed that only the secondary qualities were subjective: so far as perceived size, shape, solidity, and the like were concerned, these too were sensible qualities and were not to be attributed to the objects which caused our ideas of them.
>
> (Mandelbaum 1964, p. 101)

So rather than Boyle's pin illustration being a conflation of bodily sensation with sense impressions, on Mandelbaum's view, Boyle considers them to be strictly identical. But this supposed equivalence in the nature of the epistemic access to all the qualities of bodies is to be rejected. Basic to the categorisation of the sensible qualities is that they are 'explicated by a *relation to our senses*', as Boyle tells us in the *Forms and Qualities* (*Works*, III, p. 23, *S*. p. 32). This is what sets them apart from the other non-mechanical qualities, which themselves are different from the primary affections. The sensibles are a specific subgroup of qualities that pose a unique problem for the corpuscular hypothesis. In fact, in that work Boyle claims that it is the 'chiefest' difficulty that can be brought against the hypothesis. Thus the starting point, for Boyle, in an understanding of the sensible qualities is that they *appear* to be objective features of the world; 'at first sight', so to speak, they seem to 'have an *absolute* being irrelative to *us*'. However, we will have to wait for Boyle's final word on this issue.

Keith Hutchison holds a position that is closely related to Mandelbaum's. He argues that first, since the paradigmatic manifest qualities like colour are explained by the mechanical philosophers in terms of underlying and insensible structures, they are effectively the same as occult qualities like magnetism. In both cases we merely observe the effect of the underlying mechanisms which, being insensible, are therefore occult. Second, he claims that the acceptance of the veil of perception renders all qualities occult.

> To insist . . . that one's psychological perception of a sensible quality is of a different order of reality from the physical cause of that quality is tantamount to declaring that cause occult. So accepting Locke's distinction [between primary and secondary qualities] is equivalent to denying the existence of manifest qualities, and on this point all proponents of any

form of the mechanical philosophy were agreed, though few expressed it this way. . . . the new philosophy did not allow that bodies had attributes that were manifest in the Aristotelian sense.

(Hutchison 1982, p. 243)

On the first point Hutchison is right, many manifest qualities are explained in terms of underlying corpuscular structure. However, it does not follow that '[t]here remains thus no strict distinction in Descartes' philosophy [or Boyle's] between the occult and the manifest' (Hutchison 1982, p. 243). To be sure, Boyle did hold to the veil of appearance doctrine of perception and consequently believed that we have no *immediate* epistemic access to the qualities of bodies. But this does not entail that for Boyle the occult/manifest distinction effectively collapses, all qualities becoming occult. For, the issue about occult qualities does not turn on whether or not we have immediate perceptual access to them, but rather it has to do with degrees of perceptual access. There are many qualities of bodies to which we have perceptual access albeit mediate. But in the case of occult qualities even this is lacking – we only have mediate access to their effects.

Moreover, when Boyle does give a positive account of the perception of the primary affections of sensible matter, and this only seems to happen in passing, he alludes to no problems other than the standard point about fallibility. Thus, as we have seen, a stick in water is represented by the sense organ as bent in shape, but the mind corrects this by judging that in the light of the disparity in density of the media, it is actually straight. Presumably this correction is not required in cases of veridical perception, but some degree of judgment is still required. Because the mechanical affections are not explicated by a relation to our senses, the mind judges that sensations of them do represent objective qualities of objects.

4 The sensible qualities in *The Origin of Forms and Qualities*

It is clear then that Boyle accepts a form of representative realism with regard to the primary affections of matter. Further, we have seen that the pin illustration overstates the case for the percipient dependence of the sensible qualities by conflating all sensory impressions with bodily sensations. We are now left with the problem of whether or not Boyle accepts a form of subjectivism for the sensible qualities. Let us set up the issue in the following way. According to Boyle, we know that sensations of primary affections are caused by primary affections and that these sensations represent actual, objective primary affections of bodies. The causal relation seems to map onto the representational relation. What about sensations of sensible qualities? What are the sensations of sensible qualities caused by and what, if anything, do they represent?

In Boyle's extended discussion of the 'chiefest' difficulty for the corpuscular hypothesis, viz. the purported objective existence of sensible qualities, Boyle (unintentionally) canvasses the various answers to these questions.[35] One's initial impression upon reading the relevant section of the *Forms and Qualities* is that his discussion is muddled, even confused. But perhaps we can be a little more charitable here, for Boyle is traversing relatively uncharted terrain. To be sure, the nature of perception and the perception of the qualities of bodies had been a philosophical issue since the Presocratics and the writings of the late scholastics are replete with discussions of the problem. Yet within the mechanical/atomist 'tradition' there was virtually no precedent for a treatment of sensible qualities in the light of their relational and dispositional character and yet these are the features of the sensibles that Boyle strives to explicate. The standard discussions available to Boyle were either influenced by the scholastic discussions or took the subjectivist line of Democritus and Descartes, the view that sensible qualities are just sensations in the mind. Little attention had been given to their relational or dispositional character. It is perhaps excusable then, that Boyle's discussion lacks the philosophical rigour that is found in well-worked terrain.[36]

Let us begin with Boyle's admission regarding the sensible qualities near the beginning of his discussion that 'no man (that I know of) hath been able to give accurate definitions of them' (*Works*, III, p. 22, *S*. p. 30). Boyle is sure that all of us know what we are referring to when we speak of colours, odours etc.: '[talk of] sensible qualities [is easily understood] when . . . we add some enumeration of particular subjects wherein they do the most eminently reside' (*Works*, III, p. 21, *S*. p. 29). Further, 'it seems evident that they [sensible qualities] have an *absolute* being irrelative to *us*' and that 'bodies may be said in a very favourable sense to have those qualities we call sensible, though there were no animals in the world' (*Works*, III, p. 23 and p. 24, *S*. p. 32 and p. 33). We can now list the various options that Boyle raises in the discussion. They are not listed here in the sequence that they appear in the text, but rather are sorted for ease of explication.

First, we have a negative claim: the sensible qualities are not 'real' qualities. Just prior to the first use of the pin illustration, Boyle makes the Cartesian point that from our infancy we are inclined to attribute existence to things which are not in fact in the objects in the way in which we conceive them to be.[37] He then says, 'there is in the body to which these sensible qualities are attributed nothing of *real and physical* but the size, shape, and motion or rest of its component particles . . .' (*Works*, III, p. 23, *S*. p. 31, italics added).[38] This move in the context of a discussion of the sensible qualities naturally inclines the modern philosopher to expect Boyle to follow up with some form of projectivism or at least an error theory about the sensible qualities. But it is crucial to note that the target of the error theory is the peculiar scholastic ontological category of 'real' qualities and not accidents in general. The rejection of sensible qualities as real qualities does not entail that Boyle is committed to some form of subjectivism (see chapter 4, §6).

Second, we find that the term 'sensible quality' can have different referents. In some contexts Boyle uses it to refer to qualities of bodies and in others to refer to the ideas in the mind that the qualities of bodies cause. Thus he can say 'I do not deny but that bodies may be said in a very favourable sense to have those qualities we call *sensible*' and immediately after go on to speak of a body 'having such a disposition of its constituent corpuscles that, in case it were duly applied to the sensory of an animal, it would produce such a sensible quality which a body of another texture would not' and again 'to these operations of the objects on the sensories, the mind of man, which upon the account of its union with the body perceives them, giveth distinct names, calling the one light or colour, the other sound . . .' (*Works*, III, p. 24 and p. 23, *S*. p. 33 and p. 31). 'Sensible quality' then, clearly refers to different things: the qualities of bodies and ideas or sensations in the mind. And this ambiguity is widely acknowledged.[39] On the whole the response to it has been to note it as looseness of expression or an unfortunate lack of clarity, and that Boyle's primary sense of the term is that of a property possessed by an object. The other sense then is derivative and less common.[40] However, M. Mandelbaum and L. Keating have taken the less common sense to be the primary sense in Boyle. For them, Boyle's sensible qualities are ideas in the mind.

Now Mandelbaum's and Keating's view that sensible qualities are merely ideas in the mind caused by the mechanical affections is not a reductive view; the ideas are still entities albeit mental entities. Rather it is a deflationary view with regard to the corporeal realm. It sweeps the sensibles out of the corporeal realm and into the mental and gives them an entirely different ontological status. A variant of this view is found in Peter Alexander who wants to establish a dichotomy between the secondary qualities and the sensible qualities. For him, Boyle distinguished between secondary qualities and sensible qualities; the former denoting textures of objects and the latter ideas caused by the secondary qualities.[41] He says,

> [s]econdary qualities cause sensations in us; colours, sounds, odours and tastes are sensations and therefore correctly called *not* secondary qualities but the effects of secondary qualities on us. . . . The word 'sensible' in Boyle's 'sensible qualities' means, I suggest, not 'able to be sensed' but 'as sensed'.
>
> (Alexander 1985, p. 85)

Thus Alexander's view is that, for Boyle, the *secondary* qualities are identical to textures, whereas the *sensible* qualities are merely ideas in the immaterial mind. Alexander's distinction between the secondaries and the sensibles is almost impossible to maintain from the texts. The only place where the term 'secondary quality' appears in the *Forms and Qualities* it is clearly synonymous with 'sensible quality' which in that particular context is said to be in bodies (*Works*, III, p. 24, *S*. p. 32).[42] So an initial problem with this subjectivist interpretation of Boyle is that it simply overlooks the fact that the majority uses of 'sensible quality' in Boyle's works refer to the qualities of bodies while some remain genuinely ambiguous. Take for example Boyle's definition of taste in his *Mechanical Qualities* (1675).

> By taste considered, as belonging to the object, (under which notion I here treat of it,) I mean, that quality, or whatever else it be, which enables a body, by its operation, to produce in us that sensation, which we feel, or perceive, when we say we taste.
>
> (*Works*, IV, p. 260)[43]

By taking the 'loose sense' in Boyle's more ambiguous uses of 'sensible quality' and related terms and using it as primary, one has to ignore or dismiss as inconsistent the majority of textual material on the sensible qualities.

It may be more accurate to interpret Boyle as having two different, perhaps irreconcilable, strands to his thought on the sensible qualities, especially in the light of the other claims he makes about them in the *Forms and Qualities*. For third, we have the positive claim, related to the denial of real qualities, that sensible qualities are reducible to, or derived from, the primary affections of matter; colours and odours 'depend' upon the more primitive affections of matter,[44] or the weaker claim that sensible qualities 'are but the effects of the often-mentioned catholic affections of matter and deducible from the size, shape, motion (or rest) . . . of the insensible parts of bodies' (*Works*, III, p. 26, *S*. pp. 36–37). In modern philosophical parlance we might gloss this as the claim that the primary qualities are the categorical ground of the sensible qualities. We can almost feel Boyle hedging toward what has become known as the Lockean view, the idea that sensible qualities are dispositions or powers in bodies to cause certain sensations in percipients.

Thus it is not surprising that, fourth, we find a claim that seems to amount to there being dispositions in the objects to bring about sensations of colour etc.; 'if there were no sensitive beings, those bodies that are now the objects of our senses would be but *dispositively*, if I may so speak, endowed with colours, tastes . . . and *actually* but only with those more catholic affections of bodies – figure, motion . . .' (*Works*, III, p. 25, *S*. p. 34)[45] and again, there is no heat in a body 'distinct from the power it hath of putting the small parts of the wax into such a motion as that their agitation surmounts their cohesion' (*Works*, III, p. 26, *S*. p. 36). There is also the long digression in the *Forms and Qualities* that treats of the relative nature of the non-mechanical qualities. It is these claims, that sensible qualities are dispositions or powers and have a relational nature, that are the point of departure from the typical Cartesian subjectivist analysis of the sensible qualities and will prove to be an important key to interpreting what Boyle says on the ontological status of the sensibles in the next chapter.

Notes

1 Boyle says, 'we explicate colours, odours, and the like sensible qualities, by a *relation to our senses* . . .', *Forms and Qualities*, *Works*, III, p. 23, *S*. p. 32. For the same idea in Charleton see *Physiologia*, p. 128.

2 See R. Jackson 1968, pp. 55–58, J. Yolton 1970, p. 22, E. M. Curley 1972, J. Mackie 1976, pp. 9–15, F. J. O'Toole 1974 and P. Heimann and J. E. McGuire 1971, pp. 247–248.

3 See P. Alexander 1977 and 1985. For a summary of his view see 1985, p. 82 and for the claim that '[p]rimary qualities are powers' see 1985, p. 82 and p. 160 and 1977, p. 209. On Alexander's view (of Boyle and Locke) a corpuscle's *size is, inter alia*, its power to fit only into holes above a certain size. To this extent there is no distinction between what it is and what it can do' (1985, p. 160).

4 See M. Mandelbaum 1964, pp. 19–21, p. 101, p. 115 and p. 119 and L. Keating 1993.

5 It is not surprising therefore to find that there are only two treatments of the subject in the secondary literature on Boyle, those by M. Mandelbaum (1964) and J. J. MacIntosh (1983). Remarkably, MacIntosh 1983 does not even refer to Boyle's discussion of perception in the *Excellency of Theology*, neither does he refer to the important comments on perception in *Forms and Qualities* nor the rather puzzling passage in *Christian Virtuoso, I*. There is a very short, uncritical discussion of perception in M. Crowley 1970, pp. 90–92. For examples of fragments in the *BP*, see vol. 10, fols 29–31 (transcribed in Appendix 1) and 48v.

6 Boyle actually uses the term 'information' in a similar context: see *Christian Virtuoso, I, Works*, V, p. 539.

7 For further discussion of the common sense see chapter 2, §5.

8 For Descartes on the common sense see *Rules, CSM*, I, p. 41, *Treatise on Man, CSM*, I, pp. 105–106, *Opticks, CSM*, I, p. 164 and *Letter to Mersenne* of 24 December 1640 and 21 April 1641, *CSMK*, p. 162 and p. 180.

9 See also *Christian Virtuoso, II, Works*, VI, p. 750. Boyle, like many others in the seventeenth century, believed that the nerves were hollow, having 'inconspicuous cavities' and so allowed the animal spirits to flow through them (*Christian Virtuoso, II, Works*, VI, p. 743). See also *Languid Motion, Works*, V, p. 10.

10 See *Christian Virtuoso, II, Works*, VI, p. 742.

11 See *ibid.*, p. 748.

12 As J. J. MacIntosh has pointed out (1983, pp. 341ff).

13 See also *Forms and Qualities, Works*, III, p. 51 and 'History of Particular Qualities', *Works*, III, p. 301, *S*. p. 110 and 'Excellency of the Mechanical Hypothesis', *Works*, IV, p. 78, *S*. p. 153.

14 Though see *BP*, vol. 2, fol. 125 where he argues against some scholastics that 'Corporeal Phantasms' are not required for the soul's intellectual operations.

15 See also *Christian Virtuoso, II, Works*, VI, p. 742. Perhaps Boyle was influenced here by Hooke's theory of memory. The case for attributing a superpositional theory of memory to Descartes is found in J. Sutton 1998.

16 It is perhaps worth noting that two of Descartes' most important discussions of the nature of sensation occur in his *Sixth Meditation* and *Replies to the Sixth Set of Objections* which were published together. Boyle's *Excellency of Theology* quotes from this work twice and reveals that he had read it closely. See *Works*, IV, p. 13 and p. 28. Moreover, in the same work Boyle refers us in a footnote to his 'notes about

Sensation and Sensible Qualities', p. 40. I do not know whether these notes are still extant. Perhaps a fragment of them is to be found in *BP*, vol. 10, fols 29–31 in which the influence of Descartes is also seen. The notes refer to Descartes' discussion of pain in *Principles*, IV, §196, *CSM*, I, p. 283 and are in hand E who worked for Boyle in the 1660s. See Appendix 1.

17 In later writings Boyle expresses doubts about the role of the pineal gland. See *Christian Virtuoso*, *II*, *Works*, VI, pp. 741–742 and *BP*, vol. 2, fol. 105 and vol. 1, fol. 20.

18 These words are spoken by the interlocutor Eleutherius, repeating the description given by Boyle's mouthpiece Carneades on the previous page. Later (p. 741) Carneades defines sensation as 'an internal perception of the changes that happen in the sensories'.

19 See also *Forms and Qualities*, *Works*, III, p. 23, *S*. p. 31.

20 See also *Excellency of Theology*, *Works*, IV, p. 45 where Boyle says, 'as the Aristotelians cannot particularly show, how their qualities are produced, so we cannot particularly explicate, how they are perceived; the principal thing, that we can say, being in substance this, that our sensations depend upon such an union or permission of the soul and body, as we can give no example of in all nature'.

21 Descartes tells Gassendi in the *Fifth Set of Replies* that 'as for movement and sensation, I refer them to the body for the most part, and attribute nothing belonging to them to the soul, apart from the element of thought alone' (*CSM*, II, p. 243). It should be noted that Boyle had not read *Treatise on Man*, Descartes' most detailed treatment of the physiology of sense perception, by the time he had finished his *Excellency of Theology*.

22 See also *Forms and Qualities*, *Works*, III, p. 23, *S*. p. 31. Thus it is wrong for J. J. MacIntosh (1983, p. 345) to claim that Boyle's 'tendency seems to have been – perhaps in view of our inability to say anything worthwhile about the immaterial – to reserve the term "idea" for corporeal ideas, the ideas of the "sensible soul"'. The 'materialisation' of ideas was not a general trend in the new Cartesianism in which Boyle took a particular interest. For instance, Desmond Clarke (1989, p. 45) notes that La Forge, in his *Traité*, 'reserves the term *idée* exclusively for states of the immaterial mind'.

23 See also 'Excellency of the Mechanical Hypothesis', *Works*, IV, p. 78, *S*. p. 153: 'perceptions by the animadversive faculty of the soul are sensations'.

24 See the analogy between the innate light of the rational faculty and the eye in 'Advices', *Works*, IV, pp. 460–461.

25 All three senses are found in *Excellency of Theology*, *Works*, IV, p. 44.

26 See *CSM*, II, pp. 28ff. For a helpful discussion of Descartes' view see Ayers 1991, I, chapter 6. Boyle does mention, in the mouth of an interlocutor Eleutherius, the *formale* in the quality of heat when considered in its relation to the sense of touch. However, he remains uncommitted on the utility of this scholastic conception. See 'Nature of Cold', *Works*, III, p. 736 and 'Advices', *Works*, IV, p. 457.

27 *Pace* J. Yolton. See Yolton 1984 for an attempt to remove the veil of appearance from both Descartes and Locke. For an insightful critique see Ayers 1991, I, p. 56ff.

28 See *Principles*, IV, §196, *CSM*, I, p. 283. For Locke see *Essay*, II, viii, §13. The pin illustration is employed by Boyle three times in the *Forms and Qualities*: see *Works*, III, p. 23, p. 24, p. 25, *S*. p. 31, p. 33, p. 35.

29 See also *Forms and Qualities*, *Works*, III, p. 23, *S*. p. 31. See Descartes *Principles*, I,

§70: 'we do not really know what it is that we are calling a colour; and we cannot find any intelligible resemblance between the colour which we suppose to be in objects and that which we experience in our sensation' (*CSM*, I, p. 218).

30 In fact Boyle is possibly following Descartes here. See for example Descartes' *Optics* IV, *CSM*, I, pp. 164–166. However, the argument against 'real qualities' in objects is a recurring theme in discussions of the sensible qualities by the mechanists in general. See for example Digby, *Two Treatises*, pp. 2–3.

31 This corresponds to Descartes' third grade of sensory response. See *Sixth Set of Replies*, *CSM*, II, p. 295.

32 See *Things Above Reason*, *Works*, IV, p. 421, *S.* p. 232: 'We have a positive idea of things that are square and round, black and white, and in short of other things whose shapes and colours make them the objects of our sight.'

33 For a discussion of the same problem in Locke see M. Ayers 1991, I, pp. 214ff.

34 See Appendix 1 and *BP*, vol. 10, fol. 48v.

35 See *Forms and Qualities*, *Works*, III, pp. 22–27, *S.* pp. 30–37.

36 A nice parallel here is found in Locke's discussion of identity in the *Essay*, see M. Ayers 1991, I, p. 5.

37 See Descartes' *Principles*, I, §71, *CSM*, I, p. 219 and *Sixth Meditation*, *CSM*, II, p. 57. The point was a common anti-Aristotelian move in the early to mid-seventeenth century. See for example Digby, *Two Treatises*, pp. 2–3. For Locke see *Essay* II, viii, §24–5. For Boyle's use of the point against the vulgar notion of nature see section I of *Notion of Nature*, *Works*, V, pp. 161–167.

38 See also *Forms and Qualities*, *Works*, III, p. 25, *S.* p. 35.

39 See P. Alexander 1985, p. 79, R. Jackson 1968, p. 57, J. Mackie 1976, p. 15.

40 On a rough count I have found seventeen instances of 'sensible quality' (including one case of 'sensible phenomena') in the relevant section of *Forms and Qualities*, *Works*, III, pp. 11–44, *S.* pp. 14–64, of which eleven refer unambiguously to qualities of objects and four to sensations in mind.

41 See P. Alexander 1985, pp. 79–85.

42 See also, 'Essay on Nitre', *Works*, I, p. 364, where Boyle speaks of 'those more secondary affections of bodies, which are wont to be called sensible qualities'.

43 For one instance that is ambiguous, see the passage that L. Keating claims is a summary of Boyle's position: 'the perceptions of these impressions are by men called by several names, as heat, colour, sound, and are commonly imagined to proceed from certain distinct and peculiar qualities in the external object which have some resemblance to the ideas their action upon the senses excites in the mind . . .'. Cutting short the quote at this point is significant for Boyle goes on to say, 'though indeed all these sensible qualities and the rest that are to be met with in the bodies without us, are but the effects or consequents of the above-mentioned *primary affections* of matter . . .', *Forms and Qualities*, *Works*, III, p. 36, *S.* p. 51, underlining added. It is not clear whether 'sensible qualities' here are distinguished from or in the same category as 'the rest that are to be met with in the bodies without us'. The similarity in expression here to Digby's discussion of the sensible qualities is striking. 'Now we receiving from our senses, the knowledge that we have *of things without us; do give names unto them* according to the passions and affections, which those things cause in our senses . . .' (*Two Treatises*, pp. 242–243, italics added).

44 See *Forms and Qualities*, *Works*, III, p. 24, *S*. p. 32. See also *Essay*, II, viii, §14 and §2, §21, §3: 'do they [the sensible qualities] not depend on the Bulk, Figure, Texture and Motion of the Parts?'.

45 The way that Boyle introduces the rare and clumsy adverb 'dispositively' shows that he is not working with a well-established vocabulary of dispositions and powers. See the *OED* which cites this reference.

4 The ontological status of the sensible qualities

We have seen that according to Boyle there is a causal chain extending from the object 'perceived' to the mind. The incorporeal mind perceives impressions caused by motions in the brain that are caused by the qualities of bodies. Presumably this is the only mechanism by which the mind can 'perceive' the qualities of bodies; all the perceptible qualities of bodies are perceived in this manner. The perceptions resulting from these motions in the brain are sensations and sensations are in the mind. In the case of the sensible qualities they are those ideas we sometimes call colour, smell, taste, etc. All this is non-controversial and what one would expect from a mechanist and a dualist who is strongly influenced by Descartes. However, at times Boyle speaks as if the sensible qualities of bodies are really the very same thing as the mechanical affections of bodies. Yet on other occasions Boyle appears to speak of the sensible qualities as powers or dispositions, as if they are some ontological addition over and above the mechanical affections of bodies. It is the purpose of this chapter to explore these tensions and to attempt to settle the question of the precise ontological status of the sensible qualities.

1 The sensible qualities as powers and relations

Boyle often speaks of the non-mechanical qualities, and in particular the sensible qualities, as relations. For instance, in the work entitled 'Of Men's Great Ignorance of the Uses of Natural Things' he says,

> I consider . . . that the faculties and qualities of things being (for the most part) but certain relations, either to another, as between a lock and a key; or to men, as the qualities of external things referred to our bodies, and *especially to the organs of sense* . . .
>
> (*Works*, III, p. 479, italics added)[1]

And in the 'History of Particular Qualities' we find the claim that

> . . . the qualities commonly called *sensible* and many others too being according to our opinion but *relative attributes*, one of these now-mentioned

alterations [of texture], though but mechanical, may endow the body it happens to with *new relations* both to the organs of sense and also to some other bodies, and *consequently endow it with additional qualities*.

(*Works*, III, pp. 303–304, S. p. 115, italics added,
apart from '*sensible*')[2]

In fact, an entire subsection of the *Forms and Qualities* is devoted to discussion of the relative nature of physical qualities.[3]

Boyle also spoke of certain non-mechanical qualities as powers or dispositions. It is not unusual to find him saying such things as quicksilver 'has a quality or *power* . . . to dissolve gold and silver, and a *capacity* or *disposition* to be dissolved by aqua fortis . . .' (*Cosmical Qualities, Works*, III, p. 306, italics added). But occasionally there are stronger claims, claims that suggest that these powers are a separate category in his ontology, as for instance his comment quoted above that 'the *faculties* and qualities of things being (for the most part) but certain relations'. And this brings us to an important distinction to be observed in Boyle's use of the term 'disposition'. He uses the term in two distinct senses, both of which were in ordinary usage in his day. The most common meaning of the term in Boyle is that of the arrangement of parts. He speaks of a body as 'having such a disposition of its constituent corpuscles' where the sense is clearly referring to how the corpuscles of a body are structured. In this sense 'disposition' is synonymous with 'texture' (*Forms and Qualities, Works*, III, p. 24, S. p. 33).[4] The second sense is a tendency to bring about a certain effect or effects. In speaking of snow Boyle says 'it hath a greater disposition than coal or soot to reflect store of light outwards' (*Forms and Qualities, Works*, III, p. 24, S. p. 34).[5] Here he is using 'disposition' as a synonym of 'power' and 'capacity'. The two senses are obviously related in Boyle, for it is in virtue of the 'disposition' of its parts that snow has the 'disposition' to reflect light.[6] But it is important to distinguish them if we are correctly to interpret him.[7]

Now while there are fewer references to qualities as powers than to qualities as relations and no explicit claim to the effect that all the sensible qualities *are* powers, from what he says about powers we need to take seriously the suggestion that, for Boyle, most if not all of the non-mechanical qualities are powers. If this is so, they are powers to bring about certain effects in other bodies and, in the case of the sensibles, in percipients. This is suggested, not just from the apparent synonymy of terms such as 'quality', 'power' and 'capacity' for Boyle,[8] but, more specifically, from the way in which Boyle applies his celebrated lock and key illustration in the *Forms and Qualities*. Having discussed as powers those qualities of the key and lock of opening and being opened, he goes on to tell us that what he has said of the lock and key applies equally to the sensible and other qualities of bodies (*Works*, III, p. 18, S. p. 24). The clear implication is that the point made about the lock and key is illustrative of other qualities. So if this interpretation is correct, the sensible qualities are also powers like those of the lock and key, only in their case they are the powers of causing sensations in the percipient rather than effects in other bodies.

Given then, that the sensible qualities are spoken of as both powers and relations, some questions immediately present themselves. First, are the powers identical to relations, or are they different from relations but related to them in some metaphysically significant way? And second, in what sense does a change of texture 'endow' a body with new relations and 'consequently endow it with additional qualities'? Are the new relations a separate ontological category over and above the mechanical affections of matter, or can relations be fully reduced to the mechanical affections of their relata?

These questions can be clarified by provisionally ordering the properties that make up Boyle's ontology. First, there are mechanical properties of matter, then there are the relations between bodies and finally there are the sensible (and other non-mechanical) qualities or powers. Now, Boyle constantly says things to the effect that the sensible qualities or powers are 'derived from' or 'deduced from' the mechanical affections.[9] Thus the mechanical affections seem to have some sort of ontological priority over the sensibles. Further, the sensible qualities or powers seem somehow to be dependent upon or identical to relations. So relations seem to have some ontological priority over the sensibles. Finally, since it appears that relations cannot exist in the absence of their relata, their relata seem to have some ontological priority over the relations. Thus we can order the three constituents of Boyle's assay of properties as follows:[10]

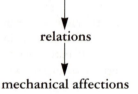

Figure 2

We can now restate the above questions by asking: are sensible qualities or powers reducible to relations? And are relations reducible to the mechanical properties of their terms? In order to answer these questions we need to digress and set up a number of metaphysical distinctions that will furnish us with some tools for interpretation. But first a caveat.

It is important to avoid the error of anachronism. Some of the following distinctions and terminology seem very far from seventeenth-century concerns. They are the fruit of more recent metaphysical reflection. Yet I believe the following relations and distinctions are helpful in interpreting Boyle's views or at least for setting parameters within which his views can be interpreted and setting up directions for further inquiry. They also give us a bearing on the historical significance of his views. We can use them to compare and contrast

Boyle with Locke, Hume and others on the questions of powers, relations and reducibility.

2 Ontological reduction

What is ontological reduction? A first stab might say that it is *explaining* one part of our ontology in terms of some other part. But what is involved in this notion of *explaining*? Most examples of ontological reduction involve establishing the kind of relations in which one part of our ontology stands to other parts. If the entity to be reduced stands in a particular relation to another entity, then it is said to be reduced to that entity. For example a certain relation might stand in such a way to its relata that it is said to be reduced to its relata. The reduction relation is then said to be explanatory. If one entity is not reducible to another it is said to be ontologically distinct.

For example, easily the most economical form of reduction involves the relation of *identity*. Identity is strict or absolute identity. Everything is identical to itself and nothing else, not even its 'identical' twin. It is a reflexive, transitive and symmetrical relation. It holds for every kind of entity in an ontology, and so every property is identical to itself. It may sound like a fairly vacuous relation, but there are interesting and important instances of apparently distinct properties standing in this relation. For instance, Boyle sometimes speaks as if heat is identical to the motion of corpuscles[11] and some contemporary philosophers believe that colours are identical to certain complex structural properties of objects.[12] Any entities that are non-identical are ontologically distinct.

Another relation that is relevant here is *dependence*.[13] Some entities can be dependent on other entities for their existence. Dependence is a relation between properties and between properties and substances. If F is ontologically distinct from G then, if F is dependent on G, F cannot exist if G does not exist. For example, many philosophers believe that external relations, e.g. spatio-temporal relations, are entities that are distinct from their terms. That is, the relation is something over and above its relata. If Simmias is taller than Socrates, then there exists the individual Simmias, the individual Socrates and the relation 'taller than'. But the relation 'taller than' while being ontologically distinct is dependent on certain non-essential properties of its relata, viz. the respective heights of Simmias and Socrates. Without these properties the relation would not exist. So we say that the relation 'taller than' stands in a dependence relation to its terms. *Independence* is the converse of dependence. Independence is a relation between properties (and facts). F is independent of G if F can exist and G not exist. To use a Boolean example, a corpuscle might be cubical and in motion or at rest. That is, the shape of the corpuscle is independent of its motion.

One further distinction is relevant here. Relations can be either unilaterally reducible or multilaterally reducible.[14] That is they can be reduced to the (non-relational) properties of either one or all of their terms. For example, if the relation 'self-identity' is reducible it will be so unilaterally because its terms are the very same thing.[15] However almost all relations, if they are reducible, appear to be multilaterally reducible.

Let us return to our problem of determining just what are the relations between Boyle's mechanical properties, relations and sensible qualities or powers. Let us call the reduction relation R and the distinctness relation D. We have four possibilities for the ontological status of Boyle's sensible qualities: powers are reducible to relations and relations are reducible to their relata; powers are reducible to relations but relations are distinct from their relata; powers are distinct from relations but relations are reducible to their relata; and powers are distinct from relations and relations are distinct from their relata.

(a)   R (Power, Relation)   and   R   (Relation, Relata)
(b)   R (Power, Relation)   and   D   (Relation, Relata)
(c)   D (Power, Relation)   and   R   (Relation, Relata)
(d)   D (Power, Relation)   and   D   (Relation, Relata)

It is clear that (a) collapses powers into relations which in turn collapse into their relata, that is, corpuscles having the mechanical affections. Thus we wind up with a single level ontology of properties. There are no properties over and above the mechanical affections of bodies. The next two possibilities, (b) and (c), both yield two-tiered ontologies of properties, (b) having mechanical properties and relations only, and (c) having sensible qualities or powers and mechanical properties. The fourth possibility, (d), yields a three-tiered ontology of sensible qualities or powers, relations and the mechanical properties of matter. The task remains then to determine which if any of (a), (b), (c) or (d) Boyle held, keeping in mind that it is not possible to hold more than one of these four theses consistently. We will proceed by first considering the case for the fully reductive thesis (a) and then considerations against (a) and for one of the theses that involve distinctness: (b), (c) or (d).

3 The case for reduction: explicit references

The case for the reductive thesis (a) initially appears to be quite strong. The thesis is that, for Boyle, the sensible qualities of bodies are nothing over and above the shape, size and motion of corpuscles. On this view powers are identified with relations, which are in turn identified with the mechanical affections of their relata. An important exponent of a version of this view is Peter Alexander who claims that the central notion here is texture.[16] On his view, there is an additional tier in Boyle's ontology, that of textures. Boyle's 'secondary' qualities are identical to textures which are structural properties of a body. Moreover, the powers that bodies have to affect others are just textures. These in turn are themselves nothing more than the various arrangements of the constituent 'compound' corpuscles of a body which are ultimately made up of atomic corpuscles or particles, which, by definition, lack texture but have the mechanical affections of shape, size and motion. Thus textures, which are identical to 'secondary' qualities, are ultimately reducible to the mechanical affections of bodies.[17]

This interpretation of Boyle attributes to him what amounts to an early form of categorical realism about the sensible qualities. It is the view that qualities like colour, taste and smell are to be identified with their categorical grounds, that is, with certain complex structural properties of the agent.[18] Similar though more sophisticated categorical realisms are still held today.[19]

Now while I have set up the issue of ontological reduction in Boyle as being between powers and relations and between relations and the mechanical properties, it is apparent that most of the time Boyle seems to ignore the relational aspects of powers and speaks neither of the 'power-relation' relation nor of the 'relation-relata' relation, but of the 'power-mechanical property' relation. And the most compelling evidence for attributing the reductive thesis to Boyle is the host of passages that seem unambiguously to state that the sensible qualities (and other non-mechanical qualities) of bodies are identical to the mechanical affections of those bodies. A number of these passages are found in the *Forms and Qualities*.[20] For instance he says of powdered glass,

> though the powers of poisons be not only looked upon as *real* qualities, but are reckoned among the *abstrusest* ones, yet this deleterious faculty, which is supposed to be a peculiar and superadded entity in the beaten glass, is really nothing distinct from the glass itself . . . as it is furnished with that determinate bigness and figure of parts which have been acquired by comminution.
>
> (*Works*, III, p. 19, *S*. p. 25)[21]

In addition to such apparently overt statements of the reductive thesis, there is some more specific textual support for reduction. Consider the relation of powers to relations. Was Boyle committed to the reducibility of powers to relations or are powers ontologically distinct from relations? There are a few unambiguous passages in which Boyle *identifies* powers with relations. An important example is the following passage (already quoted) from the 'Uses of Natural Things'):

> I consider that . . . the *faculties* and qualities of things being (for the most part) but certain relations, either to another, as between a lock and a key; or to men, as the qualities of external things referred to our bodies, and especially to the organs of sense . . .
>
> (*Works*, III, p. 479, italics added)[22]

What about the relation of relations to their relata? Did Boyle believe that relations are some ontological addition over and above the corpuscles and their mechanical affections or that they are reducible? If we could find some unambiguous passages that posit the reducibility of relations to their relata the case would appear to be settled in favour of reduction, i.e. (a) above.

4 For reduction: the traditional view of relations

From the work of Olsen and Weinberg[23] it appears that the question of the ontological status of relations in the centuries leading up to Boyle's day was dominated by Aristotle's remark in the *Metaphysics* that 'the relative (πρός τι) is least of all things a real thing or substance, and is posterior to quality and quantity' (N, 1088ª24, quoted from *Barnes*, II, p. 1719). Weinberg goes so far as to claim that '[t]he medieval views about the nature of relations appear to determine the views of the seventeenth-century philosophers' (Weinberg 1965, p. 112). And since this is true for Suárez, Descartes, Gassendi and Hobbes, all of whom could have influenced Boyle on this matter, it appears safe to say that there was no precedent in the writings of those who influenced Boyle for taking relations to be a separate ontological category.

Moreover, further evidence that Boyle did not consider relations to be a separate ontological category may be found in the fact that he seems not to have clearly distinguished between relations and relational properties. For example, in the *Forms and Qualities* he speaks of relations such as 'father of' and 'husband of' and tells us that we should not conclude that with regard to these 'capacities or relations' there are 'so many real and distinct entities in the person so variously denominated' (*Works*, III, p. 17, *S.* pp. 22–23). Just what Boyle means by 'real qualities' will be discussed below (§6), but his talk of the relation 'father of' rather than the property of 'being a father' as not being 'in the person' as a real quality is most naturally interpreted as a failure to distinguish between relations and relational properties. This is entirely consonant with one who is influenced by the traditional Aristotelian treatment of relations. And when we couple this with Boyle's self-confessed aversion to metaphysical disputation, it is quite understandable that there is no sustained treatment of the ontology of relations in his writings. The upshot is that, while it is difficult to decide from his explicit references to relations whether or not Boyle thought relations were reducible to or distinct from their terms, the most likely conclusion, in the light of these historical considerations, is that he held that they were so reducible ((a) or (c) above).

5 For reduction: Boyle on colour

Further evidence for the reducibility thesis is found in some of Boyle's works that deal with specific sensible qualities. A good example of this is found in Boyle's most important work dealing with a particular sensible quality, the *Experiments and Considerations touching Colours*. In this work Boyle identifies colour with modifications of light because it plays the *primary causal role* in the process leading to the perception of colour. He calls it the 'more immediate cause of colour'. He acknowledges that there is in bodies a 'certain disposition of the superficial particles, whereby it sends the light reflected, or refracted to our eyes thus and thus altered'. (By 'disposition' he means arrangement of corpuscles.) In this sense colour 'depends upon the visible body'. And this is the place in which colours are usually thought to reside. In fact, so much of *Colours* concerns the ways in which the mechanical properties of bodies can affect the incident beams of light, that on a superficial reading of the work one might gain the impression that Boyle thought that colours *are* textures and thus are reducible to the mechanical properties of the external object.[24] However, it is not the position that he adopts. For according to Boyle it is light itself that 'produces the sensation of a colour, but as it produces such a determinate kind of local motion in some part of the brain' (*Colours, Works*, I, p. 671).

Boyle believes that if colour is thought to be a characteristic of light, one can easily explain certain troublesome phenomena such as rainbows and spectra created by glass prisms. There was some debate in Boyle's day as to whether such phenomena were real colours or mere 'apparent' colours. On Boyle's view these phenomena are real colours because they are simply coloured light refracted. Thus Boyle's view can be seen to be a precursor to the kind of 'wave-length realism' (as Keith Campbell calls it, 1993, p. 254) that was inspired by Newton's work on the colour spectrum. But what according to Boyle is light?

Initially in *Colours* he suggests a particle theory of light as a tentative hypothesis. He says,

> . . . much less do I pretend to determine, or scarce so much as to hope to know all that were requisite to be known, to give you, or even myself, a perfect account of the theory of vision and colours. For in order to such an undertaking, I would first know what light is, and if it be a body (as a body or the motion of a body it seems to be) what kind of corpuscles for size and shape it consists of, with what swiftness they move forwards, and whirl about their centers.
>
> (*Colours, Works*, I, p. 695)

But by the end of the *Colours* he is speaking unreservedly in corpuscular terms[25] and this continues into his treatment of blackness and whiteness, the two colours he explores with detailed experiments. The properties of light can be reduced to shape, size and motion.[26] Thus Boyle's identifying colour with characteristics of light is an important example of the identification of a sensible quality with the mechanical affections of the agent. This, combined with the other evidence we have marshalled above, appears to establish a *prima facie* case for (a), the view that powers are reducible to the mechanical affections.

Why then are there scholars who, like R. Jackson and F. J. O'Toole, resist the reductive thesis and posit that for Boyle the sensible qualities are irreducible powers? The reason is that there is textual evidence and some important philosophical considerations that militate against the reductive thesis in Boyle. First, there are a number of significant passages in which Boyle speaks explicitly in non-reductive terms about the sensible qualities and other non-mechanical qualities. Second, there is Boyle's peculiar notion of a disposition that has led one scholar (O'Toole) to resist the reductive thesis. And finally, there are problems of consistency for the reductive thesis in the light of Boyle's voluntarism. The following sections deal with each of these issues in turn. But before we proceed to them there is some important 'ground clearing' to do.

6 The case for distinctness: Suárez's real qualities

It might be thought that the case for (a) can be strengthened by the standard reading of the polemics of the *Forms and Qualities*, particularly when we consider how Boyle introduces the digression on the 'relative nature of physical qualities'. Early in the *Forms and Qualities* when Boyle is writing in a polemical mood against the philosophy of the schools, he admonishes us not to multiply entities beyond what is necessary. He tells us that 'not only diversity of *names*, but even diversity of *definitions*, doth not always infer a diversity of *physical entities* in the subject whereunto they are attributed' (*Works*, III, p. 17, *S*. p. 22). He then explains this point using examples of relations commonly attributed to men such as 'father of' and 'husband of'. He says,

> the same man, who, in respect of differing capacities or relations to other things, is called by differing names, and described by various definitions, which yet (as I was saying) conclude not so many real and distinct entities in the person so variously denominated.
>
> (*Ibid.*, *S*. pp. 22–23)

This leads immediately into the 'excursion about the relative nature of physical qualities' and the extended discussion of the lock and key. So it seems natural to think that the thought that led Boyle into the discussion of the relative nature of certain qualities was the Ockhamist point that just as relations are nothing over and above their terms, so the sensible qualities are nothing over and above the mechanical affections. More points for thesis (a) above!

However, a closer inspection of both the terminology involved and the dialectical context reveals that this passage does not provide conclusive support for (a). The crucial passage comes a page earlier and it is important here to appreciate the exact polemical nature of Boyle's discussion. Boyle is at pains to argue that the sensible and like qualities are not 'real qualities' in the sense popular amongst some modern scholastics. He says,

> but one thing the modern Schools are wont to teach concerning accidents is too repugnant to our present doctrine to be in this place omitted: namely, that there are in natural bodies store of *real qualities* and other *real accidents*, which not only are no moods of matter, but are real entities distinct from

it, and, according to the doctrine of many modern schoolmen, may *exist separate* from all matter whatsoever.

(*Ibid.*, p. 16, *S*. p. 21)[27]

This is the main theme of the famous excursion about the relative nature of physical qualities. He prefaces this excursion by saying that in order to avoid this grand mistake (of Suárez and other schoolmen) it is worth digressing to discuss the relative nature of qualities (*ibid.*, p. 18, *S*. p. 23). Then towards the conclusion of the digression Boyle says, 'I have said thus much, Pyrophilus, to remove the mistake that *everything men are wont to call a quality* must needs be a real and physical entity . . .' (*ibid.*, p. 21, *S*. p. 28). Boyle then ends the excursion, but continues reiterating this point throughout the next few sections.

Now what must be emphasised here is that Boyle is arguing that the sensible qualities (and others) are not real qualities where the term 'real qualities' has a *very specific sense*. He is not claiming that since they are not real qualities they are therefore unreal, that is, that they have no ontological status over and above the mechanical properties. To read Boyle in this way, as some have done, is to miss the dialectical context entirely.[28] Boyle's denial that the sensible qualities are 'real qualities' in no way implies the reductive thesis. Rather, as the title of the excursion indicates, Boyle had an alternative understanding of the sensibles, namely that they are relative attributes. Now before we examine Boyle's objections to real qualities it is important to have before us a thumbnail sketch of the differences between Boyle's substance/attribute distinction and that of the schoolmen, and in particular Suárez.[29]

The centrepiece of Suárez's ontology is his substance/attribute distinction. For Suárez substance is that which exists in itself (*in se*) and by itself (*per se*). It is a subject in which accidents can inhere, but which itself inheres in nothing.[30] And it is *beings* that are substances, that is, such things as dogs and people. Accidents, by contrast, are just those entities which may or may not inhere in a subject. They are a genus of which quality is a species and they are related to substance by inherence. But Suárez admits a special type of accident called 'real qualities'. They can exist without inhering in a subject. A further category in his ontology, one which Suárez effectively introduced into early modern discussion, is that of mode (*modus*). A mode is that which modifies entities such as substances or accidents. There are substantial and accidental modes. They, unlike real qualities, cannot exist separately from that which they modify.

Finally Suárez has three types of distinction that pertain to different elements in his ontology. Two are relevant here. The first is the *real distinction* that holds between entities. And the second is the *modal distinction* that holds between the modes themselves and between modes and that which they modify. There is a real distinction between substances and between accidents and between the same accident that inheres in different substances. And there is a modal distinction between, say, quantity and its inherence in a subject.

Now Boyle, following Descartes, also has a substance/attribute distinction, but one which differs significantly from that of Suárez. Often Boyle uses the term 'substance' to denominate particular things, like men or kinds of stuff, like water. But when he considers it as a fundamental ontological category he speaks in Aristotelian terms. For Boyle a substance is 'a self-subsisting entity, or that which needs no other created being to support it or to make it exist'. It is the 'subject of accidents', that in which accidents inhere.[31] In fact there are two types of substances: material and immaterial substances.[32] But what is important in this context is that (following Descartes) accidents are identical to modes. Now for Boyle accidents, and therefore modes, are those things 'needing the existence of some substance or other in which they may be, as in their subject of inhesion'. As such it is definitional that an accident *'cannot exist separately* from the thing or subject wherein it is . . .' (*Forms and Qualities, Works*, III, p. 17, S. p. 21).[33] A consequence of this identification is that Boyle does not have the Suaracian distinction between substantial and accidental modes. Further, on the Cartesian view only substances are really distinct. However, Boyle speaks at times as if the modes themselves (shape, size and motion)[34] are really distinct too. In fact, in the *Forms and Qualities* the real and modal distinctions found in Descartes seem to have coalesced.[35] This brings us to the relation between modes and qualities. One of Boyle's aims in his *Forms and Qualities* is to explain the origin of qualities in terms of the modes of matter. So there is an important ontological distinction that is to be maintained between the two. This is nowhere more evident than in Boyle's explicit resistance to calling modes or mechanical affections qualities. It contrasts markedly with Berkeley's later use of 'mode' and 'quality' as synonyms.[36]

Let us return then to the polemics of the *Forms and Qualities*. The real qualities of the schools, Boyle says (in the quote above), are 'no moods of matter', that is they are not like the primary affections which Boyle has just denominated 'moods' of matter (where 'moods' is a variant of 'modes'). Real qualities are 'real entities distinct from' matter and may exist separate from matter or may be 'super-added' to it.[37] The real qualities of the schools are ontologically distinct and independent of material substance. And Boyle goes on to show how real qualities cannot belong to any of Aristotle's nine categories of accident. It is only substance that is a 'real entity or thing that needs not any (*created*) being, that it may exist'. And so, to Boyle, it seems as if the schoolmen are attributing the ontological status of substance to the sensible qualities.[38] This is intolerable, for it is definitional of qualities that they need 'the existence of some substance or other in which they may be, as in their subject of inhesion'. And to illustrate this point he gives us the example of whiteness. It is extremely difficult to conceive how whiteness could exist independent of some subject (*Works*, III, p. 17, S. p. 21).[39] Thus to Boyle the real qualities are rather peculiar entities. They are altogether different from any entity that he admits into his ontology. In fact, he finds them completely unintelligible. So much so that he sets himself the task, in the excursion about relative qualities and beyond, to dismiss the notion that the sensible qualities are such entities and to establish their relative nature. He repeats six times claims to the effect that,

> they are not in the bodies that are endowed with them [the sensible qualities] any *real or distinct entities*, or differing from the matter itself furnished with such a determinate bigness, shape, or other mechanical modifications.
>
> (*Ibid.*, p. 18, *S.* p. 24, italics added)

Yet all this serves to tell us what the sensible qualities are not. It in no way implies that since they are not real they are therefore reducible to the mechanical affections of matter. And yet it furnishes us with no idea of what their ontological status is. Moreover, the issue is further complicated by the fact that very occasionally Boyle uses the term 'real' with a different sense to describe shape, size, motion and texture. For instance, in the *Forms and Qualities* he says, 'there is in the body, to which these sensible qualities are attributed, nothing of real and physical but the size, shape and motion or rest, of its component particles . . .' (*Ibid.*, p. 23, *S.* p. 31). But he has already told us that real qualities are not modes whereas the mechanical affections are modes.

Having discussed the meaning of 'real quality' we are now in a position to examine the famous discussion of the lock and key in the *Forms and Qualities*. This passage has become something of a *locus criticus*, for its interpretation seems to be a benchmark in the secondary literature by which other passages are interpreted. The passage runs as follows:

> when Tubal Cain . . . had made his first lock . . . that was only a piece of iron contrived into such a shape; and when afterwards he made a key to that lock, that also in itself considered was nothing but a piece of iron of such a determinate figure. But in regard that these two pieces of iron might now be applied to one another after a certain matter, and that there was a congruity betwixt the wards of the lock and those of the key, the lock and the key did each of them now obtain a new capacity; and it became a main part of the notion and description of a *lock* that it was capable of being made to lock or unlock by that other piece of iron we call a *key*, and it was looked upon as a peculiar faculty and power in the key that it was fitted to open and shut the lock: and yet by these new attributes there was not added any real or physical entity either to the lock or to the key, each of them remaining indeed nothing but the same piece of iron, just so shaped as it was before. And when our smith made other keys of differing bignesses or with differing wards, though the first lock was not to be opened by any of those keys, yet that indisposition, however it might be considered as a peculiar power of resisting this or that key, and might serve to discriminate it sufficiently from the locks those keys belonged to, was nothing new in the lock, or distinct from the figure it had before those keys were made. To carry this comparison a little further, let me add that,

though one that would have defined the first lock and the first key would have given them distinct definitions with reference to each other, yet (as I was saying) these definitions, being given but upon the score of certain respects which the defined bodies had one to another, would not infer that these two iron instruments did physically differ otherwise than in the figure, size, or contrivement, of the iron whereof each of them consisted. And proportionably hereunto, I do not see why we may not conceive that, as to those qualities (for instance) which we call *sensible*, though, by virtue of a certain congruity or incongruity in point of figure or texture (or other mechanical attributes) to our sensories, the portions of matter they modify are enabled to produce various effects upon whose account we make bodies to be endowed with qualities, yet they are not in the bodies that are endowed with them any real or distinct entities, or differing from the matter itself furnished with such a determinate bigness, shape, or other mechanical modifications.

(*Ibid.*, p. 18, *S*. pp. 23–24)

Peter Alexander interprets this passage in this way. 'We can describe the lock's physical characteristics completely in terms of the shapes and sizes of the pieces of metal composing it and their relations to one another.' The same applies to the key. 'The lock and key are nothing beyond what can be so described.' We can add to the description of the lock and the key that they have the capacities of opening and being opened. But it is a mistake to claim that this is any ontological addition. 'To discover a power, in this situation, is not to discover any new part of a body but merely to discover what the parts previously known will do, that is, to discover that the description we formerly gave *implied* that power.' In fact, Alexander (1985: pp. 71–72) claims that Boyle here is 'attacking an idea of powers, held by some modern schoolmen and chemists, that makes powers occult. At the end of his previous section he has discussed such an idea of powers.'[40]

A number of points require comment here. First, it is true that this passage is set within the critique of the scholastic notion of real qualities, but *pace* Alexander, it is not concerned with occult qualities (which are not even mentioned) and neither is Boyle's polemic against real qualities an attack on powers *per se*. These two claims misrepresent the polemical context of the passage. Some real qualities were powers for the schoolmen, but many were not. Second, Alexander uses this interpretation as the basis of his claim that Boyle identified powers with both textures and primary qualities and therefore that powers and the mechanical qualities of bodies are not distinct. In his important book *Ideas, Qualities and Corpuscles* (1985) he discusses none of the other passages referring to the dispositional or relational character of the sensible qualities apart from Boyle's discussion of the sensible qualities in the *Forms and Qualities*. So, much hangs on the interpretation of this passage for the whole of Alexander's understanding of Boyle's view of powers. However, the question as to whether powers are reducible to the primary qualities is just the point at issue here. It is not enough to declare that they are reducible and then use this passage as an interpretative 'key'. Why not, for instance, interpret this passage in the light of those from 'Uses of Natural Things' and *Cosmical Qualities*, both of which imply a belief in powers as ontologically distinct from the mechanical qualities?

Third, and this is the import of the foregoing discussion, a clear exposition of the doctrine of real qualities reveals that the denial that powers are real qualities or physical attributes like the mechanical affections does not entail that powers have no ontological status over and above their categorical grounds. To be sure, in this passage Boyle does say of the powers of the lock and key that 'by these new attributes there was not added any real or physical entity' and of the sensible qualities that 'they are not in the bodies that are endowed with them, any real or distinct entities, or differing from the matter . . .'. But these comments need to be considered in the light of both the specialised meaning of 'real quality' as a quality that can exist separated from any substance and that physical entities are the modes of matter.[41] A denial of powers as 'real qualities' does not entail that they are identical to the mechanical affections. Boyle's comment that sensible qualities are not 'real and distinct entities' can quite naturally be interpreted as referring to scholastic real qualities. And we still need to make sense of Boyle's claim that 'the lock and key did each of them obtain a new capacity', particularly in the light of similar comments in his 'Uses of Natural Things'. In short, the lock and key passage *may* sustain the interpretation that Alexander gives it, but this must be determined by interpreting it in the light of other relevant passages.

This criticism is even more telling against Laura Keating. For she argues for a fully reductive interpretation of the lock and key passage and then uses this interpretation to dismiss the view based on other passages that Boyle considered powers to be distinct from their grounds. Of the lock and key passage she claims that 'Boyle thinks that it is clear that the attribution to the key of the quality or power of being able to open the lock does not require the existence of a distinct entity in the key' (Keating 1993, p. 308). Then against the claim that 'objects have powers which are to be distinguished from their shape, size, motion and texture', she appeals to her interpretation of the lock and key passage: 'as we have seen in the example of the lock and key, Boyle does not want the distinction between corpuscles and their operations on other bodies to be the basis of a distinction between the material constitution of a body and some other feature or entity' (Keating 1993, p. 314). But this is just the point at issue in the interpretation of the lock and key passage! In the light of what Boyle says elsewhere, should we interpret this passage as claiming reduction? Clearly what is needed is not only a more subtle grasp of the polemical context of Boyle's lock and key analogy, but also an examination of the other passages in which Boyle speaks of qualities as relations and powers. It is to them that we now turn.

7 For distinctness: relative qualities

Surprisingly, much of what Boyle has to say about the relative nature of the sensible (and other) qualities in the *Forms and Qualities* is not to be found in the excursion, but comes after in sections V and VI. It is in these sections that Boyle emphasises and elaborates the point made in the excursion that if we are to understand the origin of qualities, 'we must consider each body not barely as it is in itself an entire and distinct portion of matter, but as it is a part of the universe' (*Works*, III, p. 20, *S*. p. 26).[42] Having restated this point at the beginning of section V he goes on to discuss it in relation to the sensible qualities in particular and tells us that the ideas we have of the sensible qualities are

> either the effects of our prejudices or inconsiderateness, or else to be fetched from the *relation* that happens to be betwixt those primary accidents of the sensible object and the peculiar texture of the organ it affects . . .
>
> (*Ibid.*, p. 23, *S*. pp. 31, italics added)

Unfortunately much of the force of this point in this section is lost because Boyle at the same time reverts to dealing with the 'real qualities' objection. But a similar thought is expressed more clearly in chapter IV of the 'History of Particular Qualities' where Boyle says,

> there may be certain other attributes [than texture] that we call *extra-essential*, which may be common to that body with many others, and upon which may depend those more external affections of the matter which may suffice to give it this or that relation to other bodies, <u>divers of which relations</u> we style *qualities*.
>
> (*Works*, III, p. 302, *S*. p. 113, underlining added)

He then goes on in this chapter to make the familiar point about the need to consider each body not in isolation, 'but as it is placed in and is a portion of the universe' (*Works*, III, p. 303, *S*. p. 114). However, that Boyle believed he had achieved an explication of the relative nature of the qualities of bodies in the *Forms and Qualities* is evidenced in a passing comment in the *Cosmical Qualities* where he tells us that

> I have in the Origin of Forms touched upon this subject already, . . . that which I principally (and yet but transiently) take notice of [there] is, that one body being surrounded with other bodies, is manifestly wrought on by many of those among whom it is placed . . .
>
> (*Works*, III, p. 307)

The purpose of the *Cosmical Qualities* was to take this point further and to consider qualities not simply as relations between the agent, patient and other surrounding bodies, but as relations where some of the relata are 'unheeded' or unknown, such as the invisible causes of magnetism. Now the import of all of these passages, not to mention the discussion of relative qualities in the 'Uses of Natural Things', is that Boyle considered the sensible (and other) qualities to be relations between the agent and the percipient (or patient) and that they are not simply dyadic relations, but often involve many more relata than simply the agent and patient. Now if this was Boyle's view, and as we have seen there is some textual evidence for it, then he can be seen to have been an early advocate of a relational account of the sensible qualities. In fact, to my knowledge, if this interpretation were to be correct, he would be the first proponent of the relational view.[43]

But what of the ontological status of the relations that are constitutive of the sensible qualities and what of their relation to powers? At times he speaks unambiguously as if powers and relations are different things. When speaking of the lodestone and needle in the 'Uses of Natural Things' he says,

> for a steel needle, being applied to a loadstone, manifested itself to be capable of constantly shewing the north and south in all seas . . . to navigators, who, by this property, which *depends upon the relation* that iron has to one only stone, have been able to discover the new world . . .
>
> (*Works*, III, p. 480, italics added)

And, as we have already seen, in the 'History of Particular Qualities' where Boyle especially has the sensible qualities in mind, he speaks of bodies being endowed with additional qualities *as a consequence* of standing in new relations (*ibid.*, p. 304, *S.* p. 115).[44] The most natural way to take both of these passages is that they imply distinctness; the powers seem to be something over and above the relations on which they depend. Such passages count against the reductive interpretation of Boyle (i.e. for (c) and (d) above).

However, there is a way in which the upholder of the reductive interpretation can reply to this relational interpretation. With regard to the distinctness of powers and relations they could, at the risk of anachronism, claim that Boyle quite understandably is here evidencing confusion because he lacks the distinction between supervenience and identity. On the one hand he recognises that powers seem to depend on relations and on the other he seems to think that they are the very same thing as relations. What better way to express this than to say that the power supervenes on the relation? But, they could continue, Boyle did not have the distinction between identity and supervenience and so his view is ostensibly inconsistent. Moreover, given the historical considerations outlined above (§4), even if Boyle held that the sensible qualities are relations, he most likely held a reductive account of those relations. It seems then, that these explicit references to the relational view in Boyle do little more than counter-balance the explicit references that support the reductionist thesis. Is there more to the case for distinctness?

8 For distinctness: Boylean powers and dispositions

One line of argument that O'Toole mobilises against the reductive thesis in Boyle has to do with what Boyle says about the nature of powers. In fact what Boyle has to say about powers and dispositions has sufficient intrinsic interest to make it worth digressing here to consider powers and dispositions in detail. In the *Forms and Qualities* and elsewhere Boyle speaks of the necessity of the existence of other bodies for the presence of a power. That is, both relata must be present and standing in some kind of relation for there to be a power in the agent. Boyle says that when Tubal Cain made his first lock,

> that was only a piece of iron contrived into such a shape; and when afterwards he made a key to that lock, that also in itself considered was nothing but a piece of iron of such a determinate figure. But in regard that these two pieces of iron might now be applied to one another after a certain manner, and that there was a congruity betwixt the wards of the lock and those of the key, the lock and key did each of them now *obtain a new capacity* . . .
>
> (*Works*, III, p. 18, S. p. 23, italics added)

This point is brought out more forcefully in the 'Uses of Natural Things' where Boyle says,

> . . . so most of those powers and other attributes, that we call qualities in bodies, depend so much upon the structure or constitutions of other bodies, that are disposed or indisposed to be acted on by them, that *if there were no such objects in the world*, those qualities in the bodies, that are said to be endowed with them, would be but aptitudes to work such effects . . . As if there were no lock in the world, a key would be but a piece of iron of such a determinate size and shape.
>
> (*Ibid.*, pp. 479–480, italics added)[45]

It is clear from these passages that Boyle saw the necessity of both relata for the presence of the power. Thus, supposing that powers are reducible to relations ((a) or (b) above), the primary affections of both the agent and the patient are, to use a modern expression, the categorical grounds of the power. Change the primary affections of either the agent or patient and you change the power of the agent. Boyle says that, 'that, which we consider, in a key, as the power or faculty of opening or shutting, supposes, and *depends upon* the lock, whereto it corresponds' ('Uses of Natural Things', *Works*, III, p. 479, italics added). Therefore, if one is to reduce this relation it will have to be reduced multilaterally.

All this sheds light on another feature of Boyle's discussions. He often speaks of both the agent and the patient as having powers. The key has the power to open the lock and the lock has the power to be opened by the key. Hence there is a symmetry in the manifestation of any power. Powers come in pairs. The patient is passively 'disposed' to be affected and the agent manifests its power to cause the effect. And so when they stand in a relation to each other Boyle can say that 'the lock and key did *each of them* now obtain a new capacity'.

But Boyle's extending of the grounding of dispositions to include all the relata led to, what might seem to us, a false view of the necessary conditions for the attribution of a power to a body. Boyle knew that if powers were to manifest themselves certain conditions must pertain. He also saw that dispositions can be unmanifested while certain conditions necessary for manifestation are present, in particular the existence of the relevant relata. And sometimes he even speaks of powers as if they are in some sense present even in the absence of one of the relata. He says,

> I do not deny but that bodies may be said in a very favourable sense to have those qualities we call *sensible*, though there were no animals in the world. For a body in that case may differ from those bodies which now are quite devoid of quality, in its having such a disposition of its constituent corpuscles that, in case it were duly applied to the sensory of an animal, it would produce such a sensible quality which a body of another texture would not . . .

Yet he concludes this paragraph by saying that when the percipient is absent, one can speak of the sensible qualities of an object as being there 'dispositively', that is potentially but not actually:

> if there were no sensitive beings, those bodies that are now the objects of our senses would be but *dispositively*, if I may so speak, endowed with colours, tastes and the like, and *actually* but only with those more catholic affections of bodies – figure, motion, texture, &c.
>
> (*Forms and Qualities, Works*, III, p. 25, *S*. pp. 33–34)[46]

E. M. Curley (1972, pp. 446ff) was the first to notice a tension here in Boyle's view of powers; a tension between the need for single or multiple categorical grounds. This is indicative of the fact that Boyle was 'feeling his way' so to speak in unchartered terrain here. Curley suggested a creative solution by drawing a distinction between individual and sortal powers. But regardless of how we might resolve the tension, the most frequently occurring view in Boyle is that the power is only present in the object in the presence of all the relevant relata. The repeated claim is that the power of the key to open the lock was only there when the key stood in an external relation to the lock, for 'if there were no lock in the world, a key would be but a piece of iron of such a determinate size and shape' ('Uses of Natural Things', *Works*, III, pp. 479–480).[47]

But why should this be? Why is the presence of the patient necessary for the existence of the power? In the light of the popular construal of dispositional properties today it might seem that Boyle has inadvertently linked a feature of the epistemology of power properties with the ontology of powers. It looks as though he thought that because the presence of the lock is necessary for our *knowledge* of the power of the key, it follows that the presence of the lock is necessary for the power to be there at all. In other words, Boyle has conflated the cause of knowledge of the power with the cause of the presence of the power. However, this is wrong. On the interpretation offered here, Boyle simply had a broader conception of what a disposition actually is than is current today. For Boyle, whose life was given over to the observation of chemical reactions and other complex natural phenomena, dispositions were exactly those active and passive powers that were grounded in the structural properties of both the agent and the patient (and possibly their relation to each other) when they exist together.

Moreover, if this is correct then Boyle had a rather different set of conditions of difference and continued existence for dispositions than those that are commonly accepted today. On the popular modern view, a particular differs in dispositional properties (in the same world) at different times if and only if there is a difference in underlying categorical properties. On Boyle's view a body with exactly the same structural properties (in the same world) at t_1 as at t_2 can differ in its dispositional properties if it stands in different relations.[48] As regards conditions for continued existence, the standard view has it that an unmanifested dispositional property is capable of continuing in existence in virtue of the continued existence of the primary properties of the agent. But on Boyle's view, not only is this condition required, but the continued existence of the disposition also depends upon the continued existence of the primary affections of the patient. However, with respect to the conditions for the manifestation of a disposition, Boyle's view and the modern view are identical.

Further, it is important to note that on this view of dispositions the sensible qualities are percipient-dependent. The powers of bodies to cause ideas of sensible qualities in us are only present when percipients exist. This is why Boyle says that the sensible qualities are explicated by a relation to our senses. But, returning to our main line of argument, even though Boyle seems to have thought that powers were grounded in both the agent and patient, this, *pace* O'Toole, is not enough to show that he could not have held some sort of reductive thesis about the sensibles. To be sure, Boyle would deny that powers were reducible to the mechanical affections of the *agent*. But that is just to say that Boyle denied unilateral reducibility. Given what Boyle says about powers, there is nothing preventing him from accepting their multilateral reducibility. This part of O'Toole's case against reduction fails.

There is, however, a rejoinder for O'Toole. We have seen above (§7) that there are some texts in which Boyle seems to treat powers and relations as ontologically distinct. They provide some grounds for the claim that, for Boyle, it is not only the relata that are necessary for the grounding of a power. If Boyle rejected the reducibility of powers to relations, ((c) or (d) above), then it may also be necessary that they stand in some spatio-temporal relation. On this view it is not enough, for Boyle, that the key should exist in one world and the lock in another. There needs to be a (external) relation between the two objects, say the lock and key, for any one of them to have a power. So, when Boyle says that 'powers depend upon' relations he is thinking of the relation as a ground of the power over and above the agent and patient as grounds of the relation. But notice that it is the distinctness relation (D) between the power and the relation that resists reduction and not the fact that Boyle's relations are multilaterally reducible. And we saw above that these 'apparent' references to the distinctness of powers and relations can be accommodated by a proponent of the reductive thesis. Is there a more decisive argument against (a) available?

9 For distinctness: Boyle's voluntarism

There is a strong argument for the ontological distinctness of sensible qualities from the mechanical affections of bodies and it resides in Boyle's theological voluntarism. In Boyle's voluntarism we find that the laws of nature are contingent and are expressions of the divine will.[49] They bear no necessary relation to the natures of objects and therefore to their mechanical affections. Boyle says,

> the laws of motion . . . did not necessarily spring from the nature of matter, but depended upon the will of the divine author of things . . .
>
> (*Christian Virtuoso, I, Works,* V, p. 521)

Thus God can deprive an object of a sensible quality merely by altering the laws of nature, as he does in the case of miracles. Boyle tells us that God has performed miracles 'sometimes by suspending the natural actings of bodies upon one another, and sometimes by *endowing* human and other bodies *with preternatural qualities*' (italics added). And he claims that this should not surprise us because

> it cannot be incredible that the most free and powerful Author of those laws of nature, according to which all the phenomena of qualities are regulated, may (as he thinks fit) introduce, establish or change them in any assigned portion of matter . . .
>
> ('Possibility of the Resurrection',
> *Works,* IV, p. 201, *S.* p. 207)[50]

This counts decisively against the reduction of powers to mechanical affections, that is against (a) above. For it shows that the existence of the mechanical affections of the agent is not sufficient for the existence of any non-mechanical property. Boyle believed that, given that the laws of nature are held constant, powers are 'deducible' from the natures of things. In fact, it was a desideratum of natural philosophy to discover what the natures of things were so as to under-stand and explain their powers. But all this is contingent on God's upholding of the present laws of nature – change the laws and the powers of bodies will change too.[51] Thus the sensible qualities of matter cannot be identical to the mechanical affections because they are contingent upon the laws of nature. It is clear then that (a) is inconsistent with Boyle's voluntarism. But his voluntarism is consistent with each of (b), (c) and (d).

10 Conclusion

Where does all this leave us? When Boyle says 'whereas we explicate colours, odours, and the like sensible qualities, by a *relation to our senses*, it seems evident that they have an absolute being irrelative to us . . .', he has nicely summed up the two seemingly incompatible views of the sensible qualities that are to be found in his works. First there is a version of categorical realism, (a), that posits that the sensible qualities are objective physical properties of bodies, properties that are reducible to the mechanical affections of matter. And then there is the relational view, (b), (c) or (d), that the sensible qualities are powers that relate the agent to the percipient. The first of these views finds support in explicit references in Boyle's works, in his treatment of particular qualities such as colour and in the deflationary view of relations that Boyle most likely held. But it is inconsistent with Boyle's theological voluntarism. The second view also finds support in explicit references and is consistent with both the detailed exegesis of the *Forms and Qualities* offered above and the theory of laws of nature that is such an integral part of Boyle's natural philosophy.

But how are we to reconcile the two views in Boyle? A first suggestion might be to claim that the incompatibility is merely apparent, that Boyle's talk of properties in categorical and relational/dispositional terms simply reflects different ways of talking about the same properties. Perhaps Boyle held the 'Janus-faced' view of properties advocated by C. B. Martin, holding that every property has a categorical and dispositional side.[52] But this is at best speculative and at worst anachronistic. And this two-sided notion of properties itself is desperately in need of further explication. Moreover, even if this were the case, there remains the problem of harmonising what Boyle says about the sensibles with his voluntarism.

A more promising line is to ask what was Boyle's project and aim in his discussions of the sensible qualities? And which of the two views is most consistent with those aims? Here we can take the *Forms and Qualities*, the 'History of Particular Qualities' and the *Cosmical Qualities* as a unit. They are part of a larger project of Boyle's to provide a systematic, theoretical account and an experimental history of the qualities of bodies. The two latter works both refer back to the *Forms and Qualities*[53] and the aim of *Forms and Qualities*, reiterated in part in the 'History of Particular Qualities', is to give an account of the origin of qualities that is consistent with the corpuscular hypothesis. This involved a polemical component, arguing against the schoolmen and the chemists, a theoretical component and an experimental component. Boyle is at pains to emphasise that he intends to show how the qualities of bodies '*may* be produced mechanically' solely by changes in the '*texture*, or *motion*, or some other *mechanical affection*, of the body wrought upon' (*Forms and Qualities*, *Works*, III, p. 13, *S.* p. 17). This would incline one to think that Boyle aims systematically to reduce the non-mechanical to the mechanical qualities. And yet it is in these very works that he spells out the relational nature of the qualities. I infer from this that Boyle's discussions of the relational nature of the sensible qualities are neither peripheral nor tangential to his overall project, but rather an integral part of it. It seems then, that in unravelling Boyle's views on the sensible qualities, we have uncovered two incompatible and irreconcilable aspects of his thought. If the foregoing analysis is correct, then there is little prospect of offering a fully consistent interpretation of his doctrine of the sensible qualities without turning a blind eye to important texts. I conclude that with regard to the ontological status of the sensible qualities, it is unlikely that there is a definitive Boylean view of the matter.

What then can be gleaned from our discussion of Boyle's views on the ontological status of the sensible qualities? There are three points that I would like to make in conclusion. First, it is clear that much of the secondary literature on this topic has been too narrow in its scope, both with regard to the selection of texts on which to base interpretations and with regard to its appreciation of the range of philosophical issues that arise out of Boyle's discussions. Second, it is hoped that, for anyone with even a superficial knowledge of Locke's *Essay*, the foregoing discussion has illustrated just how great is the difference between Locke and Boyle in their approaches to the issue of the nature of the sensible qualities. Boyle's interest in the sensibles arose out of his desire to explicate all the qualities of bodies according to the corpuscular hypothesis and to present experimental histories of those qualities. For he firmly believed that a corpuscular account of the qualities was at least as coherent, if not more so, than that offered by the chemists and the schools. Thus Boyle's aim in explicating the sensible qualities was not epistemological, though at times in the *Forms and Qualities* epistemological considerations intrude. By contrast, Locke's discussions are all in an epistemological context. Moreover, this has an important bearing on how we should conceive the history of the primary and secondary quality distinction to bear on the current debate over secondary qualities. A. D. Smith has recently argued (1990, p. 222 and p. 223) that the categorical realist position of D. M. Armstrong and J. J. C. Smart

> is out of touch with the traditional distinction. For the principal concern of writers such as these is with the question of, for example, whether the objects that are agreed to be red share an objective scientifically specifiable physical property.

And that 'the issues they address are but tangentially related to what the notions of primary and secondary qualities have meant to the history of philosophy'. Yet as we have seen this is precisely the issue that Boyle took upon himself to address. Far from being tangential, the recent advocates of categorical realism should be seen as reviving an approach to the issue that was explored in depth by Boyle.

And this brings us to my third and final point. I hope that it is evident from the foregoing discussion that Boyle's works, while not furnishing us with a definitive view as to the ontological status of the sensible qualities, are a remarkably fertile source of discussion of many of the central issues that pertain to the nature of the sensible qualities. Boyle was the first English speaker to explore the contours of the problem, the first to be pulled at one time toward dispositionalism and at another toward categoricalism. And for that reason alone his works repay careful study.

Notes

1 In the very next paragraph Boyle says 'I take most of the qualities of natural bodies to be but relative things.'

2 See also *Works*, III, p. 302, *S.* p. 113.

3 See *Forms and Qualities*, *Works*, III, pp. 18–22, *S.* pp. 23–30.

4 See also *ibid.*, p. 22, *S.* p. 30: 'a certain disposition or contrivance of parts in the whole, which we may call the *texture* of it'. This sense is equivalent to the sense of *dispositio* among the scholastics and is ultimately derived from Aristotle's *Metaphysics* V, 1022^b1ff, *Barnes*, II, p. 1614.

5 In this instance 'disposition' refers to an active power. But in most uses of the word with this sense akin to the modern 'dispositional property' he has in mind passive powers such as mercury's 'disposition to be dissolved by aqua fortis'. For a juxtaposition of these two different senses of 'disposition' see *Cosmical Qualities*, *Works*, III, pp. 306–307. For an instance of the use of 'disposition' in the sense of power in a passage that does not concern the corpuscular philosophy see *Final Causes*, *Works*, V, p. 438 where Boyle speaks of 'the disposition of the cameleon to change colours'. For the same two senses of 'disposition' in Charleton see *Physiologia*, pp. 186–187.

6 There is an interesting etymological question as to whether the sense of 'disposition' in 'dispositional property' is derived from the use of the word to mean texture or arrangement. Consider for example this passage from Charleton: 'For, as the several *Pipes* in an Organ, though in themselves all equally *Insonorous*, or destitute of sound, have yet an equal Disposition, in respect of their Figuration, to yield a sound, upon the inflation of Wind from the Bellows' (*Physiologia*, p. 186). If so, then the idea of a property base of a disposition in the sense of power was built into the usage of the word in the sense of power from the outset. It would also be interesting to ascertain whether Charleton is the first writer in English to use the word in both senses. A further question that warrants investigation is the extent to which Boyle's notion of dispositions derived from Descartes' doctrine of *dispositio*.

7 The distinction is noted by F. J. O'Toole 1974, p. 306 and L. Keating 1993, p. 315.

8 See the highlighted quotes above.

9 See for instance *Forms and Qualities*, *Works*, III, p. 24, p. 26, p. 28 and p. 36, *S.* p. 32, p. 36, p. 40 and p. 51, and *Mechanical Qualities*, *Works*, IV, p. 260.

10 Boyle also admitted substances into his ontology. He held a substance/attribute distinction that was very similar to that of Descartes. See *Forms and Qualities*, *Works*, III, p. 40, *S*. p. 57, 'Advices', *Works*, IV, p. 461 and *Christian Virtuoso*, I, *Appendix*, *Works*, VI, p. 697 which probably draw on Descartes' *Principles*, I, §51, *CSM*, I, p. 210.

11 See for example *Forms and Qualities*, *Works*, III, p. 21, *S*. p. 27.

12 D. M. Armstrong 1987 and F. Jackson and R. Pargetter 1987.

13 A further relation, supervenience, is frequently appealed to in modern discussions of ontological reduction. Since Boyle had no such relation it will not be discussed here.

14 This distinction is found in R. Langton 1993, pp. 72–73 who has adapted some terminology from K. K. Campbell 1990, pp. 104–106.

15 *Pace* R. Langton who claims that 'The thesis that no relations are unilaterally reducible is true, and analytically so' (1993, p. 74). Langton's claim however does seem true for external relations.

16 It should also be pointed out that it is consistent with J. Bennett's suggested interpretation of Locke on relations. See Bennett 1971, p. 254. For a useful critique of this interpretation of Locke see R. Langton 1993.

17 P. Alexander 1985, p. 80–82. A. Pyle 1995 follows Alexander (see pp. 544–546). M. A. Stewart agrees with P. Alexander on the reduction of powers to textures (see his 1987, pp. 114–115 and his 1991, p. xiv and p. xviii for his general acceptance of the reductive thesis). Another exponent of the reductionist interpretation is E. McMullin (see his 1978a, pp. 36–38). See also L. Keating 1993, pp. 308–309 and p. 314 though of course she does not believe that the sensible qualities are so reducible.

18 A precedent for the view may be found in Descartes' comment in the *Principles* that 'the properties in external objects to which we apply the terms light, colour, smell, taste, sound, heat and cold . . . are, so far as we can see, simply various dispositions [*diverses figures, situations, grandeurs et mouvements de leur parties*] in those objects which make them able to set up various kinds of motions in our nerves which are required to produce all the various sensations in our soul' (*CSM*, I, p. 285; the French is from *AT*, VIII, p. 323).

19 D. M. Armstrong, F. Jackson and R. Pargetter have already been instanced as proponents of this view (see n. 12).

20 See F. J. O'Toole 1974, pp. 309–310.

21 See also *Forms and Qualities*, *Works*, III, p. 25, *S*. p. 35.

22 See also *Cosmical Qualities*, *Works*, III, p. 306.

23 K. Olsen 1987, chapter 2 and J. Weinberg 1965, pp. 61ff.

24 Boyle says, 'after all I have said of colour, as it is modified light, and immediately affects the sensory, I shall now remind you, that I did not deny, but that colour might in some sense be considered as a quality residing in the body that is said to be coloured; and indeed the greatest part of the following experiments refer to colour principally under that notion . . .', *Colours*, *Works*, I, p. 674.

25 See *ibid.*, *Works*, I, p. 706 and p. 708.

26 See *ibid.*, p. 695. Perhaps the 'unimaginably subtle corpuscles that make up the beams of light' (p. 689) for Boyle are atomic. If so, then texture would play no role in their reductive analysis.

27 Note the close parallels of expression in Cudworth's *True Intellectual System*, I, Preface, p. 54: 'the qualities and forms of inanimate bodies are no entities really

distinct from the magnitude, figure, site and motion of parts' (note that 'sight' in this edition has been corrected by 'site' which is original).

28 See for example L. Keating 1993, pp. 307–308, p. 310 and p. 314. As for P. Alexander's view (1985, pp. 48–51) that Boyle was accusing the schoolmen of assimilating real qualities to substantial forms, he seems to have it the wrong way around. Rather than the scholastics identifying form with accidents, this was precisely the move that Boyle himself (following Descartes) made. He identified form with figure which is an accident of bodies. In fact, contrary to what Alexander claims, Boyle acknowledges that the schoolmen were careful 'lest they should make forms to be but accidents' (*Forms and Qualities*, *Works*, III, p. 39, *S*. p. 55). The only sense in which Boyle thinks that the forms of the schoolmen are like accidents is that their dependence on matter is somewhat analogous to the dependence of accidents on substance (*Forms and Qualities*, *Works*, III, p. 40, *S*. p. 57). But it is the lack of this very dependence which is the distinguishing mark of the real qualities. Another who misses the dialectical context entirely is F. J. O'Toole who says '[t]he theory of qualities which Galileo and Boyle rejected is essentially the view of scientifically unsophisticated common sense' (1974, p. 301).

29 I have chosen to focus on Suárez first, because he is the Aristotelian whom Boyle quotes and was renowned for his doctrine of real qualities, and second, because of his profound influence on Descartes who in turn influenced Boyle.

30 See Suárez, *Disputationes Metaphysicæ*, 33, §1.

31 See *Forms and Qualities*, *Works*, III, p. 40, *S*. p. 57 and pp. 16–17, *S*. p. 21. Thus J. Williamson (1990) is wrong to claim that for Boyle substance is just homogeneous matter. Substance/attribute ontologies were widely held in Boyle's time. Hobbes, for instance, in his *A Short Tract on First Principles*, claims that 'Everything is either substance or accident' (see R. S. Peters 1962, p. 164).

32 See *Forms and Qualities*, *Works*, III, p. 40, *S*. p. 57 and *Notion of Nature*, *Works*, V, p. 241 and p. 243.

33 See *Forms and Qualities*, *Works*, III, p. 27, *S*. p. 37 where the mechanical affections are in view.

34 See *ibid.*, p. 16, *S*. pp. 20–21. Boyle's modes differ from those of Descartes. For Descartes modes are those accidents which are subject to variation, whereas for Boyle the shape and size of elementary corpuscles are modes but remain invariant. See the discussion of Descartes' modes in A. Gabbey 1980, p. 237. For Digby's rejection of modes see *Two Treatises*, p. 40.

35 For Descartes see *Principles*, I, §60, *CSM*, I, p. 213. For Boyle's lapse on this point see *Forms and Qualities*, *Works*, III, p. 23, *S*. p. 31.

36 For Boyle's resistance to calling modes qualities see especially 'History of Particular Qualities', *Works*, III, p. 292, *S*. p. 97 and chapter 2, n. 1. For Berkeley see *The Principles of Human Knowledge*, §7 and §9, in Berkeley 1965, pp. 47–48. Whether or not Berkeley knew of the rich history of the terms, his usage is entirely consonant with his collapsing of the primary and secondary quality distinction.

37 The view that accidents can exist separately from substance can be traced back at least as far as Suárez. See his *Disputationes Metaphysicæ*, 40, §2, 8, pp. 255ff. See *Forms and Qualities*, *Works*, III, p. 7, *S*. p. 8 n. *a* for Boyle's reference to this doctrine in Suárez.

38 In section V of *Notion of Nature* (*Works*, V, p. 190), which was written in the early 1660s most likely before the publication of *Forms and Qualities* (M. Hunter and E. B. Davis 1996, pp. 230–231), Boyle claims that some schoolmen call real

qualities 'semi-substantia'. This category is supposedly intermediate between the corporeal and incorporeal. There Boyle tells us that 'I acknowledge no such chimerical and unintelligible beings.'

39 From a Cartesian viewpoint Boyle is correct in rejecting real qualities. However, as it stands this is not an argument against real qualities, but merely a statement of the difference between the two ontologies, his and Suárez's. For Descartes' arguments against real qualities see his *Replies to the Sixth set of objections*, *CSM*, II, p. 293 and his *Letter to Mersenne* of 26 April 1643 in *CSMK*, p. 216. We should also note here in passing that if Boyle intends to give a fully reductive account of the sensibles it is highly inappropriate of him to use the quality whiteness to illustrate the nature of accidents. For a colour quality would just be identical with some mechanical properties of an object. But Boyle uses colour as a contrast to 'real' qualities. It is a property with its own ontological status, but not the status of a substance.

40 See also P. Alexander 1974, p. 233.

41 It is important to note that in Locke the term had lost its Suaracian connotations to the extent that, in the *Essay*, he could speak of the primary qualities as real qualities. He says, '[t]he particular *Bulk, Number, Figure, and Motion of the parts of Fire, or Snow, are really in them*, whether any ones Senses perceive them or no: and therefore they may be called real Qualities, because they really exist in those Bodies . . .' (*Essay*, II, viii, §17).

42 P. Alexander is incorrect when he claims that one of the points of the digression about the relative nature of the qualities is that 'all qualities are relative to something material that has them; he is denying "that a quality or other accident may subsist without a subject"' (1974, p. 231). If this was Boyle's point it would apply equally to the mechanical affections of matter, whereas the section deals specifically with 'the qualities', that is the non-mechanical qualities of matter.

43 For a recent relational account of colour see E. W. Averill 1992.

44 See also 'History of Particular Qualities', *Works*, III, p. 302, *S*. p. 113.

45 The word 'depend' in the second line of this quote is incorrectly written as 'depends' in *Works*. I have changed it to 'depend' which is the reading found in *Works (1744)*, III, p. 192. See also *Notion of Nature*, *Works*, V, p. 247 where Boyle says 'a key may acquire or lose its power of opening a door'.

46 Pages 23–27 (*S*. pp. 32–35) of the *Forms and Qualities* deal specifically with this issue. See also 'Uses of Natural Things', *Works*, III, p. 479.

47 Boyle's view is contrasted with that of Charleton who claims that objects in the dark 'have a *Disposition* to exhibit this or that particular Colour, upon the access of the Producent, Light' (*Physiologia*, p. 186).

48 *Pace* P. Alexander 1974, p. 230. See *Cosmical Qualities*, *Works*, III, p. 306.

49 See for instance *Christian Virtuoso*, I, Appendix, *Works*, VI, p. 714: 'the laws of nature, as they were at first arbitrarily instituted by God, so, in reference to him, they are but arbitrary still'. See also *ibid.*, p. 679 and *Notion of Nature*, *Works*, V, p. 170, *S*. p. 181. For a more detailed discussion of the contingency of laws see chapter 7, §6.

50 In one of his notebooks Boyle tells us that there is 'no cause why blew & yellow for instance should make a green & not a pink nor a purple colour, but the laws which God freely establisht' (*Royal Society MS 185*). I am indebted to Michael Hunter for this reference.

51   Margaret Wilson (1979) and Edwin McCann (1985a) find a similar doctrine in Locke, but Wilson has overlooked its presence in Boyle. For criticisms of Wilson and McCann's interpretation of Locke see M. Ayers 1991, I, pp. 145–153.
52   See C. B. Martin 1993, p. 184.
53   See 'History of Particular Qualities', *Works*, III, p. 292 and p. 296, *S*. p. 97 and p. 103 and *Cosmical Qualities*, *Works*, III, p. 307.

Part II
Matter in motion

5 Natural and violent states and motions

Having set out Boyle's theory of the qualities of bodies, we are now in a position to embark on an exposition of how the various components of his corpuscular hypothesis fit together. We are now well placed to map out the nature and scope of Boyle's mechanism. In order to do so we will first examine Boyle's understanding of the nature of motion with particular reference to his rejection of the scholastic distinction between natural and violent states. We will then turn to his conceptions of space, laws of nature and finally to the issue of mind/body interaction.

An examination of these issues will enable us to determine the extent to which Boyle broke from scholastic physics and embraced and championed the mechanical philosophy. It will also enable us to see that Boyle's mechanism was not simply created in the image of Descartes' but had its own distinctive stamp and idiosyncrasies. For example, our discussion of his views on the nature of place and laws reveals that Boyle's cosmology was decidedly non-Cartesian and that the self-styled Christian virtuoso developed a unique account of the relation of God to the created order. This is an account that invokes a peculiar conception of laws of nature and one that is particularly sensitive to the theological problems that beset the mechanical philosophy.

Our immediate concern however is with Boyle's understanding of the concept of motion. And here, surprisingly, we encounter an issue of some interest to historians of science. For Boyle stands in a transitional phase in the emergence of a clear conception of motion, in particular a clear concept of inertial motion. Much ground had been made by Galileo and Descartes, but in a number of areas scholastic conceptions still muddied the waters in the mid-seventeenth century. The distinction between natural and violent motions still held sway in many quarters and a related distinction between natural and violent states was widely held. Both of these distinctions would have to be completely expunged before a clear conception of inertial motion could emerge. Indicative of this transitional phase is the fact that writers like Hobbes, Wallis and even Boyle often articulate laws of nature that seem at first sight to be approximations of, or precursors to, Newton's first law. For example in the *Boyle Papers*, when discussing problems with the Epicurean concept of *motion*, Boyle speaks of one of the most fundamentall Customes or Laws of nature, which is *that every undivided Body will alwayes continue in that state wherein it is, unless it be put* out of it by some Externall force . . .

(*BP*, vol. 2, fol. 6)

When pressed, however, it is clear that inertial motion is not in the minds of these writers at all. What we do find in Boyle, is a concerted attack on the notions of natural and violent motions and natural and violent states. And although there is no evidence that this had any influence on the young Newton, what is does show is Boyle's involvement in another phase of the assault on scholastic physics; a phase that, to my knowledge, has not been documented and a phase which forms another strand in the articulation of the mechanical philosophy.

1 Sources of Boyle's views on motion

Boyle certainly saw himself as a recipient of a long tradition of theorising about the nature of local motion. In criticising Hobbes he asks why Hobbes

sends us to his own writings for the doctrine of motion; as if, to omit antienter authors, such great personages as *Galilæo, Mersennus, Verulam, Des Cartes, Gassendus, Balianus, Johannes Marcus Marci, Honoratus Fabri* (not to mention other moderns, nor those of our own assembly, as the eminently-learned Sir *Kenelme Digby*, and the others, whom their modesty forbids me here to name) . . .

(*Examen, Works*, I, p. 233)

This list gives us some insight into the sources of his own views on motion. We know that he read Galileo in Italian,[1] that he read Mersenne, Gassendi and Hobbes, but without a doubt his conception of motion owed most to Descartes. He read, amongst other works, Descartes' *Principles* to which he frequently refers. In addition to the work of Galileo and Descartes, significant developments in the field of mechanics occurred during Boyle's lifetime,[2] and there is evidence that Boyle read some of these. He was in a good position to get access to much of this work. For example, he knew Wallis personally,[3] he corresponded with Newton and he would have kept abreast of developments in the field from Oldenburg and the *Philosophical Transactions*. But Boyle's scientific concerns were more closely tied to the explication of the qualities of bodies and he did not have a sustained interest in the quantitative aspects of mechanics. His interest in motion arose in so far as his corpuscular hypothesis aimed to furnish explanations of the qualities in terms of mechanical principles which included motion.

In the final analysis, Boyle seems to have adopted the attitude that the explication of motion is an ongoing philosophical problem that is best left to the experts, that is, the mathematicians and specialists in mechanics.[4] Yet the concept of motion was central to his corpuscular philosophy. Motion and matter are the two grand principles of that philosophy. He tells us a number of times that, 'local motion seems to be indeed the principal amongst second causes, and the grand agent of all that happens in nature' (*Forms and Qualities*, *Works*, III, p. 15, *S*. p. 19)[5] and that he is endeavouring 'to resolve the phenomena of nature into matter and local motion' (*Languid Motion*, *Works*, V, p. 2).

2   The concept of motion

Boyle is not known to have made any contribution to the development of the concept of motion and it certainly seems that he never attempted to. The only experiments he appears to have made merely confirm the observations of others.[6] The reasons for this are twofold. First, as noted above, the primary focus of Boyle's corpuscular philosophy was the explication of the qualities of bodies instead of the development of a mechanics.[7] Second, in contrast to Descartes, Boyle's views on motion were set in a far less ambitious scientific epistemology. Where Descartes considered his own notion of motion to be perfectly clear,[8] Boyle saw the concept of motion and the closely related concepts of space and time as both rich and difficult to explicate. He speaks in numerous contexts of how hard it is to get a clear notion of each of them. Of local motion he says,

> as for that most familiar thing local motion, though modern as well as ancient philosophers and mathematicians have bestowed much time, and great pains, to explicate the nature of it; yet by arguing even about a thing, that those who have not examined it presume they know very well, we may bring our understandings into perplexities from whence they will scarce be able to extricate themselves . . .
> (*Christian Virtuoso*, *I*, *Appendix*, *Works*, VI, pp. 692–693)[9]

In fact he sometimes uses these difficult concepts as examples when discussing incomprehensibility and things that are above or beyond human reason.[10] And yet he thought that these notions were the fundamental or 'primordial' conceptions in terms of which most other phenomena are to be explicated (*Christian Virtuoso*, *I*, *Appendix*, *Works*, VI, p. 692).

Thus Boyle should not be taken to have had a naive conception of motion, nor to have thought that the notion is unproblematic. To be sure, he does not engage the sort of philosophical questions that occupied Gassendi, Charleton and the young Newton in any depth or with a view to reaching a definitive position (i.e. as to whether matter is infinitely divisible, as to whether atoms are to be considered as mathematical points, as to whether time is unitary or continuous). But this is not to say Boyle was ignorant of these disputes. He frequently mentions them, yet he never discusses them in any depth nor sides with a particular view. As we have seen (chapter 2, §2.1), he prefers to 'sit on the fence' in the dispute over divisibility of matter. He was well aware of the problems posed by the Zenonian paradoxes of motion. But he took a very pragmatic, even Moorean, attitude towards them:

> because we can walk up and down, and so remove our bodies from place to place; by this one argument, I say, we are justly satisfied, that there is a local motion in the world, notwithstanding all the specious and subtil arguments, that *Zeno* and his followers have employed to impugn that truth . . .
>
> ('Theological Distinction', *Works*, V, p. 549)[11]

Since Boyle was a mechanical philosopher it is not surprising to find that the most salient feature of his departure from the Aristotelian concept of motion is that which is virtually axiomatic for any seventeenth-century mechanist, viz. the delimiting of *motus* to local motion, or as Boyle sometimes calls it, *lation*. He claims that there are 'six kinds of motion reckoned up by Aristotle and his followers' and that one of the great virtues of the corpuscular philosophy is its economy in being able to explain the same phenomena as the Aristotelians explain, but with recourse to only one kind of motion ('History of Particular Qualities', *Works*, III, p. 297, *S*. p. 105).[12] The six kinds of motion or *kinêsis* include *generation* and *corruption*[13] which involve change of substance and *alteration* which involves change of quality. But Boyle, in contrast to Aristotle, admits only one kind of corporeal substance, matter, and denies that substantial forms are in any sense ontologically distinct from matter. Furthermore, it is constitutive of the corpuscular hypothesis that all qualitative change resulted from changes in the mechanical affections of matter. Therefore, generation, corruption and alteration are all reduced to the transposition of corpuscles. Of generation he says,

> no new *substance* is in generation *produced*, but only that which was *pre-existent* obtains a new *modification* or manner of existence.
>
> (*Forms and Qualities*, *Works*, III, p. 32, *S*. p. 45)

As for the alteration of quantity which issues in the remaining two types of Aristotelian motion, *augmentation* and *diminution*, this is also the result of the transposition of corpuscles by local motion. Thus, in effect, the six Aristotelian motions are reducible to one, lation or local motion. Of course this reduction is predicated upon the rejection by Boyle of the Aristotelian doctrines of matter, form and substance and his acceptance, in their stead, of (something approximating to) the Cartesian definition of matter as extension and Descartes' equating of form with figure.[14] Indeed the debt to Descartes goes even further. In 'Advices', Boyle tells us that he prefers Descartes' definition of motion to that of Aristotle. The immediate context is a discussion of the fact that certain things should not be considered to be substances. Boyle has in mind such 'successive beings' as time and motion. In discussing motion, he explores the implications of the Aristotelian and Cartesian definitions for the question as to whether or not the world can move. He claims that according to some modern Aristotelians

> that approve *Descartes's* definition of local motion, (which indeed is far more intelligible than *Aristotle's*) the world may be said to move without changing of place; for it does not <u>pass from the neighbourhood of some bodies to that of others</u>, since comprising all bodies, and yet being bounded, there is no body for it to leave behind, nor any beyond it for it to approach to.
>
> ('Advices', *Works*, IV, p. 459, underlining added)[15]

Now the thought here is quite compressed, but the underlined words are clearly a loose rendering of the definition of motion given in Descartes' *Principles*, II, §25 where he says,

> motion is the <u>transfer</u> of one piece of matter, or one body, <u>from the vicinity of the other bodies</u> which are in immediate contact with it, and which are regarded as being at rest, <u>to the vicinity of other bodies</u>.
>
> (*CSM*, I, p. 233, underlining added)[16]

Just what Boyle understood by Descartes' definition, and for that matter Aristotle's, is an issue to which we will return shortly. However, it is enough at this stage to notice Boyle's explicit preference for the Cartesian conception as opposed to the Aristotelian one.

Another aspect of the Aristotelian doctrine of motion about which Boyle has much to say and which he explicitly rejects is the distinction between natural and violent *motions*. This is important because the doctrine of natural and violent motions is antithetical to the principle of inertia and was a major stumbling block to the emergence of a clear understanding of inertia until late in the seventeenth century. The Aristotelian doctrine of natural and violent motions was predicated on two notions. The first was that there is a terminus to every process of change in the terrestrial realm and that change of place, i.e. local motion, is a process of change. Therefore all local motion must come to an end.[17] One can easily see the importance of the rejection of this principle by comparing the idea of a terminus to the principle of inertia. This latter principle is that a body in a state of uniform rectilinear motion (or rest) in the absence of other forces, is not undergoing change and will continue in motion (or rest) forever. The second notion on which Aristotle's doctrine of natural and violent motions was predicated is that every body has a natural place. This chapter will focus on Boyle's rejection of the first Aristotelian notion, that of the terminus. Boyle's rejection of natural places will be discussed in the following chapter.

The distinction between natural and violent motions was widely held throughout the seventeenth century.[18] It was a crucial constituent of any scholastic's armoury, but a version of it was also upheld by the likes of Gassendi and Charleton, two staunch opponents of the peripatetic philosophy. A measure of just how ubiquitous the distinction was can be seen in the way Boyle, who actually rejected the distinction, still adverts to the natural and violent terminology to describe motions and how the young Newton recorded his early musings on motion under the title 'Of violent motion'.[19] The term 'violent motion' remained in common parlance amongst natural philosophers until late in the century. Opposition to the distinction can be traced back at least to Galileo who claimed that it was incoherent and that it admitted exceptions.[20] Yet his view was closer to Aristotle's than the rhetoric suggests.[21] Another who rejected the distinction was Descartes. So when we come to discuss Boyle's position, I believe that it is best to conceive of him as continuing a line of opposition that was gathering strength and would, in Newton, find its ultimate vindication.[22]

Now what is interesting in Boyle's discussion of the distinction between natural and violent *motions*, is the extremely close parallels it has with his discussion of another scholastic distinction, one that also played an important role in seventeenth-century philosophy. It is the distinction between natural and violent *states*. In fact, one cannot understand Boyle's views on the latter without unpacking what he has to say on the former. I aim to show below that in Boyle's mechanical philosophy we can discern a shift from the scholastic notion of the perseverance of the *status* of a body, toward the Newtonian concept of a body persevering in a state of motion or rest.

This was no trivial matter in the emergence of a clear conception of inertial motion. It may be that Boyle was not clear on the primacy of rectilinear motion over circular motion and that he had no significant conception of force, but his thought on motion represents a transitional stage in the emergence of a new conception of the state of a body. And while this was simply a concomitant of the application of his corpuscular philosophy to natural phenomena and not the product of an intentional quest to clarify the concept of motion, it represents one of the few ways in which British mechanism made an important, though minor, contribution to the clarification of the concept of motion before Newton. For it provided one more piece of the complex intellectual fabric that formed the context within which Newton worked. To be sure, much of the groundwork had already been laid out by Descartes. As Koyré (1965, p. 69) has pointed out, Descartes was the first to speak of '*states* of motion and rest' in anything like the modern sense. But it took a number of generations for the full implications of Descartes' insights to be exploited and for the underlying Cartesian conceptual framework to be transformed.[23] And this is where the corpuscularianism of natural philosophers such as Robert Boyle played its part.

I begin by setting Boyle's views in some historical context. In doing so I hope to clarify the nature of the doctrine Boyle was opposing and to reveal what were the positive influences on Boyle's thought. First, I shall sketch the Aristotelian doctrine of natural and violent motions and then discuss how Gassendi and Charleton modified it to suit their atomism. I shall then proceed to outline the grounds for Descartes' opposition to the distinction and will discuss his comments on natural and violent states. Finally, I shall turn to

Boyle. He has a whole series of objections to both distinctions. We shall look at each in turn, and then make an assessment of the significance of Boyle's discussion.

3 The Aristotelian distinction

The distinction between natural and violent motions was a central plank of Aristotle's physics. It pertains to local motion and is fully integrated into both Aristotle's doctrine of the four elements and his cosmology with its theory of natural place. The doctrine, as outlined in *Physics*, VIII, is rather complicated because Aristotle, in explicating the difference between natural and violent motions, is attempting to do three things. First, he wants to distinguish between the motion of animate and inanimate bodies; second, he wants to explain what it is that causes inanimate objects to move, either naturally or violently; and third, he wants to argue for the Platonic doctrine that nothing moves without a mover. On the first count, Aristotle distinguishes between the natural motion of animate things and the unnatural motion of inanimate things by claiming that for the former, their motion is derived from themselves, it is internal. By contrast the motion of inanimate objects is derived from something else, it is external. Animate bodies have within themselves the source of their own natural motion, the soul, and this sets them apart from inanimate bodies which lack souls. It remains then to explain the motion of inanimate bodies.

It is perhaps best to begin our brief sketch of the motion of inanimate bodies with the four element theory and Aristotle's cosmology. The cosmos, for Aristotle, contains the sub-lunary sphere which is made of terrestrial matter. It is to be sharply differentiated from the celestial realm. The matter and motion of the celestial realm differ from that of the cosmos. Everything in it moves in circular motion and is made of a fifth element not found in the terrestrial sphere. The celestial realm is importantly related to the terrestrial, but it is only to the latter that the distinction between natural and violent motions pertains.

For the Stagirite there are four elements in the terrestrial realm: earth, air, fire and water. Each of these has its natural place within the cosmos. Earth has its natural place in the centre, or rather, the centre of the cosmos is where earth is. Fire's natural place is on the outer ring of the cosmos and water and air are the intermediate elements with their natural places in between earth and fire. The idealised form of this cosmology is best conceived as four concentric spherical layers, each one representing a different element.[24] Now Aristotle tells us that '[w]hen these things [elements] are in motion to positions the reverse of those they would properly occupy, their motion is violent: when they are in motion to their proper positions – the light thing up and the heavy thing down – their motion is natural . . .' (*Physics*, VIII, 4, 255ᵃ3–5, *Barnes*, I, p. 426). The obvious question then is, in virtue of what do bodies move to their natural place? Here Aristotle has a number of answers.

On the one hand natural places exert a certain influence on the elements. Perhaps this is best thought of as a final cause of their motion.[25] But another reason why bodies move to their natural places is because of their own inner nature. Aristotle asks 'how can we account for (διὰ τί) the motion of light things and heavy things to their proper places? The reason for it is that they have a natural tendency toward a certain position; and this is what it is to be light or heavy, the former being determined by an upward, the latter by a downward tendency' (*Physics*, VIII, 4, 255^{b}13ff, *Barnes*, I, p. 427). But this natural tendency is not to be thought of as an active cause of their motion, because this would furnish inanimate bodies with some sort of internal source of motion and therefore undermine the distinction between the motions of animate and inanimate bodies. So Aristotle regarded the internal natures of elemental bodies as being passive causes. However, it is important to note that by the seventeenth century the passivity of the internal cause of motion had been lost sight of. Instead, bodies were thought to possess a form or appetite which was an active cause of their movement.[26] But Aristotle, in order to provide an active cause of the motion of inanimate bodies, introduces both a generating cause – the person who boils the kettle in the case of water boiling – and an obstacle-removing cause – the person who pulls away the pillar and so 'causes' the object to fall.[27]

So much for the causes of natural motion in inanimate bodies. What of the cause of unnatural or violent motion? Here Aristotle furnishes us with a notoriously unsatisfactory answer. Since he is committed both to the Platonic principle that every motion has a mover and the impossibility of action at a distance, he believes that the motor must be in constant contact with the thing moved. So when a projectile is thrown, its first motor is the hand of the thrower, then having been released, the air behind the object becomes the motor because the hand imparts to the adjacent layers of air a power to keep the projectile in motion. There is thus a kind of chain of transfer of power to each successive layer of the medium as it comes in contact with the projectile.[28] Aristotle's theory was seen to be inadequate and was eventually replaced by Philoponus' theory of impetus, of which the central idea was that a force to remain in motion is imparted from the original motor into the projectile itself rather than a power to set something in motion being imparted to the medium. But the issue remained alive down to the time of Newton and so we find that it is the subject of his youthful 'Of violent motions'.

Now there are three features of Aristotle's doctrine of natural and violent motions which will play an important role in our ensuing discussion. The first is the idea of a *terminus*. According to the Stagirite, all motion tends to a terminus. That is, all local motion, whether violent or natural, comes to an end in nature. Violent motion is 'opposed' by nature. In fact it is a principle of nature that *nullum violentum durabile* – nothing violent endures. Violent motion terminates when an object is held in a non-natural place or it terminates by becoming natural motion, as when a projectile ceases to ascend and starts to descend. All natural motion, while not opposed by nature, comes to an end when the element in question arrives at its natural place. The second feature is this: the only sense in which bodies naturally persevere in nature is when they are at rest in their natural places. Once this is achieved, Aristotelians would say that the body is in its 'natural state of rest'. The third feature of Aristotle's distinction that is important to note is the manner in which it is related to another process of change called *alteration*. For Aristotle any process of change involves *kinêsis*. Local motion is merely one species of change or *kinêsis*. Another species of change which is common in nature is alteration.

While local motion is change of place, alteration is change of quality. In particular, it is change of one of the first four qualities – hot, cold, wet or dry. Aristotle explained alteration by appeal to forms. Very roughly, the *form* of each corporeal object has a certain essential combination of the first four qualities. When the body undergoes alteration, the proportions of these qualities change. But since all change has a terminus, and all bodies have form, there is a tendency in nature for the form of all bodies to be actualised. Thus he was able to explain the phenomenon of reversible alteration, where a body, say water, when heated 'naturally' returns to be cold. Now, since *kinêsis* is any kind of change, local motion and alteration, for Aristotle, are really two species of the same genus of change. So it is not surprising to find him mixing up illustrations of alteration in his discussions of natural and violent motions.[29] The importance of this connection between reversible alteration and natural and violent motions will emerge in our discussion of natural and violent states.

4 Gassendi and Charleton

Having outlined Aristotle's doctrine of natural and violent motions, we now turn to the views of some of the leading seventeenth-century figures whom Boyle read. First, we treat of Gassendi and his English disciple Charleton. Gassendi saw his revival of Epicurean atomism as a direct challenge to the Aristotelian orthodoxy of the day and set himself in self-conscious opposition to scholastic physics. Like Epicurus, he rejected the four element theory of matter and the Aristotelian cosmology. In its place he admitted homogeneous atomic matter and the void. Yet, surprisingly enough, both he and his English populariser Charleton upheld a version of the distinction between natural and violent motions.[30] It will be instructive for us to see what the rudiments of their view are in order to compare it with the Aristotelian, Cartesian and Boylean views.

Gassendi and Charleton adopted and modified Epicurus' theory of motion. On Epicurus' view, matter has an inherent source of motion, gravity, in virtue of which it incessantly moves. For Epicurus, matter had eternally existed and had always been in motion. Whereas Gassendi, in 'baptising' Epicurus, had attributed the source of motion to an initiating act of God. Thus, for Gassendi 'the prime cause of motion in natural things is the atoms, for they provide motion for all things when they move themselves through their own agency and in accordance with the power they received from their author in the beginning'.[31] A second departure was that, where Epicurus posited a non-isotropic space with a rain of atoms all moving in a downward direction, Gassendi argued for isotropic space with no 'natural' directions and no natural places.[32] But he did posit natural motions. These were simply motions of uniform speed and direction.

Further, according to Gassendi and Charleton, when an atom in motion suffers some repugnancy, i.e. when it speeds up, slows down or changes direction, then it suffers violent or non-natural motion. But when atoms form concretions which can in fact be quiescent, their being in motion is far more natural than their being at rest.[33] The chief source of repugnancy that bodies suffer is gravitational attraction. Thus any vertical motion is violent because of the effect of the earth's gravity. By contrast, horizontal motion is natural. It perseveres in the absence of any intervening forces. Horizontal motion has no terminus.[34] Finally, it appears that Charleton believed that the celestial orbs moved with a natural circular motion.[35]

5 Descartes

Descartes' physics also represents a radical departure from Aristotle's. Like Gassendi, he posited a homogeneous matter, and he saw himself as providing an alternative to Aristotelianism. However, unlike Gassendi and Charleton he denied atomism; he was a plenist; and he adamantly denied the distinction between natural and violent motions. To Mersenne he wrote, 'I do not accept any difference between violent and natural motions' (*Letter to Mersenne*, 11 March 1640, *AT*, III, p. 39).[36] And yet it is ironic that the grounds of his denial, at least as it is found in the *Principles* and his correspondence, lie in his reworking of certain ontological categories of the Aristotelian Suárez.[37] Following Suárez (and ultimately Aristotle), Descartes held a substance/attribute ontology. In Suárez's ontology, modes were an additional category of being, over and above substances and attributes. They were a category of being which modified entities such as substances or accidents. But for the Descartes of the *Principles*, modes were identical to a certain type of accident, viz. those accidents that are subject to variation.[38] As such they only modified substances and not accidents. And most importantly for our discussion, motion and rest were modes of matter.[39] (See chapter 4, §6.)

Now the idea that motion is a mode of matter is rather problematic. This was pointed out to Descartes by Henry More, who asked him how one body can transfer one of its modes to another body, since Descartes was committed to the doctrine of transmission of motion.[40] A further conceptual difficulty has been pointed out more recently by Garber (1992, pp. 172ff). Motion in Descartes' system is really a relative notion, and yet modes appear to be essentially monadic properties of substances. Yet regardless of these difficulties, Descartes adopted this Suaracian category and put it to work in his physics. It may seem that this notion of motion as a mode of matter is not essential to Cartesian physics and that Descartes' views on motion would be better expounded without it. Yet, in addition to the fact that Boyle took over Descartes' notion of motion as a *mode* into his mechanism,[41] there are two pertinent reasons for considering it here. First, the notion is related to Descartes' conception of the state (*status*) of a body, and second, Descartes explicitly appeals to the notion of modes to argue against the central tenet of the natural/violent motion distinction. Let us examine both of these facets of his use of the notion of modes, as these will prove to be important preliminaries for our exposition of Boyle's arguments against the distinction between natural and violent motions.

First then, Descartes actually *identifies* states and modes. This is nicely brought out in another letter from Descartes to Mersenne dated 26 April 1643, not long before the publication of the *Principles*. In it Descartes says that it is a principle of physics that

> whatever is or exists remains always in the <u>state</u> in which it is, unless some external cause changes it; so that I do not think that there can be any *quality* or *mode* which perishes of itself.
>
> (*Letter to Mersenne*, 26 April 1643, *CSMK*,
> p. 216, underlining added)[42]

What is important here is his explication of what it is for a body to remain in a state in terms of maintaining its modes. Clearly states are equivalent to modes. Having made this identification, and remembering that motion and rest are modes of bodies, the next step in the rejection of the natural and violent motions distinction is straightforward.

The second step in Descartes' rejection of the distinction is based on the following metaphysical grounds. Modes do not have within themselves a principle of their own destruction or change. That is, the physical axiom that 'whatever is or exists remains always in the state in which it is' applies to all modes. The mode of shape in a body has no tendency to change, so why should the mode of motion? Rather, (because of the immutability of God) all modes continue to exist unchanged in the absence of external forces. And since motion is a mode, so the motion of a body also continues to exist in the absence of other forces. That is, 'what is once in motion always continues to move' (*Principles*, II, §37, *CSM*, I, p. 240).[43] Therefore the central thesis underlying the natural/violent motion distinction is false, viz. that there is always a terminus to any process of change and that change of place is a process of change. The letter to Mersenne continues,

> If a body has a certain shape, it does not lose it unless it is taken from it by collision with some other body; similarly if it has some motion, it should continue to keep it, unless prevented by some external cause.

Descartes goes on to explain how this is derived from the immutability of God. The same line of reasoning is found in his explication of the first law of motion in *Principles*, II, §37 where he concludes that the idea that 'it is in the very nature of motion to come to an end' is 'a false preconceived opinion' (*CSM*, I, p. 241).[44] In short then, states persevere and since states are identical to modes and motion is a mode, motion perseveres.

But there is another sense of the word 'state' that is occasionally found in Descartes. The term was employed in discussions of another issue that was apparently widely debated in the seventeenth century. It was the question as to whether or not certain substances had *natural states*.[45] In fact, many spoke of a distinction between natural and violent states which was an analogue of the natural/violent motion distinction. So we find Descartes replying to Mersenne in 1638:

> You ask whether I think that water is in its natural state when it is liquid or when it is frozen. I reply that I do not regard anything in nature as violent, except in relation to the human intellect . . . It is no less natural for water to be frozen when it is cold, than to be liquid when it is less cold, because the causes of each are equally natural.
>
> (*Letter to Mersenne*, January 1638 (?), *CSMK*, p. 79)

What is interesting about this reply is first, that Descartes naturally contrasts the natural state of water with something violent and, second, the dismissal of the natural/violent state distinction on the grounds that it is a purely relative distinction. This very argument, as we shall see, turns up again in Boyle.

The basic idea of a natural state was that a certain substance, water being the paradigm, naturally tends towards a particular disposition of its constituents, where these constituents do not just involve spatial parts but also qualities such as hot and cold. For example, water was said to be in its natural state when it was liquid and cold. A substance was said to be in a non-natural or violent state whenever the particular 'natural' disposition did not pertain. It may be in the process of changing its disposition – ice melting – or its disposition may remain static – water boiling, but until it reaches its 'natural state' it is in a violent state. What in fact was observed was the behaviour of particular substances within systems that tend toward equilibrium. This is now explained in terms of the laws of thermodynamics, but in the seventeenth century there was a range of explanations of these phenomena.

One of the issues for the natural philosopher was to explain the sense in which substances 'naturally' tended toward a particular disposition. Many thought that there was some principle called *Nature* at work which ensured that substances tended toward their natural states. It can be seen that the phenomena described by the distinction between natural and violent states is co-extensive with that described by the Aristotelian account of reversible alteration. The natural/violent state distinction is merely an extension of the natural/violent motion distinction to cover a different form of *kinêsis*. In both, the process of change invariably has a terminus and in both, nature 'opposes' what is violent.

But for mechanists like Descartes and Boyle, the issue was to explain the phenomena in terms of their own theories of matter and motion. I hope to show that the manner in which they did this is of particular interest and importance for the emergence of the concept of inertial motion. The line of reasoning is fairly simple. Let us keep in mind that, early in the century, philosophers spoke quite naturally about natural and violent states and natural states of rest, whereas by late in the century the terms 'state of rest' and 'state of motion' had become technical terms in Newtonian dynamics.[46] How are we to account for this shift of emphasis in the meaning of the word 'state' (*status*, *état*)? The natural (or violent) state of a body is, for the mechanists, a particular disposition of its qualities and parts.[47] We can dub this the 'thick' sense of 'state'. The 'thin' sense of 'state' then, is simply state of motion or state of rest. The thick sense of 'state' is that which pertains to the natural/violent state distinction. The thin sense pertains solely to the modes of motion and rest. Now at first sight the two distinctions, that between natural and violent states and that between natural and violent motions, appear orthogonal. Ostensibly they are discrete. But once they are examined, one discovers two important connections between them.

First, given that the thick sense of 'state' has to do with a body's particular disposition of qualities and parts, it must be borne in mind that for the mechanist Descartes, all the qualities of bodies are to be analysed in terms of shape, size and motion. Descartes says that '[a]ll the properties which we clearly perceive in [matter] are reducible to its divisibility and consequent mobility in respect of its parts . .' (*Principles*, II, §23, *CSM*, I, p. 232).[48] Shape, size and motion are modes of bodies,[49] but natural and violent states of bodies are to be analysed in terms of modes and, in particular, in terms of motion which is the salient mode in a mechanistic universe. Therefore, talk about states of bodies is ultimately reducible to talk of states of motion or rest. Second, the natural/violent state distinction bears many parallels with the natural/violent motion distinction and, as we shall see, these parallels are not present by accident. There is an important conceptual dependence of one distinction upon the other. Not surprisingly, Boyle's arguments against one distinction almost exactly parallel his arguments against the other.

6 Boyle on natural and violent states

Our aim in this section is to examine the grounds upon which Boyle rejected the natural and violent state distinction and to reveal some of the parallels between this distinction and that between natural and violent motions. This is not for its own sake, but rather it is with a view to unravelling the rather complicated network of ideas about states and motions that Boyle inherited from his scholastic and mechanist forebears. There are two works in which Boyle treats of the distinction between natural and violent states. They are 'A Paradox of the Natural and Preternatural State of Bodies' and section VI of *Notion of Nature*.[50] There is a substantial amount of overlap between the discussions both in the arguments used and in the examples given. Moreover, section VI of *Notion of Nature* is not well structured and it contains some repetition of arguments and examples. Here our discussion will focus on both works.

Boyle's general objection to the doctrine of natural and violent states is not with the notion of a natural state *per se*, but that 'the common distinction of a natural and violent state of bodies has not been clearly explained, and considerately settled, and both is not well grounded, and is oftentimes ill applied' ('A Paradox', *Works*, III, p. 782). In fact, says Boyle, often the classification of states as violent or natural is nothing more than arbitrary and casual and is not derived from the systematic application of the distinction.[51] But when Boyle moves on to more substantial criticisms we find, as is often the case with his criticisms of Aristotelianism, that it is not so much a misapplication of the natural/violent state distinction that is the point at issue, but the fact that Boyle is starting from a different conceptual framework. He is working with different presuppositions and it is these, supported by relevant empirical observations, that set him at odds with the distinction between natural and violent states.

Boyle's first philosophical argument against natural states is derived from his doctrine of insensible matter. He says, 'matter being confessedly devoid of knowledge and sense, I see no reason, why we should not think it uncapable of being concerned to be in one state or constitution, rather than another . . .' (*Notion of Nature*, *Works*, V, p. 205). The point is that because matter is insentient there is nothing within it that could be the cause of its 'endeavour-ing' to reach one state rather than another. He has already used this argument in *Notion of Nature* against the Aristotelian doctrine of natural place.[52]

There are two points of interest about Boyle's presentation of this argument. First, the notion of bodies having an 'appetite' to return to their natural states has no parallel in Aristotle's doctrine of natural and violent motions. For Aristotle, the internal nature of the body was only a passive cause of its motion toward its natural place. The extension of this thesis to the claim that bodies have appetites to be in a particular state is a scholastic development.[53] Second, in 'A Paradox' Boyle's discussion reveals an important parallel between the doctrines of natural and violent states and natural and violent motions. He says that he will discuss examples that are alleged to show that 'a state is natural to a body, and that being put out of it by *external causes*, it will, upon the cessation of their violence be restored thereunto . . .' ('A Paradox', *Works*, III, p. 783). Recall that Aristotle distinguished between natural and violent *motions* in terms of internal and external causes. Here the same criterion is applied to natural and violent *states*. This parallel between the two distinctions is our first piece of evidence of the dependence of one upon the other.

The next argument that Boyle mobilises against the distinction is the argument from relativity that we have seen already in Descartes. Take water, says Boyle, it is 'extremely difficult to determine what degree of coldness is natural to water, since this liquor perpetually varies its temperature as to cold and heat, according to the temper of the contiguous or the neighbouring bodies, especially the ambient air'. The so-called 'natural' temperature of water varies with the seasons and across different regions. In fact, Boyle had heard from none less than 'the Russian Czar's chief physician' that in some parts of Siberia 'water is so much more cold, not only than in the torrid zone, but than in *England*, that two or three foot beneath the surface of the ground, all the year long . . . it continues concreted in the form of ice' (*Notion of Nature*, *Works*, V, p. 206).[54] Boyle continues in his customary manner to heap up empirical observations to reinforce the point that the notion of a natural state for a particular body is a relative one. Two examples that occur in both of the works under discussion are the compression of air and the forcible bending of a sword. In both cases he thinks it is 'far more likely, that the cause should be mechanical, than that the effect proceeds from such a watchfulness of nature as is pretended' (*Notion of Nature*, *Works*, V, p. 207).

Part of the problem, according to Boyle, is the widespread acceptance of the axiom *nullum violentum durabile* – nothing violent endures. That is, what is violent, being contrary to nature, cannot last long. This is, of course, one of the two key notions upon which the doctrine of natural and violent motions is grounded. Yet here Boyle is challenging what he sees as a central tenet of the natural/violent *state* distinction. And so we have a further parallel between the two distinctions. Moreover, Boyle acknowledges that this axiom also applies to the distinction between natural and violent motions. In fact, having mentioned it in discussing states in *Notion of Nature*, Boyle slips naturally into a discussion of motions rather than states. He immediately goes on to mention another criterion by which 'the schools and even some modern philosophers' distinguish natural and violent motions (*Works*, V, p. 208). According to them, natural motions are distinguished from violent ones in that 'the former are perpetual, or at least very durable'.

Now this is not the Aristotelian doctrine! Aristotle's natural motions come to an end. So who does he have in mind when speaking of the schools and other modern philosophers? Boyle does not tell us; however we know that the doctrine of perseverance was accepted by some Aristotelians such as the Coimbrans earlier in the century.[55] Boyle's comment here furnishes us with important evidence that the notion was gaining ground amongst Aristotelians in the mid-seventeenth century.

We have then two arguments against the natural/violent state distinction. The first is from the insensible nature of matter and the second an argument from relativity. How do these arguments compare with Boyle's criticism of the natural/violent motion distinction?

7 Boyle on natural and violent motions

The sub-section on natural and violent motions in *Notion of Nature* continues that work's sustained polemic against the 'vulgarly conceived notion of nature'.[56] This was also the rationale behind the discussion of natural and violent states. Not surprisingly, we find here parallels between the two distinctions themselves and in the arguments used against them. Boyle believes that by undermining the distinction between natural and violent motions, he is able further to disarm those who claim that there is some mysterious principle at work in the world over and above matter, minds, angels and God. He tells us,

> There is a distinction of local motion into natural and violent, that is so generally received and used, both by philosophers and physicians, that I think it deserves to have special notice taken of it in this section; since it implicitly contains an argument for the existence of the thing called nature, by supposing it so manifest a thing, as that an important distinction may justly be grounded on it.
>
> (*Works*, V, p. 209)

His first claim against the distinction, similar to the point made against the natural/violent state distinction, is that it is usually ambiguous: it is often used in such an obscure way that the distinction is unclear. But those few who use it intelligibly 'define natural motion to be that, whose principle is within the moving body itself; and violent motion that, which bodies are put into by an external agent or cause' (*Notion of Nature*, *Works*, V, p. 209). This could be straight from Aristotle's *Physics*, and it presupposes the Platonic principle that *Quicquid movetur ab alio movetur* (whatever is moved is moved by something else).

Now, continues Boyle, on the one hand it seems as if most, if not all, motion is violent because 'the immense firmament itself, and all the planetary orbs' (compared to which terrestrial matter is a mere point) are moved by a prime mover, that is, they are set in motion by some external principle. Yet on the other hand, once moving, it seems as if all matter is in natural motion.[57] This is because, 'for instance, an arrow, that actually flies in the air towards a mark, moves by some principle or other residing within itself'. It is intriguing to determine just what Boyle had in mind here. First he tells us that the motion cannot depend upon the bow because the motion would continue even if the bow were annihilated. In other words, it is not a case of action at a distance. Second, he tells us that it does not depend upon the medium, as Aristotle claimed. In fact, Boyle goes on to make Galileo's[58] point that the medium's contribution is actually to resist the arrow's motion rather than to cause it. So, concludes Boyle, if we suppose that the medium be annihilated, 'I see not why the motion of the arrow must necessarily cease'. Boyle asks why there need be any terminus to the motion at all. Yet as we have seen the central tenet of the doctrine of natural and violent motions is that there is a terminus to any process of change and that local motion is a process of change.

Boyle now seems to lose his way in the argument. He continues to argue for the universality of natural motion: do not springs and bows have within them some principle in virtue of which they return to their original shape when compressed? But then he switches back to violent motions and claims that 'external agents are requisite to many motions that are acknowledged to be natural'. Here the point seems to be that the distinction is difficult to draw. And he follows this up with some seemingly ill-chosen empirical observations. For instance, onions, leeks and potatoes require the heat of the sun in spring in order to germinate. What these illustrations show is just how broad was Boyle's conception of the applicability of the so-called distinction between natural and violent motions. It pertained to all natural phenomena and not simply to such standard examples as the projectile motion of an arrow. Boyle then goes on to gesture against the Epicurean position on natural and violent motions (*Works*, V, p. 210). He does not seem to have Gassendi or Charleton in mind when he claims that motion does not belong essentially to matter, for he fails to mention the Gassendist criterion of repugnancy and he ends up saying nothing with which Gassendi or Charleton would disagree. Moreover, the argument against Epicurus is not fully formed. The implicit conclusion is that, since there is no inherent motive force in matter, motion is not 'natural' to it. But Boyle drops Epicurus at this point and moves on.

Next, Boyle claims, with some degree of novelty, that natural and violent motions 'are very hard to distinguish'. Yet surely he has already made this point, though here he illustrates it with many more examples. He then moves on to reiterate his point about the relativity of natural and violent motions and introduces some arguments that serve further to undermine the doctrine, but he does not develop these ideas. The arguments are first, that matter is insensible and is therefore, *contra* Aristotle, indifferent to its destination. (This point was made against the natural/violent state distinction.) And second, that all motion can be considered natural in that the direction of motion is determined by the laws of nature. Repeating the point that all motions 'may in some respect be said to be natural, and in another violent', he goes on to say that

> as very many bodies of visible bulk are set a moving by external impellents, and on that score their motions may be said to be violent, so the generality of impelled bodies do move either upwards, downwards, &c. toward any part of the world, in what line or way soever they find their motion least resisted; which impulse or tendency being *given by virtue of* what they call the *general laws of nature*, the motion may be said to be natural.
>
> (*Notion of Nature*, *Works*, V, p. 210, italics added)[59]

The point is not just that all motion is law governed and therefore natural. It appears to be that the 'cause' of bodies moving in particular directions is the laws of nature (and by implication not natural places or appetites within matter). The inner natures and natural places in Aristotle's explanation of motion are replaced in Boyle's mechanical philosophy by laws of motion.

8 Inertial motion and the perseverance of states

The crux of Boyle's case against both of the natural/violent distinctions is his claim that bodies will persevere in their present state. That is, he denies the doctrine of the terminus. But we must remember that Boyle has two different types of state in mind when he makes this claim. In the case of natural and violent states he has the thick sense in mind. He is thinking of the disposition of a body's qualities and parts.[60] Whereas in claiming that bodies will persevere in their present state in the case of the natural and violent motions distinction, he has the thin sense in mind. The thin sense is something akin to the Newtonian concepts of 'state of motion' and 'state of rest'.[61] So we have seen four types of state in Boyle: natural states, violent (or preternatural) states, states of motion and states of rest. And to complicate matters further, there is a fifth type of state discussed by Boyle and which was popular amongst scholastics in the mid-seventeenth century. It is the idea of a body being in its 'natural state of rest'.[62] A body was said to be in its 'natural state of rest' when, as a result of being in natural motion, it arrives at its natural place and so remains at rest. Such rest is a 'natural state'. In Aristotelian terms, since motion is a process of change, it is the only possible 'natural state', in the thin sense, that a body can be in.

So it was common before Newton for scholastics and others to speak of states of rest. In fact, the Keplerian concept of inertia can be seen as an attempt to quantify this property of bodies. For Kepler, inertia was that innate property of all bodies in virtue of which they resist changing from a state of rest and in virtue of which, if in motion, they endeavour to return to a state of rest. But this thin conception of 'natural state of rest' is markedly different from the Newtonian one. It is not in contradistinction to a 'natural state of motion', for that is a contradiction in terms, for both Kepler and the scholastics. And for the scholastics it is set within a physics of natural and violent motions and natural places.[63] Even for some mechanists who had dispensed with natural places, the notion that rest was a natural state for bodies and that bodies tended to remain in that state, was a central tenet of their physics. For example, Hobbes tells us in *Concerning Body* (1655) that '[t]hat which is at rest will always be at rest, except it be moved by some external thing' (*English Works*, I, p. 115). But, more importantly, the notion is found in one of Boyle's earliest published works, 'Fluidity and Firmness' (1661), where Boyle tells us of ice that, 'every part actually at rest must by the *law of nature* continue so, till it be put out of it by an external force capable to surmount its *resistance to a change* of its present state' (*Works*, I, p. 387, italics added).[64]

Thus we have a complicated semantic range for the word 'state' in Boyle's works. We have seen five senses of the word, some of them having links to his scholastic heritage and others no doubt were part of an emerging mechanistic vocabulary in Britain.[65] We also find in Boyle's works the concept of the perseverance of a state, but one which applies to states in every sense. I will conclude this chapter by discussing two issues that, I believe, will help us clarify this diversity of meanings of the word 'state'. The first issue we need to clarify is the extent to which Boyle can be said to have understood the nature of inertial motion, keeping in mind that all of Boyle's relevant published works predate the publication of Newton's *Principia* in 1687. The second is to point out a discernible shift in the understanding of the notion of the *perseverance of a state* that is evident in Boyle. Let us turn then to inertial motion.

In some contemporary discussions of the concept of inertia in the mid-seventeenth century the precise meaning of the term 'inertia' is unclear. Some commentators claim that Boyle must surely have understood the principle of inertia.[66] One goes so far as to claim that it played an integral role in his corpuscular philosophy and even his understanding of disease (Kaplan 1993, pp. 63–64 and p. 103).[67] As the notion is related to the concept of the state of a body and the idea of the perseverance of states, it is important to be clear about the precise meaning(s) of the term. Perhaps the best starting point is with Newton's first law:

> Every body perseveres in its state of resting or of moving uniformly in a straight line, except insofar as it is compelled by impressed forces to change that state.

> (Quoted from Gabbey 1980, p. 291)

It is this law that is commonly termed the *principle of inertia*. But the principle of inertia is not the same thing as inertia. In fact the law does not even employ the word 'inertia'. Following J. Barbour (1989, pp. 678–680), I believe that it is helpful to distinguish two senses of the term 'inertia' and its cognates. The first sense takes the term as a substantive and is that which derives from Kepler. It refers to a *force* within a body that resists changes of state. This is a scalar property of material objects and was (roughly) the sense in which Newton employed the term. (For Kepler the relevant change of state was from rest to motion, for Newton it was change of motion.) The second sense, which is actually the adjectival form of the word, refers to a particular (thin) *state* of a body. A body moving in uniform rectilinear motion (in the absence of other forces) is in a state of 'inertial motion'.[68] So we have the *principle of inertia* which refers to Newton's first law; the *property of inertia* which is a force of resistance to change of state; and the *state of inertia* which is uniform rectilinear motion or rest.

Now sometimes when Boyle suggests that a body will continue in its present state, as he does in *Notion of Nature* (*Works*, V, p. 206)[69], he is not referring to the state of inertial motion, nor is he speaking of an instance of the principle of inertia, nor a force within a body. His conception of state is far broader than that which pertains to 'inertial motion'. For Boyle is thinking of 'the instance afforded by water', that is, its temperature. We have dubbed this the 'thick' sense of 'state'. The 'thin' sense of 'state' is simply a state of motion or a state of rest. The thick sense of 'state' is that which pertains to the natural/violent state distinction. The thin sense pertains to the principle of inertia.[70]

But what of Boyle's claim, when arguing against the natural/violent motion distinction, that 'I see not why the motion of the arrow must necessarily cease'? Boyle could hardly have had thick states in mind here. But neither was he thinking of uniform rectilinear motion. All that Boyle has expressed from the Newtonian principle of inertia is the possibility of the indefinite *perseverance* of motion. He here seems to accept, as he does elsewhere, the truth of the third word in Newton's law, *perseverae*. Yet this is far from expressing the principle of inertia. The notion of the perseverance of motion in the absence of other forces is certainly essential to the principle of inertia and as we have seen it is antithetical to Aristotle's doctrine of natural and violent motions (though it was accommodated by many late scholastics). But it is only one aspect of Newton's first law and the thought had been 'in the air' at least since Buridan.[71] Boyle would have encountered it in Galileo, Descartes, Gassendi and Charleton and of course Wallis.[72] However, rather than having a conception of inertial motion, most of these writers retained a conception of impressed force or impetus in their doctrines of motion. In fact, R. S. Westfall (1973, p. 185) has commented that '[m]ost of the students of mechanics during the seventeenth century employed a concept of impetus in their dynamics'. A good example is Wallis, who in a letter to Boyle spoke of the law that 'a Body in motion is apt to continue its motion, and that in the same degree of celerity, unless hindred by some contrary Impediment; (like as a Body at rest, to continue so, unless by some sufficient mover, put into motion' (*Phil. Trans.*, 16, p. 268). He then goes on to elaborate on it explicitly using a conception of impetus. It is most likely then that Boyle too held a simple impetus conception of motion and some of his comments seem to betray this. He says in *Notion of Nature* that,

> it may be said, that all bodies, once in the state of actual motion, whatever cause first brought them to it, are moved by an internal principle: as, for instance, an arrow, that actually flies in the air towards a mark, moves by some principle or other residing within itself . . .
>
> (*Works*, V, 209)[73]

The most natural reading of this passage is to take the 'internal principle' as a type of impetus. So, from the passages we have examined, it is incorrect to claim that Boyle states, or even understood, the nature of inertial motion. However, he certainly understood the doctrine of the perseverance of motion and he found it quite credible. (For more on perseverance see chapter 7, §2.)

9 Conclusion

What is of particular interest in Boyle's discussion of his corpuscular hypothesis is the way in which the notion of the perseverance of a state is undergoing a crucial twofold shift. On the one hand it is shifting from being associated solely with the state of rest to that of state of motion. And on the other, the importance of the notion is shifting from the thick, scholastic senses of 'state' to the thin Newtonian senses of that word. In Boyle we find an undermining of the superstructure upon which the scholastic doctrine of the perseverance of thick states was built, and the emergence of an increasing role for the doctrine of the perseverance of thin states. That is, we find Boyle arguing against the natural and violent state distinction and rejecting the doctrines on which the scholastic notion of 'natural state of rest' was founded (the doctrines of natural and violent motions and natural places). And at the same time, while Boyle continues to employ thick states (such as solid and liquid) these are not states *simpliciter*, but are in a sense derivative, since they are now analysed exclusively in terms of the thin states of corpuscles. Any thick state of a body is, according to the corpuscular hypothesis, fully explicable in terms of the thin states of its constituents and its neighbouring bodies. For example, we can explain the freezing of water, not in terms of its being in a 'violent state', but in terms of the (thin) states of motion or rest of its component particles.[74] To be sure, in the early 'Fluidity and Firmness' Boyle begins the work by raising the issue (which he tells us he will not discuss) of '[w]hether philosophers might not have done better in making fluidity and firmness rather states than qualities of bodies', implying that he sees a role for the thick sense of 'state' (*Works*, I, p. 378). But he goes on in the work to explicate these 'states, qualities or affections of matter' in corpuscular terms.

What is happening in Boyle (and others) is that the concept of the *state* of a body is undergoing its final extrication from Aristotelianism. I am not claiming that Boyle was aware of his role in this transition. It was simply a corollary of the application of his corpuscular hypothesis to the scholastic distinctions and the phenomena of nature. Nor am I claiming that there is any dependence of Newton upon Boyle with regard to the notion of the state of a body. For the thin notion of state Newton could go straight to Descartes.[75] But I do believe that Boyle's works reveal the extent to which the concept of state was in transition in the mid-seventeenth century. The insights of Descartes had not been fully digested because the notion of states continued to be clouded by the thick senses of that word. A nice example of this is found in Louis de La Forge's reference to Descartes' first law of motion in the Descartes' *Principles* where he speaks of 'the force that each thing has to maintain itself in whatever state [*l'estat*] it is in, namely those that move to remain in motion and those at rest to remain at rest, separated things to remain separated and united things united' (La Forge 1974, pp. 141–142).[76] Uniform rectilinear motion is certainly not the only thing in mind here.

Furthermore, we have seen the many close parallels between the two distinctions; the way in which both were founded on the same axioms, the role of internal and external causes and the doctrine of appetites. And we have seen the two parallel sets of arguments that are employed by Boyle to undermine the distinctions; the argument from insensible matter, the arguments against the doctrine of the terminus and the relativity argument. These parallels are clear evidence for a close conceptual dependence of the distinction between states upon the distinction between motions.

So we find in Boyle's mechanism that the thick senses of 'state' were effectively collapsed into one by the rejection of the natural/violent state distinction. And the remaining thick notion of the qualitative state of a body was sharply differentiated from the thin senses by the rejection of the natural and violent motions distinction. What emerged from this differentiation of the senses of 'state' and the denial of the natural/violent motion distinction was first, a uniform conception of motion, second, the demise of the notion of a natural state of rest, and finally, a heightened awareness that the salient notion of perseverance in the mechanical philosophy was that pertaining to states of motion and states of rest. It was these thin states that Boyle's corpuscular hypothesis invested with explanatory power. After all, motion was the grand agent of all that happened in nature. But this is not to say that Boyle completely rejected the notion of a state of a body in any sense other than that of being in a state of motion or rest. On the contrary, he saw it as a desideratum of natural philosophy to construct a history (in the Baconian sense) of the 'States of Matter, as Fluid, Firm, Animate & Inanimate &c' (*Boyle to Oldenburg*, 13 June 1666, in *Oldenburg*, III, p. 165).

Notes

1 See *Philaretus*, *Works*, I, p. xxiv, M. Hunter 1994b, p. 19. Boyle also read Galileo in French (see *Usefulness*, *II*, *sect. 2*, *Works*, III, p. 459).
2 See R. S. Westfall 1971a, chapters 3 and 5.
3 On 25 April 1666 Wallis wrote to Boyle,

> How much the world, and the great bodies therein, are managed according to the laws of motion and static principles, and with how much clearness and satisfaction many of the more abstruse phænomena have been solved on such principles within this last century of years, than formerly they had been, I need not discourse to you, who are well versed in it.
>
> (*Works*, I, p. lxxxvi and *Phil. Trans.*, 16, p. 264)

4 See *Languid Motion*, *Works*, V, p. 2.
5 See also 'History of Particular Qualities', *Works*, III, p. 300, *S*. p. 109 and *Forms and Qualities*, *Works*, III, p. 31, *S*. p. 44.
6 See *Usefulness*, *II*, *sect. 2*, Essay VIII, *Works*, III, pp. 459–461. Gabbey's comment that '[t]he advancement of mechanical or atomistic ideas did not necessarily entail a special interest or competence in the technical business of mathematising motions' (1998, p. 673) is certainly confirmed by the case of Boyle.
7 This is well illustrated by Boyle's *Languid Motion* which was 'written, as you know, to facilitate the explicating of occult qualities', *Works*, V, p. 2.
8 See *The World*, *CSM*, I, p. 94.
9 See also *Notion of Nature*, *Works*, V, p. 211.
10 See *Christian Virtuoso*, *I*, *Appendix*, *Works*, VI, p. 692, 'Theological Distinction', *Works*, V, pp. 543–544. This contrasts with Descartes' presumption that all natural phenomena are explicable.
11 See also *BP*, vol. 1, fol. 38.

12 See also 'Excellency of the Mechanical Hypothesis', *Works*, IV, p. 70, *S.* p. 141. For the same point in Descartes see *Principles*, II, §24, *CSM*, I, p. 233 and *The World*, *ibid.*, p. 94 and in Charleton see *Physiologia*, pp. 437–438. For a discussion of the scholastic view of local motion see R. Ariew and A. Gabbey 1998, §VI, pp. 440–444.

13 Strictly speaking Aristotle and many of his followers regarded generation and corruption as 'mutations' and not as motion. See *Physics*, V, 1, 225ª12–ᵇ9, *Barnes*, I, pp. 380–381.

14 For Boyle on the Cartesian definition of matter see chapter 2, §2 above and for a discussion of Descartes' doctrine of figure see D. Des Chene 1996, pp. 109ff. For the same doctrine of figure in Charleton see *Physiologia*, p. 436. Needless to say Charleton adopted Epicurus' definition of motion rather than Descartes', see *ibid.*, p. 439.

15 See also *Notion of Nature*, *Works*, V, p. 211.

16 Boyle's Descartes is almost always that of the *Principles*. Thus the question as to whether before the *Principles* Descartes entertained a more 'vulgar' notion of motion is not relevant here.

17 Of course, for Aristotle, the movements of celestial bodies have no terminus. See *Physics*, VIII, 8, 261ᵇ26ff, *Barnes*, I, pp. 437ff.

18 *Notion of Nature*, *Works*, V, p. 209; see also p. 167.

19 For Boyle's use of the terms see *Languid Motion*, *Works*, V, p. 5, p. 24 and p. 26 and for the young Newton see *Questiones*, in J. E. McGuire and M. Tamny 1983, pp. 366–371.

20 Galileo's earliest criticism of the distinction is found in *De motu locali* (1590) (see A. Koyré 1978, p. 59 n. 142 for the relevant extract and p. 155, p. 176 and p. 181 for further discussion). For Hobbes' criticisms see *Concerning Body*, IV, 30, §2, *English Works*, I, pp. 509ff.

21 See A. Chalmers 1993b.

22 Thus I side with Z. Bechler against those who interpret Newtonian physics as continuous with Aristotle's, that is, those who understand Newton's non-inertial and inertial motions as forms of enforced and unenforced motions respectively. See Bechler 1991, chapter 10 and 1992. In fact, I suggest that the ensuing discussion of Boyle's rejection of the natural/violent motion distinction provides indirect evidence for Bechler's interpretation of Newton.

23 It might be added that it is also instructive to note just how much Boyle did *not* understand about the nature of motion and Cartesian physics.

24 See E. J. Dijksterhuis 1961, p. 25.

25 See *Physics*, IV, 1, 208ᵇ10–11, *Barnes*, I, p. 355. The suggestion that the *dunamis* of natural place is a final cause is R. Sorabji's: see his 1988, pp. 186–187.

26 See for example Boyle's account of what the 'school-philosophers' teach in *Notion of Nature*, *Works*, V, p. 243.

27 For a detailed account of Aristotle's theory see R. Sorabji 1988, chapter 13, pp. 219ff.

28 See *Physics*, VIII, 10, 267ª2–12, *Barnes*, I, p. 445.

29 See *Physics*, VIII, 4, *Barnes*, I, pp. 425ff.

30 See Gassendi's *De motu*, First Letter, *Brush*, pp. 125–132 and Charleton's *Physiologia*, pp. 444ff. So too did Digby, and he also rejected Aristotelian natural places (*pace* B. J. T. Dobbs 1971, p. 3) and the Epicurean innate motive force. See his *Two Treatises*, chapter IX, p. 70 and chapter X, p. 76 and p. 78.

31 See *Syntagma philosophicum*, *Physics*, 1, 4, quoted from *Brush*, p. 422.

32 See *Physiologia*, pp. 122f.

33 See *ibid.*, p. 445.

34 It is interesting to note here the contrast with Galileo for whom downward (vertical) motion was the only form of natural motion. He also held that unimpeded horizontal motion had no terminus: see A. Koyré 1978, pp. 176–181 and pp. 198–200.

35 See *Physiologia*, p. 448 and p. 466.

36 See also *Letter to More*, August 1649, *CSMK*, pp. 380–382.

37 Since Boyle's Descartes was the Descartes of the *Principles* I will continue to speak of the physics of this work as if it is the definitive Cartesian view. However, the reader should note that the Suaracian categories that are worked into the *Principles* are not to be found in the physics of *The World*.

38 See *Principles*, I, §56, II, §56 and *Letter to *** 1645 or 1646, *CSMK*, pp. 279–280.

39 See *Principles*, II, §27, *CSM*, I, p. 234. See also A. Gabbey 1980, p. 237.

40 See *More to Descartes*, 23 July 1649 in AT, V, p. 382. For Descartes' response to More see *Letter to More*, August 1649, *CSMK*, pp. 380–382.

41 I am not claiming that Descartes was Boyle's only source for the notion of modes, for Boyle read Suárez and the notion was widely discussed in the seventeenth century.

42 See also *The World*, *CSM*, I, p. 93. Descartes puts it slightly differently in his comments on Regius' broadsheet. There he speaks of, not the state of a body, but the state of a mode which he defines as 'nothing other than its inhering in the thing of which it is a mode', *CSM*, I, p. 303.

43 See also *Letter to More*, August 1649, *CSMK*, p. 381.

44 In fact, as A. Koyré has pointed out (1965, p. 69f), the notion of a state of motion is present in *The World*, see *CSM*, I, p. 93. But it is only in the period of the publication of the *Principles* that this is explicated in terms of modes. It should also be noted that there is more to Descartes' rejection of the natural/violent motion distinction than has been alluded to above; in particular there is his theory of place and his doctrine of inert matter.

45 Boyle claims that the distinction between natural and violent *states* is very widely held and that it arises in part from a misconceived notion of nature. See *A Paradox*, *Works*, III, p. 782. For an Aristotelian discussion see Suárez's *Disputationes Metaphysicæ*, disputation 15. It is almost certain that Boyle read this disputation for he cites it in the considerations about subordinate forms in the second edition of *Forms and Qualities*, see *Works*, III, p. 117. For further discussion see D. Des Chene 1996, pp. 73ff.

46 A. Koyré points out that neither Huygens, Wallis nor Hooke used the terms 'state of motion' or 'state of rest' and that Newton's first use of these terms was in the unpublished scientific paper *De motu sphaericorum corporum in fluidis* (1684?), 1965, p. 190. But Hobbes speaks of a body remaining 'in the same state it was, which is at rest' as early as 1637 in *A Short Tract on First Principles* (see R. S. Peters 1962, p. 165) and Boyle's free and unselfconscious use of the terms suggests that they were in common use by mid-century.

47 See *Forms and Qualities*, *Works*, III, p. 36, *S.* p. 52.

48 He expresses it better in *The World* when he says of hot, cold, moist and dry, 'not only these four qualities but all the others as well, . . . can be explained without the need to suppose anything in their matter other than the motion, size, shape, and arrangement of its parts', *CSM*, I, p. 89.

49 See *Principles*, I, §48, *CSM*, I, pp. 208–209 and *Third Meditation*, *CSM*, II, p. 31, but for the denial that size is a mode see *Letter to* *** 1645 or 1646, *CSMK*, p. 280.

50 Boyle has an extended discussion of the notion of natural states in *Forms and Qualities*, *Works*, III, pp. 41–45, *S*. pp. 59–65, but he does not mention the natural/violent state distinction. The context is a critical discussion of the doctrine of substantial forms. He urges four arguments against the notion of a substantial form preserving the natural state of a body (such as water returning to room temperature). First, there are better alternative mechanical explanations; second, he presents an argument from the relativity states; third, he gives counter-examples in which bodies do not return to their natural state; and fourth, he argues *ad hominem* that if the Aristotelians' elements do not have substantial forms but tend to their states in virtue of their first qualities (hot, cold, etc.), why should not other bodies do the same since they, according to the Aristotelians, are made up of the elements?

51 See 'A Paradox', *Works*, III, p. 783.

52 See *Notion of Nature*, *Works*, V, p. 203. He also uses it in 'A Paradox' against states, see *Works*, III, p. 783.

53 This is not to say that the notion that natural places could exert a force on objects had been replaced by appetites. See for instance Boyle's 'Requisite Digression', *Works*, II, p. 39, *S*. p. 160.

54 Exactly the same illustration is used in 'A Paradox', *Works*, III, p. 784.

55 For references and discussion see D. Des Chene 1996, pp. 272ff.

56 One of the meanings of the word 'nature' that Boyle lists in section II of the *Notion of Nature* and which he goes on to discuss in section VI is 'an *internal principle of local motion*', *Works*, V, p. 169.

57 Francis Bacon said of the natural violent motion distinction that it is 'a distinction which is itself drawn entirely from a vulgar notion, since all violent motion is also in fact natural; the external efficient simply setting nature working otherwise than it was before' (*New Organon*, book I, Aphorism LXVI, *The Works of Francis Bacon*, I, p. 177).

58 Actually this objection to Aristotle's view can be traced back to antiquity.

59 See also *Notion of Nature*, *Works*, V, p. 208.

60 So he says in the *Forms and Qualities*, 'when there is no competent destructive cause, the accidents of a body will by the law of nature remain such as they were' (*Forms and Qualities*, *Works*, III, p. 43, *S*. p. 63).

61 For Boyle's early uses of 'state of rest' and 'state of motion' see 'Requisite Digression' (c.1659), *Works*, II, p. 42, *S*. p. 165, *Forms and Qualities* (1666–7), *Works*, III, p. 15, *S*. p. 19, *Sceptical Chymist* (1661), *Works*, I, p. 557 and 'History of Particular Qualities' (1671), *Works*, III, p. 297, *S*. p. 105.

62 See *Languid Motion*, *Works*, V, p. 26.

63 It is not clear that Boyle had fully extricated himself from the notion of 'natural state of rest' for on his account of the creation of the world God first made matter undifferentiated and at rest. It then required God to set it in motion, which suggests that its rest, being chronologically prior, was in some sense its natural state.

64 See also p. 402, *Sceptical Chymist*, *Works*, I, p. 570 and *Forms and Qualities*, *Works*, III, p. 43, *S*. p. 62 and *Works*, III, p. 123. Of course, Boyle qualifies this in the appendix to this work on absolute rest, see 'Intestine Motions', *Works*, I, pp. 444ff.

65 In one place Boyle speaks of *transient* and *permanent* states of bodies which appear to be alternatives to the scholastic natural and violent states. See *General History of Air*, *Works*, V, p. 613.

66 For example, J. J. MacIntosh 1991, p. 211.

67 Kaplan can only be thinking of the perseverance of states in the 'thick' sense.

68 Of course the pressing question for the correct interpretation of Newton's physics is just how the state of inertial motion (or rest) is related to the force of inertia. See Z. Bechler 1992.

69 See also *Forms and Qualities*, *Works*, III, p. 43, *S*. p. 63. A. Chalmers rightly notes that it is 'overgenerous' to call this the law of inertia, 1993a, p. 554.

70 Thus B. Kaplan 1993 (following D. Shapere 1966) is wrong to speak of the concept of inertia in Boyle in the following terms, 'the body as a viable, organized system of interacting components will maintain itself until something intrudes to alter the status quo . . .', (p. 121). See also p. 63 and p. 103.

71 See M. Clagett 1961, p. 524 for references and commentary. Of course, Buridan accepted the natural/violent motion distinction.

72 Another source is Henry Power who, following Descartes, says, 'Motion may be translated from one Body to another; but when it is not transfer'd it would remain in that Body for ever', in the Preface to *Experimental Philosophy*, 1663, in M. B. Hall 1970, p. 125.

73 Boyle says there is 'an inward principle, by which they are moved, till they have attained their position', *ibid*. Elsewhere he speaks of bodies 'which can neither excite themselves into motion, nor regulate and stop the motion once they are in' (*High Veneration*, *Works*, V, p. 141).

74 As early as the 'Proëmial Essay' to *Certain Physiological Essays*, published in 1661, Boyle was speaking of 'obvious and familiar qualities or *states* of bodies, such as heat, cold, weight, fluidity, hardness, fermentation, &c.' and claiming that they most likely depend upon the size, shape and motion of the constituent corpuscles, *Works*, I, p. 308.

75 We can find a similar transition in Descartes' treatment of the notion of state. Compare *The World*, *CSM*, I, p. 93 with *Principles*, II, §37, *ibid.*, p. 240.

76 Later in this work La Forge illustrates the same law by reference to the configuration and pattern of the animal spirits at the exit of the pineal gland (see 1974, pp. 225–226).

6 The nature of place

Our broad aim is to become clear on the nature and scope of Boyle's mechanical philosophy. This has required an exploration of Boyle's views on motion. But the concept of motion is intimately linked with those of place and time. This is seen both in the centrality of the doctrine of natural place in Aristotle's doctrine of natural and violent motions, and in Descartes' definition of motion. So, in order to further our inquiry into Boyle's views on motion, we must proceed by discussing Boyle's views on place, since Boyle has very little to say on the nature of time. First we will discuss Boyle's dismissal of Aristotle's doctrine of natural place, as this is closely tied to the last chapter where we discussed Boyle's arguments against the distinction between natural and violent states and motions. We will then examine other views of which Boyle was aware and use our discussion of these views as a springboard to determine what his own view on space and time actually were. The figures discussed are Aristotle and the scholastics, Descartes and Gassendi. We will examine each in turn with a view to determining the extent of their influence on Boyle's view of space. There are five central philosophical issues about which we need to become clear in order to determine Boyle's views on place. They are its dimensionality, the existence of extra-cosmic void, the finitude of space, the relation of space to matter, and the question as to whether space is relative or absolute.

1 Against natural places

Once again Boyle's *Notion of Nature* is our source. He begins section VI, the same section we have discussed above, with a discussion of natural place. He says,

> the first argument [for the vulgar notion of nature], . . . may be taken from the general belief, or, as men suppose, observation, that divers bodies, as particularly earth, water, and other elements, have each of them its natural place assigned it in the universe; from which place, if any portion of the element, or any mixt body, wherein that element predominates, happens to be removed, it has a strong incessant appetite to return to it; because, when it is there, it ceases either to gravitate, or (as some schoolmen speak)

to levitate, and is now in a place, which nature has qualified to preserve it, according to the axiom, that *locus conservat locatum*.

(*Works*, V, p. 203)

We should note in passing that the doctrine of appetites mentioned here was a scholastic development of Aristotle's view. Moreover, although he argues against natural places, there is a sense in which Boyle agrees that at least some bodies 'should have places adequate to their bigness'. Of course this arises from his view that the universe is designed and that the sun and planets etc. have been arranged by God in a particular manner. However, having granted this, Boyle goes on to dismiss the notion of natural places by arguing from the doctrine of insensible matter.

For Boyle, following Descartes, 'inanimate bodies having no sense or perception, . . . it must be all one to them in what place they are'. The insensible nature of matter undermines the notion that any sort of body should strive to return to its proper place. Such appetites are 'the prerogative of animadversive beings' only. After all, who informs matter of its proper place 'and that it may better its condition by removing into another? And who informs it, whether that place lies on this hand of it, or that hand of it, or above it, or beneath it?' (*Notion of Nature*, *Works*, V, p. 203).[1] Boyle continues to dismiss natural places by enumerating empirical observations that are counter-examples to the doctrine, but these need not detain us here. Furthermore, there are other arguments from his doctrine of matter that he could have mobilised but ignored. For instance, he could have argued against the doctrine of the four elements. However, it appears that the notion of insensible matter is sufficient for the refutation.

It is interesting to note that Boyle also uses the same argument against what he took to be the 'modern' thesis that 'an inanimate body should have an appetite to rejoin homogeneous bodies' (*Notion of Nature*, *Works*, V, p. 203).[2] In fact, Boyle spends more time arguing against this view than against the standard Aristotelian position. He mobilises a number of simple empirical observations against it, such as the observation that gold filings will not stick to a gold bar, that wood chips thrown from the side of a ship fall directly to the water without being attracted to the wood of the ship's hull, that while bubbles of air rise in water, sometimes they cannot break the surface of the water and 'rejoin' the ambient air above and so on. He also refers us to his *Hydrostatical Paradoxes* where he adduces empirical arguments against the view that 'water does not weigh in water' or when it is in its natural place (*Works*, II, pp. 786–791).

Now in rejecting natural places, Boyle is arguing from the nature of matter. But could he have also argued against natural places from his own understanding of the nature of place? He was certainly aware of a variety of views on place and he tells us that he has considered the nature of place quite deeply. He says that while we all have a superficial idea of what it is, if we go about to pry narrowly, and dive deep into the matter, we shall find the nature of space to be a very abstruse thing, and even the most received notions about it to be liable to such difficulties and objections as are exceeding hard to be solved, if they be not altogether unanswerable by our imperfect reason; as those will scarce deny, that have, with me, attentively and impartially considered this subject.

(*Christian Virtuoso, I, Appendix, Works*, VI, p. 692)[3]

So let us turn to his discussions of the views on place and time of other philosophers. There is a short, but rich, passage in his 'Advices' in which Boyle discusses the views of Aristotle, Descartes and Gassendi. This passage will be the focal point of our inquiry.

2 Aristotle and the scholastics on place

In the context of arguing that not all the rules or dictates of reason apply equally to every subject within a particular philosophical system, Boyle adduces several examples from the systems of prominent natural philosophers. Each example shows some inherent contradiction or paradox. First, he finds one in Aristotle's theory of place. He tells us that,

The generality of philosophers, after *Aristotle*, conceive place to be the immoveable and immediately contiguous concave surface of the ambient body, so that it is a kind of vessel, that every way contains the body lodged in it; but with this difference, that a vessel is a kind of moveable place, . . . but place is an immoveable vessel . . .

('Advices', *Works*, IV, p. 459)

This seems to be an accurate statement of the Aristotelian view, emphasising the two-dimensional nature of place and the criterion of immovability.[4] Boyle then goes on to point out two familiar problems with this view. The first is that, for Aristotle, since there is no space beyond the outermost firmament, the firmament itself must not be in a place.[5] Second, if the outermost firmament were propelled by God in a straight line, 'there should ensue a motion without change of place' which contradicts Aristotle's definition of motion ('Advices', *Works*, IV, p. 459).

Of course, this latter argument does not apply to Aristotelian physics because Aristotle's heavenly spheres only move in circular motion and because for him there is no extra-cosmic space. Yet as Grant has shown (1981a, pp. 108–110), the ideas of an extra-cosmic space and the possibility that God could move the world in rectilinear motion became increasingly accepted after the Condemnation of 1277. It is not surprising therefore, that we see Boyle here manifesting a familiarity with scholastic disputes, though without any original insights and, it seems, without clearly discriminating between the system of Aristotle and that of the scholastics.

And this is not all, for if we look beyond the 'Advices' we find that there are other aspects of the scholastic disputes concerning the nature of place (and time) about which Boyle shows some familiarity. For instance, Boyle certainly knew of the scholastic notions of internal place, or *ubi*, and Maignon's notion of virtual extension. For he discusses Linus' use of virtual extension to explicate rarefaction in his *A Defence of the Doctrine touching the Spring and Weight of the Air* and the notion of *ubi* is criticised in the short appendix to that work entitled 'An Explication of the Rota Aristotelica'.[6] This appendix also contains a critical discussion of Linus' time atoms.[7] While its author is now known to have been Robert Hooke,[8] Boyle acquiesced in its contents and approved of its inclusion in his book.

It is clear then, that Boyle was familiar with the Aristotelian doctrine of place and many of the subsequent scholastic discussions and developments of it. Yet there is nothing in his writings that suggests that he accepted Aristotle's two-dimensional view of place. In fact, Boyle's arguments against Linus' theory of rarefaction presuppose three-dimensional place. So it is not in the scholastics that we are to find the main sources for Boyle's view of space. Rather it is in the writings of Descartes and Gassendi.

3 Descartes on place

Returning to our passage in the 'Advices', after raising some problems for Aristotle's view of place, Boyle goes on to argue against Descartes' definition of motion. I will quote the passage in full because I want to refer to it to illustrate three features of the Cartesian account of place that are relevant to our exposition of Boyle's view. They are first, the question of the existence of an extra-cosmic void. Second, the identification of space with extension. And third, the scholastic distinction between external and internal space. Boyle argues that given the Cartesian definition of motion,

> the *world may be said to move without changing of place*, for it does not pass from the neighbourhood of some bodies to that of others, since comprising all bodies, and yet *being bounded*, there is no body for it to leave behind, nor any beyond it for it to approach to. And though the Cartesians in their hypothesis of the *indefiniteness of the world*, do partly avoid the force of what I have been saying; yet, besides what may be rationally urged to shew, that if the world be not more than indefinite, it must be really *finite*, I consider, that the Cartesians, though upon grounds of their own, must allow what I was observing; namely, that though every particular body in the universe is naturally capable of local motion, yet the universe itself is not . . .
>
> (*Works*, IV, p. 459, italics added)[9]

3.1 *Extra-cosmic void*

What are Boyle's arguments against Descartes here? His first argument exploits the fact that, in Descartes' definition of motion, some body is transferred from the vicinity of one body considered to be at rest, to the vicinity of another body.[10] Boyle's point is that if God should move the aggregate of all bodies, then there will be neither a stationary body in relation to which the world is moving, nor a body for the world to move to. The argument contains the suppressed premise that there is extra-cosmic space, an opinion that was widely held in the mid-seventeenth century, but which Descartes adamantly denies.[11] It is worth observing how naturally Boyle implicitly appeals to this extra-cosmic space. He has already assumed it in his preceding argument against the Aristotelian doctrine of motion and he carries the assumption on into his treatment of the Cartesian position.

Is this evidence that Boyle accepted the existence of extra-cosmic void space, that is empty space beyond the limits of the corporeal world? And is he uncritically arguing against Descartes from his own framework? The answer to the first question is one we have come to expect. For, often when Boyle mentions extra-cosmic space he does so by positing it in a hypothetical way, mentioning it as a scholastic doctrine in passing, with the implication that it is not his own doctrine. For example, in his discussion of the *horror vacui* in section VII of *Notion of Nature* he says in a parenthetical note that 'I here meddle not with the imaginary spaces of the schoolmen, beyond the bounds of the universe' (*Works*, V, p. 227).[12] In other places he freely employs 'imaginary spaces' in thought experiments.[13] But, as is usual with Boyle on the fundamental philosophical issues of physics, he reserves judgment. He is not prepared to say whether or not there actually is an extra-cosmic void.[14]

It might be thought that Boyle's discussions of other worlds must commit him to a doctrine of the plurality of worlds and that the space between those worlds will be empty. However, a careful reading of Boyle's discussions of other worlds reveals that he reserves judgment on them too. For example, in concluding his important discussion of another world with different laws in his *High Veneration*, he excuses himself from entertaining 'such suspicions' (*Works*, V, p. 140). Thus it would seem that the answer to the second question is settled too. Boyle is not uncritically arguing against Descartes from his own framework. But here, I believe, we have the phenomenon of a Boyle who, in spite of his reserving judgment on the matter, allows his 'preferred view' to direct his thought. This is an instance of Boyle losing sight of his measured philosophical nescience and arguing from premises that he actually, though not 'officially', believes.

Evidence of this is found in his immediately ensuing discussion of the argument against Descartes that he has just presented. The question of the existence of extra-cosmic space is intimately related to a further issue, viz. whether the world is bounded or infinite. And in our passage from the 'Advices', Boyle goes on to mention a possible response to his argument against the Cartesian definition of motion. The point is this: one premise in Boyle's argument was that the world is bounded, but the Cartesians notoriously claimed that the world was indefinite, that we cannot know whether it is bounded or not. And if it is infinite, then Boyle's argument does not go through.

Descartes himself, in his correspondence with Henry More, initially denied that he could know whether the world is bounded,[15] preferring to say that its extent is *indefinite*. That is, he could not determine whether it has limits or not. By the end of the correspondence, however, he finally confessed that 'I think it involves a contradiction, that the world should be finite or bounded; because I cannot but conceive a space beyond whatever bounds you assign to the universe; and on my view such a space is a genuine body.'[16] So Boyle's argument is based on a premise that Descartes explicitly rejects. Now if Boyle is genuinely agnostic about the existence of extra-cosmic space and the finitude of the world,[17] why does he run the argument against the Cartesians, (not to mention a similar argument against Aristotle) especially since he must have known of Descartes' position on the finitude of the world?[18] This is not conclusive evidence that Boyle believed in the existence of imaginary space. We encounter this phenomenon again and again in Boyle and it is further evidence of that implicit distinction between an 'official' position of nescience and an 'unofficial' position which Boyle actually preferred or even believed.

3.2   *Place as extension*

It is very likely that Boyle knew of Descartes' denial of extra-cosmic void and that he understood the grounds of this denial. For Descartes, the impossibility of such a void follows from his definition of matter as extension. In the *Principles* he tells us of the spaces beyond the boundaries of the world that,

> it follows that these spaces contain corporeal substance which is indefinitely extended. For, as has already been shown very fully, the idea of the extension which we conceive to be in a given space is exactly the same as the idea of corporeal substance.

> (*Principles*, II, §21, *CSM*, I, p. 232)

The crucial point here is the identification of extended space with extended substance. As Garber has shown, this is based on the metaphysical principle that 'nothing has no properties'.[19] So if space has extension, and extension is essential to body, then extended space is just extended substance. But what of the claim that extension is essential to body? This represents a decisive departure from the scholastic view of extension. For the late scholastics, such as Suárez and Toletus, defined extension as a *proper accident* of body; that is an accident that occurs in an entire species alone (in this case body) and yet a particular member of that species may lack it.[20] By contrast, for Descartes, extension was *the* essential attribute of body, one that no body can lack and still be a body.[21]

Did Boyle accept the Cartesian identification of space with extended substance? As we have seen (chapter 2, §2.1), on this question Boyle, notoriously, preferred to keep an open mind. He tells us that he has been pressed by many, including some of his best friends, to declare his hand on the famous controversy regarding the vacuum, but that he refuses to,

> since the decision of the question seems to depend upon the stating of the true notion of body, whose essence the Cartesians affirm, and most other philosophers deny, to consist only in extension, according to the three dimensions, length, breadth, and depth or thickness; for, if Mr. Des Cartes's notion be admitted, it will be irrational to admit a vacuum, since any space, that is pretended to be empty, must be acknowledged to have three dimensions, and consequently all that is necessary to essentuate a body . . .
>
> (*Notion of Nature, Works*, V, p. 227)[22]

Over and again Boyle refuses to commit himself on this issue. Although he finds Descartes' view attractive, he has reservations because the definition of matter is connected both with the question of divisibility and that of the existence of a vacuum and on both of these questions Boyle is agnostic. One important reservation that Boyle has with Descartes' notion of matter is that it implies a limit on God's omnipotence.

> *Des Cartes*, in making the nature of a body to consist in extension every way, has a notion of it, which it is more easy to find fault with, than to substitute a better; yet I fear, it will appear to be attended, not only with this inconvenience, that God cannot, within the compass of this world, wherein if any body vanish into nothing, the place or space left behind it, must have the three dimensions, and so be a true body, annihilate the least particle of matter, at least without, at the same instant and place, creating as much . . .
>
> (*Excellency of Theology, Works*, IV, p. 43)[23]

Another typical expression of this agnosticism is found in the 'Possibility of the Resurrection' where Boyle claims that 'the true notion of body consists either alone in its extension, or in that and impenetrability together' (*Works*, IV, pp. 198–199, *S*. pp. 202–203).[24] So it is clear that Boyle does not deny the necessity of extension for material substance. However, Boyle does question the sufficiency of extension as the defining characteristic of matter. And the denial of this sufficiency would undermine any commitment to the identification of extended substance with extended space.

3.3 Internal space, external space and position as a mode

Now there is another feature of Descartes' theory of place that we have not yet discussed. It marks an important point of contact between Descartes and his scholastic heritage. It is the distinction between internal and external space. For Descartes, as for Aristotle, external space is the surface immediately surrounding a body.[25] Internal space is identified with body, but we can abstract from the extended body and conceive of the extension generically. Thus, when a body moves, there is a sense in which it takes its particular place with it. But its internal (generic) space remains to be filled by another body (or bodies). As such, Descartes' internal space is very similar to the concept of *ubi* found in the scholastic Toletus.[26] And as for the ontological status of these two types of space, external space is a *mode* of the surrounded and surrounding bodies whereas internal space is a substance, extended matter.[27]

What was Boyle's view of this distinction? We have already seen that in the *Examen* and the 'Explication of the Rota Aristotelica' Boyle has little time for this scholastic distinction as it is found in Linus, particularly the concept of *ubi*. But there is one aspect of Descartes' view that Boyle may have adopted. It is the notion of position as a mode. For Descartes, when we abstract from external place and consider that place relative to other bodies, we derive the notion of position. The other bodies provide a reference frame for the position of the body in question. He says, '[w]hen we say that a thing is in a given place, all we mean is that it occupies such and such a position relative to other things' (*Principles*, II, §15, *CSM*, I, p. 229). Boyle seems to have taken over this abstracted and relative notion of position without appropriating for himself the notion of two-dimensional external place upon which it is founded in Descartes. And whereas for Descartes it is external place that is a mode of body, for Boyle it is relative position that is a mode. In the *Forms and Qualities* he says,

> there being actually in the universe great multitudes of corpuscles . . . there arise, in any distinct portion of matter which a number of them make up, two new accidents or events: the one doth more relate to each particular corpuscle <u>in reference to the (really or supposedly) stable bodies about it</u>, namely its *posture* . . .; and when two or more of such bodies are placed one by another, the manner of their being so placed . . . may be called their *order* . . . and indeed posture and order seem both of them reducible to situation. And when many corpuscles do so convene together as to compose any distinct body . . . then from their other <u>accidents (or modes)</u>, and from these two last mentioned, there doth emerge a certain disposition or contrivance of parts . . . which we may call the *texture* of it.
>
> (*Works*, III, p. 22, *S*. p. 30, underlining added)[28]

Of course there is a tension here in Boyle's notion of position (or situation) as a mode. It is a close relative of the tension found in Descartes' ascription of modal status to motion. For position as Boyle defines it, is a relative notion, whereas modes are monadic 'modifications' of substances. But we have already seen that while Boyle adopts much of the Suaracian terminology into his theory of matter that he found in Descartes, he does so in a very simplified manner.

And one should not be taken in by the scholastic nomenclature that Boyle employs, for underlying it is a thoroughly mechanistic ontology purged of powers, forms and subtle distinctions.

It is an interesting question to determine the extent to which Boyle was committed to a relative notion of place. And we will return to this when we discuss some claims in the secondary literature on Boyle's view of place. But for now there is another issue in the ontology of place that needs to be addressed. It is the question as to whether place is to be regarded as a substance, an attribute or something else. Patrizi was the first to hold that space was something other than a substance or an accident,[29] but the view was popularised by Descartes' antagonist Pierre Gassendi and it was through Gassendi that Boyle encountered it.

4 Gassendi's view

In the 'Advices', having treated Aristotle and Descartes, Boyle moves on to discuss Gassendi's theory of place. He tells us that Gassendi and his followers

> will not allow it [place] to be a substance, because it is neither body, nor spirit, but only somewhat, that has a capacity to receive or contain bodies, and would subsist, though God should annihilate all the substances he has created. And for the same reason it is not to be called an accident, since that necessarily requires a substance to reside in . . . whereas in case of the annihilation of the world itself, . . . their place or space would still remain . . . whence *Gassendus* wittily infers, that bodies are rather accidental in respect of place, than space in respect of bodies.
>
> (*Works*, IV, p. 460)

The novelty of Patrizi/Gassendi view is obvious. Space (and time) is an exception to the over-arching substance/attribute distinction to which Descartes, following almost all of the scholastics, was committed. For Descartes, space could be considered as either a mode of matter or as matter itself. For Gassendi, it is a pre-existent something in which created substances are positioned. Should God annihilate all substances, space would continue to exist. Moreover, as mentioned above, Gassendi's was an isotropic space, it was the same in all directions. This was in stark contrast with Epicurean space which had a downward direction in which a rain of atoms fell. Boyle objected to the Epicurean view of non-isotropic space. He claimed that because '[t]here being neither upwards nor downwards, nor center, nor circumference in Infinite Space, the Epicureans have no reason to suppose a motion of Atoms downwards . . .' (*BP*, vol. 1, fol. 38).[30] Gassendi's notion of space was not open to this objection and as such was an adumbration of Newton's concept of absolute space.[31]

Boyle finds this view quite appealing. He mentions it in various works, at one point claiming that Gassendi's view of time and place has been 'very plausibly (if not solidly) shewn' (*Reason and Religion, Works*, IV, p. 174).[32] But as we have come to expect, Boyle reserves judgment on Gassendi's view. It is no coincidence that we find his statements on Gassendi's view in his discussions of the insurmountable problems involved in explicating corporeal entities. For Boyle, the notions of space and time are two of the prime examples of notions about which it is very difficult to get a clear and consistent conception. Yet Robert Kargon has claimed that Boyle 'cannot accept the Epicurean view of absolute space and time', for according to Gassendi and Charleton, both space and time are uncreated and would survive the annihilation of the universe by God. 'Such limitation upon divine power is unacceptable to Boyle' (Kargon 1964, p. 191).[33]

However, Kargon's claim is dubious on a number of grounds. First, to my knowledge, Boyle never dismisses Gassendi's view and, as we have seen, he considered it quite plausible. Second, the passage Kargon refers us to, while mentioning Gassendi's theory of place, does not mention any objection on the grounds of a limit to divine omnipotence. In fact, one of the main objections to the Cartesian view, which was antithetical to that of Gassendi, was that it limited God's omnipotence. For it implied that God could not both annihilate a corporeal body and preserve three-dimensional empty space.[34] Boyle was only too willing to bring this objection against Descartes.[35] And Gassendi himself makes this very point in order to argue that his own view is preferable.[36] So, if anything, Boyle would have considered Gassendi's view as more tenable than Descartes' precisely because it did not imply any limit to God's omnipotence.

Third, while it is true that space for Gassendi and Charleton is uncreated and that this posed theological problems, this doctrine is not a necessary feature of the view. Boyle could readily have adopted the Gassendist ontology of space and posited that it was created by God antecedent to the creation of material bodies. Alternatively, he could have taken the line of More and identified space with God's omnipresence. What Boyle *would* have to sacrifice if he were to accept a variant of Gassendi's view is the exclusiveness of the substance/ attribute ontology. But reading Boyle's discussions of Gassendi's view leads me to believe that this is the one aspect of the view that Boyle found attractive. I conclude then, that this theological objection is simply not sufficient for Boyle to reject Gassendi's view. There would have to be features of his corpuscular hypothesis, features that implied the denial of absolute space, for Boyle to have had sufficient grounds for rejecting a modified version of the Gassendist position. Peter Alexander believes that there are such grounds. So it is to his discussion of Boyle's view on space that we now turn.

5 Did Boyle believe in absolute or relative space?

Alexander not only denies that Boyle believes in absolute space, he argues positively that Boyle believes in relative space. In his brief discussion of this issue, Alexander makes three claims. First, that '[t]here is little evidence that

Boyle believed in absolute space'. Second, that Boyle defines posture and order in relative terms. And third, that if Boyle believes in relative space it would support another interpretation of Alexander's, viz. that Boyle really attributes not simply motion and rest to corpuscles, but the property of *mobility*.[37]

Let us deal with the question of mobility first. Stewart (1987, pp. 107–108) has rightly questioned Alexander's interpretation here. There is no doubt that Boyle saw the importance of the relation between motion and rest. He believed that any corpuscle always has one or the other. But two considerations count strongly against Boyle consistently meaning mobility when he speaks of motion or rest. First, in the numerous contexts in which he discusses the primary affections of matter he never, to my knowledge, uses the term. To call 'mobility' a technical term in Boyle as Alexander does (1981, p. 28 and 1985, p. 145) is completely unwarranted. In fact, when Boyle does use the term 'mobility' it usually has the sense of 'motion' and not 'being moveable'.[38] Second, while it must be conceded that Boyle's discussion of inseparable accidents early in *Forms and Qualities* would have been much 'tidier' had he considered mobility an essential attribute of matter rather than 'motion or rest', there is a strong polemical vein in Boyle's discussion of the mechanical hypothesis that reveals that Boyle was not thinking in terms of the property of mobility. In his discussions of the difference between his corpuscularianism and Epicurean atomism Boyle is adamant, repeatedly, that motion is not essential to matter. In fact he makes this very point almost immediately before his discussion of the inseparable accidents of matter in the *Forms and Qualities* (*Works*, III, p. 15, *S*. p. 19),[39] a point that would not have carried had he been thinking in terms of mobility. I conclude that Alexander's attribution of mobility to Boyle's corpuscles is anachronistic.

This brings us then to Alexander's claim that there is little evidence that Boyle believes in absolute space. The claim comes immediately after a quote from the *Forms and Qualities* which Alexander seems to take as a lapse on Boyle's part. For the passage says,

> if we should conceive that all the rest of the universe were annihilated, except any [sc. any *one*] of these intire and undivided corpuscles . . . it is hard to say what could be attributed to it, besides matter, motion (or rest) bulk, and shape . . .
>
> (Quoted from Alexander 1985, pp. 74–75)[40]

Alexander admits that the attribution of motion to the lonely corpuscle only makes sense within the frame of reference provided by absolute space, but asserts that there is little (other?) evidence for absolute space in Boyle. However, once one begins to examine the Boylean corpus, both published and un-published, one discovers numerous passages that betray at least an implicit commitment to absolute space; that is a conception of space which allows the coherent possibility of empty space and in which space a singly existing body can be said to be at motion or rest.

First there is the casual way in which Boyle often speaks in absolutist terms when he mentions space. For instance, in 'Fluidity and Firmness' when speaking of the interactions of the particles of fluids he says, 'it can be no difficult matter . . . to thrust them out of those places, which being already in motion they [the particles] were disposed to quit, especially *there being vacant rooms at hand*, ready to admit them as soon as they are displaced' (*Works*, I, p. 387).[41] Perhaps this is just a manner of speaking, but we also need to consider that there is an entire essay, 'Intestine Motions', which is given over to a discussion of the question of whether or not there may be bodies that are in absolute or perfect rest. By 'absolute rest' Boyle means 'a continuance of a body in the same place *precisely*, and includes an absolute negation of all local motion' (*Works*, I, p. 444).[42] Boyle's use of the term 'absolute rest' suggests that he is conceiving of place in absolute terms. For a body to be at absolute rest is for it to remain in 'the same place precisely'. While these texts are not decisive on the issue, the most natural reading of them is that Boyle is assuming that place is immoveable and that, irrespective of the motions of surrounding bodies, one particular body might be 'in a state of perfect rest' in relation to an absolute reference frame.

Moreover, as already mentioned, Boyle's main argument against the Epicurean notion that motion is an innate property of matter, is that all matter may be at rest and furthermore, he surmises that after its creation but before its differentiation into various bodies, matter actually was at rest. It required God to set it in motion.[43] This presupposes an absolute conception of space. Any residual doubts about this should be dispelled by the following extract from the *Boyle Papers* where Boyle surmises that the lonely body would continue in motion.

> Suppose a Ball were in motion, & all the world should be on a sudden annihilated about it; why may not the motion of that Ball be continu'd? There being nothing to stop it; and if it be continu'd, we have a motion where the *mobile* dos not quitt the neighborhood of som' bodys and approach nearer to others.
>
> (*BP*, vol. 1, fol. 3)[44]

This extract confirms that the passage from the *Forms and Qualities* quoted above is not anomalous, but is quite consistent with other instances of the same thought experiment.

We come then to Alexander's third claim, that the definitions of posture and order in the *Forms and Qualities* are given in relative terms. It has already been pointed out above that posture and order, which are reducible to situation, are indeed relative notions as defined in the *Forms and Qualities*. Yet this does not preclude the possibility that Boyle believes in absolute space. The relevant question is whether situation is a relative attribute of bodies *simpliciter*, or whether Boyle is furnishing us with a relative notion of situation in a derivative sense. And given that just prior to defining situation he assumes an absolute frame of reference (in the thought experiment), it is only natural to take his definition as being derivative. That is, any corpuscle has a situation relative to absolute space, but the relevant notion of situation, given its role in texture and the causal interactions of bodies, is its situation relative to other bodies.

Thus I conclude, *pace* Alexander, that there is substantial evidence in Boyle that he conceives of space in absolutist terms. To my knowledge he never discusses the topic of space in terms of a choice between absolute and relative conceptions. However, just because Boyle does not explicitly discuss the issue does not mean that he is not working with a conception of absolute space.[45]

6 Conclusion

If Boyle rejected the Aristotelian cosmos what did he put in its place? Boyle saw the issue of the nature of place as very difficult, perhaps insoluble. His claims to have applied himself to it are backed up by evidence of a wide grasp of the various issues and views that were discussed in his time. But for all that, he puts forward no positive doctrine of space in his works. His official view was one of nescience on the issues of finitude, the existence of extra-cosmic void space and the possibility of intra-corpuscular void space. On this latter issue he was particularly sensitive because it was related to the twin issues of the definition and the divisibility of matter. But once we go beyond the 'official' declarations of nescience and examine his more unguarded comments and principles within his corpuscular philosophy that might betray his real view, we find, implicit in his thought, a view that was fairly standard in the mid-seventeenth century.

Boyle seems to have believed, or at least had a preference for, an infinite, absolute, three-dimensional space that contains within it a finite world of corporeal substance. Whether this world was a Cartesian plenum[46] or contained intra-corpuscular void spaces was yet to be determined by natural philosophy, though there was an ever-increasing volume of experimental evidence that suggested that void space was possible. And the *a priori* considerations against the notion of indivisibles and intra-corpuscular void space were not compelling. In short, Boyle's preferred view seems to be the Stoic view of a finite world within infinite void space.

It must be re-emphasised that Boyle shied away from metaphysical disputes. This arose, in part, from his aversion to dogmatism and systematising. And it is in part due to his '*via media*': his attempt to gain wide acceptance for the corpuscular hypothesis amongst Cartesians, atomists and all other natural philosophers. Moreover, his corpuscular philosophy was subject to the parameters set by his Christian theology. But ultimately one must concede that Boyle's physics is undermined by his decision not to come down on one side or the other in the relevant philosophical disputes: the issues of void, divisibility, infinity and the definition of matter. For instance, if he really was committed to absolute space he should have rejected the Cartesian identification of extension and space outright rather than declaring his nescience. Thus there is no prospect of unearthing a coherent physics in Boyle's works.

However, there is a sense in which the asking of technical questions with respect to space is to approach Boyle from the wrong direction. Boyle was neither a Descartes, a Leibniz nor a Newton. He was concerned with explicating the nature of qualities and establishing the corpuscular hypothesis. Boyle was first and foremost a philosopher of the qualities, not motion, space or time. The issues of the existence of a void and the divisibility of matter according to Boyle were precisely the questions that the corpuscular hypothesis did *not* need to settle. Boyle's attitude was to 'wait and see' regarding the existence of a void rather than attempting to settle it solely on *a priori* grounds.[47] But meanwhile, the corpuscular hypothesis would set up a scientific agenda that promised tangible results. This is why most of Boyle's comments on the nature of place are found in works with a theological and an epistemological orientation and why there is no sustained discussion of the nature of place in either his philosophical works on the corpuscular hypothesis or in his experimental works.

Finally, with regard to our quest to understand Boyle's mechanical philosophy, the investigation of his views on place have enabled us to make one significant advance. It follows from Boyle's implicit adoption of a framework of absolute space that he conceived of motion in absolute terms. And this is not surprising. It is entirely consistent with his attribution of the status of modes to both motion and rest, with his denial that motion is an inseparable accident of corpuscles and with his account of how God first put matter in motion after its creation. But God's role was not limited to imparting motion to matter in the beginning. According to Boyle, he has an important and ongoing role in upholding the laws of motion. But this takes us to the subject of the next chapter.

Notes

1 For the same argument see *BP*, vol. 22, fol. 105r, in M. B. Hall 1987, p. 127.

2 Boyle introduces this position earlier in section V, on p. 192. The view was a commonplace amongst Aristotelians and chemists. See for example Daniel Sennert, *Hypomnemata physica*, 1636, III, chapter 2. I thank Emily Michael for this reference.

3 See also *Things Above Reason*, *Works*, IV, p. 412, *S*. p. 219.

4 See Aristotle's *Physics*, IV, 4, *Barnes*, I, pp. 358ff.

5 This criticism of Aristotle's view was first made by Theophrastus, Aristotle's successor. See R. Sorabji 1988, pp. 192ff. See also *Christian Virtuoso*, I, *Appendix*, *Works*, VI, p. 687 and *BP* vol. 1, fol. 139.

6 See *Defence*, *Works*, I, pp. 147ff and p. 183. Digby also rejected the notion of *ubi* although he accepted Aristotle's definition of place. See *Two Treatises*, pp. 6–7 and pp. 33–34. For the claim that *ubi* is identical to virtual extension see E. Grant 1981a, p. 177. Moreover, it is worth noting that Boyle mentions the scholastic Maignon (1601–1676) in *Defence*: see p. 137 and p. 145.

7 *Defence, Works*, I, p. 183 and p. 185. See also *ibid.*, p. 149. For a discussion of this passage see J. E. McGuire and M. Tamny 1983, pp. 85–86. Linus provides an interesting contrast to Boyle, for he was a keen scholastic and yet committed to an indivisibilism of matter, place and time which are distinctively non-Aristotelian doctrines. By contrast, Boyle rejected time atoms and was non-committal on material atoms and yet was overtly anti-Aristotelian.

8 F. F. Centore (1970, p. 59) correctly claims that 'it was probably Hooke who wrote the attack on Linus' "Aristotle's Wheel"'. See *Defence, Works*, I, p. 146, and for further discussion see A. Clericuzio (1998).

9 A similar argument is found in the *Boyle Papers*, vol. 1, fol. 33 where Boyle says

> In the *Hypothesis* of the worlds being Finite, the outward Heaven cannot move in the Imaginary space, according to the notion that even the Cartesians have of local motion. And a Bullet suppos'd to be shot beyond the Convex surface of the Outwardmost Heaven, thô it do not change its Aristotelical Place, nor dos move according to the Cartesian notion of moving; dos yet goe further & further from the uppermost Heaven, which in regard of the Bullet, may be lookt upon as quiescent.

See also *BP*, vol. 5, fol. 12 and vol. 1, fol. 139.

10 See *Principles*, II, §25, *CSM*, I, p. 233.

11 See *Letter to Henry More*, 5 February 1649, *CSMK*, p. 364 and 15 April 1649, *ibid.*, pp. 374–375.

12 'Imaginary space' is a technical term amongst scholastics with a wide range of meanings from fictitious to actual: see E. Grant 1981a, pp. 117ff.

13 For a sampling of references see also *Forms and Qualities, Works*, III, p. 24, *S.* p. 32, *High Veneration, Works*, V, p. 140 and *Notion of Nature, Works*, V, p. 179, *S.* p. 190.

14 See for example *High Veneration, Works*, V, p. 138.

15 *Letter to Henry More*, 5 February 1649, *CSMK*, p. 364.

16 *Letter to Henry More*, 15 April 1649, *CSMK*, pp. 374–375. See A. Koyré 1957, chapter V for a discussion of the Descartes/More debate.

17 For Boyle's nescience on the finitude of the world see *Christian Virtuoso, I, Appendix, Works*, VI, p. 693.

18 Descartes' position on the finitude of the world in the *Principles* comes just four sections before the definition of motion to which Boyle alludes in this passage from the 'Advices', see *Principles*, II, §21, *CSM*, I, p. 232. It is interesting to compare Boyle with Newton's early discussion of this same issue in Descartes. See Newton's *De Gravitatione*, in A. R. Hall and M. B. Hall 1962, pp. 135–136. See also *Questiones*, 87.131 in J. E. McGuire and M. Tamny 1983, p. 453.

19 See D. Garber 1992, pp. 132–133. See also *Principles*, II, §16, *CSM*, I, pp. 229–230 and *Letter to Arnauld*, 29 July 1648, *CSMK*, pp. 358–359.

20 Here I am following D. Garber 1992, p. 151.

21 In this Descartes follows the Nominalists such as Ockham, see D. Des Chene 1996, p. 100.

22 See also *Spring of the Air, Works*, I, pp. 37–38.

23 Note the close verbal parallels with *ibid.*, I, p. 38.

24 See also *Excellency of Theology, Works*, IV, p. 43.

25 See *Principles*, II, §13 and §15, *CSM*, I, p. 228 and 229. In *Principles*, II, §15 Descartes modifies Aristotle's definition of external place by claiming that the surface is not part of the surrounding body, but merely the boundary between it and the surrounded body considered abstractly and relative to neighbouring bodies considered to be immobile.

26 See *Principles*, II, §10, *CSM*, I, p. 227. On Toletus see E. Grant 1981a, chapter 6 and D. Garber 1992, pp. 149ff.

27 See *Principles*, II, §15, *CSM*, I, p. 229 and *Letter to Mesland*, 2 May 1644, *CSMK*, p. 235 and 9 February 1645, p. 241.

28 See also *Works*, III, pp. 35–36, *S*. p. 51 and 'History of Particular Qualities', *Works*, III, p. 298, *S*. p. 106.

29 Patrizi's view may well have originated with some of the ancient commentators on Aristotle. See R. Sorabji 1988, pp. 29–30.

30 See also Aristotle's *Physics*, IV, 4, 215ª6–12, *Barnes*, I, p. 365.

31 There is some debate as to the extent to which Newton's conception is derived from Gassendi or More. See J. E. McGuire 1978 and E. Grant 1981a, chapter 8. For a balanced assessment see A. R. Hall 1992.

32 The primary reference is to time here, but Boyle qualifies it by saying 'which they also hold of space'. And since the arguments for space were the same as those for time it seems reasonable to conclude that Boyle found the view of place very plausible too. See also *Christian Virtuoso*, *I*, *Appendix*, *Works*, VI, p. 684.

33 See also R. Kargon 1966, p. 104. For Gassendi see *Syntagma philosophicum*, *Physics*, *Brush*, pp. 389–390 and for Charleton see *Physiologia*, p. 68.

34 For example see *Letter to More*, 5 February 1649, *CSMK*, p. 363.

35 See *Excellency of Theology*, *Works*, IV, p. 43 and *Reason and Religion*, *Works*, IV, pp. 163–164 where Boyle quotes Descartes' response to this theologically suspect implication of his theory. Boyle gives an English translation of the French version from volume II of the Clerselier edition of *Lettres de Descartes*. The original letter was written in Latin, see *AT*, V, pp. 223–224.

36 See *Syntagma philosophicum*, *Physics*, *Brush*, p. 386.

37 See P. Alexander 1985, p. 75. A. Pyle appears to follow Alexander on this point, see his 1995, p. 541 and pp. 544.

38 See for example 'Fluidity and Firmness', *Works*, I, p. 402 and 'Intestine Motions', *Works*, I, p. 447.

39 See also 'Requisite Digression', *Works*, II, p. 42, *S*. p. 165.

40 See *Forms and Qualities*, *Works*, III, p. 22, *S*. p. 30.

41 Henry Power was convinced that in 'Fluidity and Firmness' Boyle had 'demonstrated' that 'there is no such thing in the world as an absolute quiescence' ('Preface' to *Experimental Philosophy*, quoted from M. B. Hall 1970, p. 124). See also *General History of Air*, *Works*, V, p. 640.

42 See also chapter VIII of *Languid Motion*, *Works*, V, pp. 23ff.

43 See also *High Veneration*, *Works*, V, p. 140. E. A. Burtt claimed that Boyle was aided by More's conception of absolute space in denying that motion is inherent to matter. But I can find no evidence for this. See Burtt 1932, p. 168.

44 It is likely that Boyle has Descartes' definition of motion in mind here.

45 Another who has claimed that Boyle 'would have rejected the doctrine of absolute space' is J. E. McGuire. The only reason he gives is that Boyle was 'critical of the reification of concepts'. See McGuire 1972, p. 532.

46 Boyle sometimes refers to the world in Cartesian terms as 'our vortex', see for instance *Notion of Nature, Works*, V, p. 208.
47 See *Spring of the Air, Works*, I, pp. 37–38 and 'The Preface' to 'Some Specimens', *Works*, I, pp. 355–356.

7 Laws and concurrence

The next step in the explication of Boyle's mechanical philosophy is to clarify his conception of the laws of nature and to understand the functions that laws of nature have within his corpuscular hypothesis. The relation between motion and the laws of nature in Boyle's thought is of paramount importance. This is because most, if not all, of the physical laws of nature *are* laws of motion or are ultimately reducible to the laws of motion[1] and because most (if not all) of the functions of physical laws in his corpuscular hypothesis have to do with the nature of motion. Thus Galileo's law of fall which appeals to weight, would ultimately be reducible to another law or laws that appeal only to the mechanical affections of bodies. And the laws of motion apply not only in the manifest world, but also at the unobservable level.[2]

1 Boyle's conception of laws

Boyle's conception of laws of nature is set within a broader conception of laws that bears most of the hallmarks of a natural law theory. The classic features of a divine lawgiver, voluntarism and a teleological conception of the design and function of natural and non-natural objects are all present in his account. In this regard Boyle is typical of most British natural philosophers of the mid-seventeenth century. Locke's early work *Essays on the Law of Nature* (c.1660) is a paradigm example of this view, as is Richard Cumberland's *An Inquiry into the Laws of Nature* (1672). And Boyle's *Notion of Nature* is another fine example within this tradition. While it was not published until 1686, much of it was in fact written in the mid-1660s and contains the most extensive discussions of laws to be found in his published works.

Yet there is one feature of Boyle's natural law theory that diverges from the classic characterisation of this position. For Cumberland, all objects in nature, whether animate or inanimate, are subject to the laws of nature. And since all laws of nature have the same source, the distinction between moral and physical laws is derivative. In actual fact moral and physical laws are two species of the same genus – natural laws. Thus in Cumberland's *Inquiry* we find him moving quite unselfconsciously from one species to the other. He says, the whole of *moral philosophy*, and of the laws of nature is ultimately resolv'd into natural observations known by the experience of all men, or into the conclusions of true *natural philosophy*.

(Cumberland 1672, p. 41)

The point of departure for Boyle is that he posits a sharp dichotomy between moral and physical laws. He maintains that it is not strictly correct to say that matter 'obeys' laws of nature because only intelligent agents can respond to laws. Thus, those who claim that the nature of a thing is 'the law that it receives from the Creator, and according to which it acts on all occasions' (*Notion of Nature*, *Works*, V, p. 170, *S.* p. 181) are wrong.[3] Strictly speaking, when things without understanding are said to act according to laws of nature this is only a 'figurative expression'. For,

> a law being but a *notional rule of acting according to the declared will of a superior*, it is plain that nothing but an intellectual being can be properly capable of receiving and acting by a *law*.
>
> (*Notion of Nature*, *Works*, V, p. 170, *S.* p. 181)[4]

Now, while Boyle posits a sharp dichotomy between moral and physical laws, his notion of physical laws is quite different from the modern conception. It is not fully extricated from its 'anthropocentric origins'. That is to say, all laws for Boyle whether moral or physical, have a lawgiver and are to be obeyed. Where they differ is the manner in which the recipients of a law are able to respond to them. Rational and volitional agents are capable of responding to laws, inanimate objects are not. This is why Boyle says in *The Christian Virtuoso* that 'I look upon a law as a moral, *not a physical cause*, as being indeed but a notional thing, according to which, an intelligent and free agent is bound to regulate its actions' (*Works*, V, p. 521, italics added). Of course here and in the previous quote Boyle is appealing to the doctrine of insensible matter (as he does repeatedly throughout *Notion of Nature*). In fact, in *The Christian Virtuoso* he goes even further by stating that,

> inanimate bodies are utterly incapable of understanding what a law is, or what it enjoins, or when they act conformably or unconformably to it; and therefore the actions of inanimate bodies, which cannot incite or moderate their own actions, are produced by real power, *not by laws* . . .
>
> (*Works*, V, p. 521, italics added)[5]

Now if talk of laws of nature is merely metaphorical for inanimate bodies and the actions of inanimate bodies are not produced by laws, why does Boyle so often appeal to *laws* of nature? And what does he have in mind when he claims that

> it seems manifest enough that whatsoever is done in the world, at least wherein the rational soul intervenes not, is really effected by corporeal

causes and agents, *acting . . . according to the laws of motion* settled by the omniscient Author of things [?]

(*Notion of Nature, Works*, V, p. 176, *S.* p. 185, italics added)?

Hints of Boyle's answers to these questions are found in the passages quoted above. First, Boyle tells us that the actions of inanimate bodies are produced by 'real power'. Second, that they act 'according to the laws of motion settled by the omniscient Author'. It is by fleshing out the notions of real power and the role of the God in the actions of bodies that Boyle's unique understanding of laws and causes becomes clear.

2 The causal efficacy of matter

One interpretation of this issue in Boyle, that of J. E. McGuire, is to claim that the 'real power' that Boyle mentions in *The Christian Virtuoso* is none other than the power of God himself. McGuire says, 'though physical objects appear to act so as to bring about changes, in reality true causal power cannot be ascribed to them'.[6] On this occasionalist reading, Boyle's corpuscles are not only nomically impotent but causally impotent as well. Yet McGuire's view has been seriously challenged by John Milton, Timothy Shanahan and others.[7] Milton points out the lack of explicit textual support and Shanahan offers an alternative interpretation. Shanahan argues convincingly that Boyle was what he styles a 'concurrentist', holding that both matter and God make some contribution to the production of the actual causes and effects that we observe in the world.

Shanahan sets up a dialectic as follows. The Aristotelians Aquinas and Molina were attempting to find a *via media* between the Scylla of deism and the Charybdis of occasionalism. Deism, which stresses the causal efficacy of matter and the laws of nature, renders God's active and continual involvement in creation superfluous and presents difficulties providing a coherent account of miracles. By contrast, occasionalism denies any causal efficacy to matter and requires the constant causal intervention of God in every physical event. It renders the miraculous intelligible at the cost of making secondary causes superfluous. In effectively steering between these two extremes, Shanahan argues, Aquinas and Molina adopted a view that requires the immediate causal activity of both God and matter in the manifestation of every natural phenomenon. And Shanahan finds a very similar view in Boyle. He rightly points out the numerous passages in Boyle where the latter claims that God's general concourse is necessary. For instance, Boyle considers God

as the author of the universe, and the free establisher of the laws of motion, whose general concourse is necessary to the conservation and efficacy of every particular physical agent . . .

(*Reason and Religion, Works*, IV, p. 161)

This concourse 'consists in conserving these laws of motion which govern the mechanical interactions of the parts of matter'. But matter also makes a causal contribution to corpuscular interactions. 'Natural bodies can be said to possess causal powers in virtue of the motion they can impart to one another through impact, but they are incapable of sustaining the lawful order of the universe without the continued assistance of God' (Shanahan 1988, p. 567).

Now Shanahan's interpretation merits extended comment. First, with regard to Boyle's intellectual debts, to my knowledge, there is no evidence that Boyle's views were influenced by those of Aquinas or Molina. Second, while it is possible from Boyle's published works to show that he was concerned to avoid the extremes of deism, it is very difficult to demonstrate that Boyle's account of the dual causal contribution of God and matter is also a response to occasionalism. This is because Boyle does not discuss occasionalism in the contexts where he sets out the rudiments of what Shanahan styles his 'concurrentism'. Moreover, in the few places where Boyle does discuss the doctrine of occasionalism it is always in favourable terms.[8] So Shanahan's exposition of Boyle needs carefully to be demarcated from the dialectical context that gave rise to 'concurrentism'. One should not regard Boyle as consciously tapping into an established philosophical tradition that stretches back to Aquinas (and Shanahan is careful not to claim that there are any such connections). Nor can Boyle be understood to have forged his view in response to the two conflicting theological extremes. Having said this, however, I believe that Shanahan's is a very significant interpretive advance on McGuire's view and that it is the best attempt in the secondary literature at articulating the rather subtle relation between the causal contributions of God and matter in natural events.[9]

Yet Shanahan's interpretation can be fine-tuned. There is more to Boyle's 'concurrentism' than simply the dual causal contribution of matter and God to effects in the natural world. As Shanahan has noted, when Boyle says that the actions of inanimate bodies are produced by real power, he is attributing actual causal efficacy to matter. Thus he says that these actions are 'really effected by corporeal causes and agents' (*Notion of Nature, Works*, V, p. 176, *S.* p. 185). Moreover, Shanahan rightly claims that for Boyle bodies have causal efficacy 'in virtue of the motion they can impart to one another through impact'. In *Notion of Nature* Boyle tells us that God maintains 'those powers which he gave the parts of matter to transmit their motion thus and thus to one another' (*ibid.*, p. 170, *S.* p. 181).[10] Again, in *High Veneration* Boyle speaks of senseless matter being 'qualified to transfer it [motion] according to determinate rules, which itself cannot understand' (*ibid.*, p. 150). So matter is not completely inert. It does have the power to transmit motion from one body to another. Yet even this power is imparted to it by the divine author. It is not an inherent quality of matter but 'given' to the parts of matter.[11] However, we can go further than this and specify other causal powers that matter has. For it appears that a second power implanted in matter is its capacity to persevere in motion in the absence of other forces, that is, in the absence of collisions. Boyle tells us that, it may be said, that all bodies, once in the state of actual motion, whatever cause first brought them to it, are moved by an internal principle: as, for instance, an arrow, that actually flies in the air towards a mark, moves by some principle or other residing within itself . . .

(*Notion of Nature, Works*, V, p. 209)[12]

We have seen (chapter 5, §8) that this internal principle is probably a type of impetus. In addition to the powers that matter has to transmit motion on collision and to persevere in motion, Boyle seems to attribute to matter the power to change the determination or direction of motion. In an interesting discussion of mind/body interaction in his 'Advices' he says,

whereas men think they have sufficiently enumerated the ways of determining the motion of a body, by saying, that the determination must be made, either in the line, wherein the impellent, that put it into motion, made it move, or in the line, wherein it was determined to move by the situation of the resisting body, that it met with in its way; the motions of the animal spirits, if not also some other internal parts of the body, may, the body being duly disposed, be determined by the human will; which is a way quite differing from the other. And how this attribute, I mean *the power of determining the motion of a body*, without any power to impart motion to that body, should belong to an immaterial creature, which has no corporeal parts to resist the free passage of a body, and thereby change the line of its motion, is not yet, nor perhaps ever will be in this life, clearly conceived by us men . . .

(*Works*, IV, p. 457, italics added)

It is Boyle's talk of 'the power of determining the motion of a body' that is of significance here. The point at issue in the immediate context is: how can the soul have this power when it cannot even transfer motion? However, implicit in the passage is the belief that a body which does have the power to transfer motion, also has this power to 'change the line of its [another body's] motion'.[13] So we have three minimal causal powers attributable to matter that are involved in collisions. First there is the power to transmit motion, second the power to persevere in motion and third the power to change the determination of motion. And these causal powers form the first strand of Boyle's 'concurrentism'.[14]

Now it must be stressed that this is a reconstruction of Boyle's mechanism and that there is no systematic exposition in his works of the manner in which matter has causal efficacy. The interpreter has to comb rather disparate sources in order to extract the details of Boyle's understanding of the nature of matter's causal powers. However, once this is done, the reconstruction can be seen to harmonise well with the more general descriptions of the combined roles of God and matter in the manifestation of natural phenomena, the occasional claims that matter has been endowed with active powers, references to the mechanical powers of matter[15] and the more specialised topics that Boyle deals with, such as mind/body interaction (see chapter 8) and final causation.

Finally, it is worth digressing to assess a suggestion put by Alan Chalmers. Chalmers has asked (in conversation) what is the relation between the impenetrability of matter and those powers that give it causal efficacy in collisions. Could it be that impenetrability is the power property in virtue of which matter is causally efficacious? In order to explore this suggestion we need to consider each of the three causal powers attributed to matter in relation to impenetrability. And by juxtaposing a number of texts an interesting picture emerges. First, consider the power of transferring motion. In an unpublished discourse Boyle tells us that

> neither the Conarion, nor the Animall spirits, nor any part, whether gross or subtill of the Body, can mechanically act, upon the incorporeal soul; which wants Impenetrabillity, on whose account, in the subject that receives it, Local motion can be produced by the action, or motion of a Body.
>
> (*BP*, vol. 2, fol. 105)

The implication here is that local motion is produced in the patient, that is, transferred, on account of its impenetrability. It is the absence of impenetrability that renders mind/body interaction so inexplicable. Boyle does not elaborate on the relation between the transference of motion and impenetrability, but he has said enough to show that in his mind they are intimately connected. What then of the power to change the direction of motion? Here we can refer back to the passage quoted above from the 'Advices'. What Boyle finds incomprehensible is 'how this attribute, I mean the power of determining the motion of a body, without any power to impart motion to that body, should belong to an immaterial creature, which has no corporeal parts to resist the free passage of a body, and thereby change the line of its motion'. Notice how it is the inability of the soul to 'resist the free passage of a body' that renders it difficult to account for the soul's power to change the direction of a body. The implication is that material bodies which are impenetrable can change the determination of a moving body in virtue of their impenetrability. It seems reasonable then to claim that at least two of the causal powers attributable to matter are intimately related to the general power of impenetrability. Whether they are reducible to impenetrability is not a question that Boyle addressed. But if this line of reasoning is anywhere near correct, then the implication is that Boyle should have included impenetrability as a mechanical affection of matter, for it is a crucial feature of all mechanical explanations.

3 God's nomic intervention

What then is the contribution of the laws of nature? The first point to note is that Boyle denies any connection between the nature of matter and the laws of nature. He explicitly says that 'the laws of motion . . . did not necessarily spring from the nature of matter, but depended upon the *will* of the divine author of things' (*Christian Virtuoso*, *I*, *Works*, V, p. 521, italics added). This simple point is extremely important to grasp if one is to understand the workings of Boyle's corpuscular hypothesis and it constitutes another way in which we can fine-tune Shanahan's thesis. For Boyle, there is a categorical rift between the natures of things and their law-like behaviour. And this, when combined with his theism, leads him naturally to the voluntarist view that the laws of nature are expressions of the divine will for his creation. The laws depend 'upon the will of the divine author' (*Christian Virtuoso*, *I*, *Works*, V, p. 521).[16]

Given that laws arise from the divine will and not from the nature of matter, it is not surprising to find that Boyle also claims that God's constant intervention is required to maintain them. He tells us in the 'Excellency of the Mechanical Hypothesis' that the phenomena of the world are physically produced because of 'the laws of motion being upheld by his incessant concourse and general providence' (*Works*, IV, pp. 68–69, *S.* p. 139).[17] The idea is that, while matter is causally efficacious in that it can transmit its motion in collisions, the nature of that transmission and the resultant motions are determined by the immanent activity of God. Since inanimate matter cannot obey the laws he has set down for it, God himself so directs matter as to conform to those laws. It is matter itself 'in conjunction with the laws of motion, freely established, and still maintained by God, among its parts' (*Notion of Nature*, *Works*, V, p. 179, *S.* p. 191) that gives rise to the ordered world. Thus we find Boyle saying that God,

> did so guide and overrule the motions of these parts at the beginning of things, as that . . . they were *finally* disposed into that beautiful and orderly frame we call the *world* . . . And I further conceive that he settled such laws or rules of local motion among the parts of the universal matter that, <u>by his ordinary and preserving concourse</u>, the several parts of the universe, thus once completed, should be able to maintain the great construction . . . of the mundane bodies, and propagate the species of living creatures.
>
> (*Notion of Nature*, *Works*, V, p. 179, *S.* p. 190, underlining added)

If God were to cease imposing his will on the motions of corpuscles, collisions would still occur because matter is causally efficacious, but chaos would result. For

> this most potent Author . . . of the world, hath not abandoned a master piece so worthy of Him, but does still maintain and preserve it, so regulating the stupendously swift motions of the great globes, and other vast masses of mundane matter, that they do not, by any notable irregularity, disorder the grand system of the universe, and reduce it to a kind of chaos, or confused state of shuffled and depraved things.
>
> (*Christian Virtuoso*, *I*, *Works*, V, p. 519)

For Boyle, God *determines the path or tracks* that the mobile corpuscles are to follow. He often makes claims to the effect that 'God established the lines of motion, which the sun and the moon observe' (*Notion of Nature*, *Works*, V, p. 199).[18] Now at first sight it might appear that this nomic contribution of God is redundant, given the power that matter has to change the direction of motion. If matter can change the direction of motion, what role is left for the divine law-maker? Boyle's idea seems to be that while matter has the power to change the direction of a body, it is God who decrees which determinate direction is actually taken. Is it to be rectilinear or circular, and at what angle to the direction of impact? On a collision, the agent, as it were, 'empowers' the patient to change direction, but there is an element of 'indetermination' that can only be supplied by God's acting with the second cause. Thus it is God who both determines which direction results from a collision and maintains the direction of the ensuing motion. A similar idea seems to be behind Boyle's speculations about God changing the quantity of motion that is transferred in collisions. The agent is able to transfer motion to the patient, but it is God who determines just how much motion is transferred (see §6 below).[19]

4 Concurrence

Now this interpretation of Boyle's corpuscular philosophy rests heavily on the notion of divine *concourse*, where 'concourse' is taken to mean, following the sixth meaning given it in the *OED*, a concurrence (or running together) in action or causation. The English word is derived from the Latin *concursus*, which was frequently employed with this meaning in similar contexts amongst the mechanical philosophers.[20] Yet the attribution to Boyle of this meaning of the word has recently been challenged by Struan Jacobs. In an important paper he claims that in certain key contexts, 'concourse' refers to 'God's *potential* to exercise power'. He elaborates as follows:

> Boyle means that, having created the world, God at any time might interpose to suspend or alter the ordinary course of nature. So the world, as we know it, persists (is 'preserved') only on condition of God's *permission*, his 'concourse'. When nature proceeds as usual, following its ordinary course, God is giving his concourse and remaining outside the natural world as a passive onlooker. Be it noted, 'concurrence' and 'consent' were, in Boyle's time, recognized meanings of 'concourse'.
>
> (Jacobs 1994, p. 381)

The issue is one of specifying whether God's preserving concourse is immanent or transcendent, whether God is actively engaged with every physical event or a passive onlooker. I disagree with Jacobs' interpretation and believe that by divine concourse Boyle understood God as actively involved in creation. By spelling out what I take to be the problems with Jacobs' view, we can gain greater insight into just what Boyle's understanding of concourse is. But before I present them, it is worth assessing the tenability of Jacobs' semantic claim. Jacobs maintains that 'concourse' in Boyle's time could mean 'consent'. If this is true then Boyle might understand God as a detached law-giver who has given his consent to matter to interact according to his predetermined laws. Jacobs refers us to the *OED*. However, the closest meaning to consent given there is 'legal concurrence, *esp.* of an officer whose consent is necessary to a legal process'. Now since I have claimed above that Boyle's conception of laws of nature is not entirely divorced from its legal ancestry, it is just possible that he is employing a legal term when he speaks of God's concourse, as if matter has his consent so long as it obeys the laws of motion and no miraculous intervention is required. Whether or not he employs it with that sense then, must be determined on exegetical grounds.

I have four arguments against Jacobs' interpretation and will present them in order of increasing strength. I believe that their cumulative weight decisively refutes Jacob's view. The first argument is based on some very interesting historical details. There is an interpretation of Boyle that, like Jacobs, denies that Boyle believed in God's active intervention in nature once it was established. It dates back to the year 1670 and is found in the work of Jean Baptiste Du Hamel entitled *De Corporum Affectionibus*. There Du Hamel interprets Boyle's *Forms and Qualities* as claiming that God's *new concourse* is not required once the laws of nature and the bodies of animals have been made.[21] Henry Oldenburg takes Du Hamel to task on this interpretation in his review in the *Philosophical Transactions*. He claims that Boyle

> will not be found to deny that new Concourse, pleaded for by *Du Hamel*; but rather, by asserting the *continued* general and ordinary support and influence of the First Cause implyeth that that preservation and concourse ever and constantly perpetuated is *ever new*, and consequently keeps things in their pristine state and vigour, at least so far, as the Creator did once determine they should be kept . . . he doth now by his un-interrupted influence, preserve the Powers and Operations of those Principles or Springs by which they were by him once set a going.
>
> (*Phil. Trans.*, 65, 1670, pp. 2106–2107)

What is important to note here is the issue of whether 'new concourse' is required. On the more natural reading of 'concourse', new concourse is simply God's active involvement in second causes. Du Hamel interprets Boyle as claiming that this is not required, whereas Oldenburg counters that God's 'uninterrupted influence' is necessary. Yet if 'concourse' means consent, it seems very unnatural to speak of it as Oldenburg does in terms of 'uninterrupted influence'. On Jacobs' view, the only time when God influences the course of nature is when he withholds his concourse, otherwise he is a passive onlooker.

Yet here we have a close contemporary of Boyle claiming that Boyle held a view of concurrence that involves 'uninterrupted influence' in all natural phenomena. Now Boyle was an avid reader of the *Philosophical Transactions* under Oldenburg's editorship, and if he had had any objections to Oldenburg's interpretation, it is almost certain that he would have had the latter correct it. Moreover, there is a strong chance that Oldenburg's comments against Du Hamel were endorsed or even supplied by Boyle himself. The only concession we can make to Jacobs is that there is a precedent in the history of interpretation for his denial of God's active involvement in Boyle's world.[22]

The second argument has to do with Boyle's intellectual context. In this context terms like 'ordinary concourse' and 'general concourse' had a long history and an established usage. The meaning of 'concourse' amongst other mechanical philosophers and in the late scholastics, such as Suárez and the Coimbrans when they discuss God's involvement in second causes, is invariably concurrence in causation.[23] To my knowledge, the legal meaning of consent is never employed in these contexts. Witness for example Descartes in the *Principles* where he says that God 'by his regular concurrence [*concursum ordinarium*], . . . preserves the same amount of motion and rest in the universe as he put there in the beginning' and that this, like the preservation of matter itself, is done 'by the same process by which he originally created it' (*Principles*, II, §36, *CSM*, I, p. 240).[24] All this creates a presumption that Boyle is employing the term in the same sense. If he were to use a specialised legal sense, one would expect to find indications in his discussions of concurrence that he was diverging from normal usage and this brings us to the third argument.

Third, I claim that an analysis of the textual evidence reveals no indications on Boyle's part that he is employing 'concurrence' in a specialised legal sense. On the contrary there are some passages that argue decisively for the traditional meaning of 'concurrence'. We need first, in exploring Boyle's texts, to review the evidence that Jacobs gives for his interpretation. The initial text that Jacobs cites in support of his view is from the early 'Requisite Digression' of c.1659. This essay, as the title informs us, concerns 'those that would exclude the Deity from intermeddling with matter', but the essay largely focuses on accounts of the formation of the world, rather than the present state of things. It can quite naturally be divided into two parts, the first dealing with the Aristotelians and the second with the Epicureans, all of whom, on Boyle's view, exclude the Deity from 'intermeddling'. Jacobs' first quote is from the first part and the immediate context is an extended discussion of 'how mere and consequently brute bodies can act according to laws, and for determinate ends, without any knowledge either of the one or of the other' ('Requisite Digression', *Works*, II, p. 38, *S.* p. 159). Boyle goes on to tell us his preferred view which is that God having constructed the various bodies of the universe and set them in motion

> by the assistance of his ordinary preserving concourse, the phenomena which he intended should appear in the universe must as orderly follow, and be exhibited by the bodies necessarily acting according to those impressions or laws . . . as is consistent with the good of the whole and the

preservation of the primitive and catholic laws established by the supreme cause.

(*Ibid.*, p. 39, *S.* p. 160)

Jacobs claims (1994, p. 381) that 'Boyle's locution "by the assistance of his [God's] ordinary preserving concourse" refers to, not divine activity or intervention in nature, but God's *potential* to exercise power'. Two considerations count against this interpretation. First, as we have seen above, 'ordinary preserving concourse' is a set expression amongst the mechanists meaning concurrence in action or causation. There is no indication on Boyle's part that he is using the term with a different sense here. Second, it seems that the passage on its own can be read in more than one way. Talk of bodies 'necessarily acting according to . . . laws' could be taken as the strong modal claim that bodies cannot but act in a law-like manner. If so, then Boyle talks of 'the preservation of the primitive and catholic laws' as a consequence of the necessary and law-like behaviour of matter. This is apparently how Jacobs reads it. However, alternatively the modal claim can be taken in a weak sense where 'necessarily' is a derivative 'theological' necessity. This reading would have it that 'by the assistance of his ordinary preserving concourse', the phenomena that occur 'must as orderly follow' (and here the excision in the above quote is relevant) not because, as the Aristotelians claim, matter is endowed with intelligence or an *anima mundi*, but because of God's active preservation of the laws of the universe. On this reading the preservation of the laws of nature is the cause of the law-like behaviour of bodies. Now, on its own the passage can be read either way, but in an essay that concerns 'those that would exclude the Deity from intermeddling with matter' and an immediate context of a discussion of how insentient bodies cannot obey laws, the most natural reading is to interpret 'concourse' here as referring to God's active intervention in things corporeal.

The second passage that Jacobs quotes is from *Reason and Religion*. There Boyle tells us that (quoting more extensively than Jacobs),

if we consider God as the author of the universe, and the free establisher of the laws of motion, whose general concourse is necessary to the conservation and efficacy of every particular physical agent, we cannot but acknowledge, that, by with-holding his concourse, or changing these laws of motion, . . . he may invalidate most, if not all the axioms and theorems of natural philosophy . . .

(*Works*, IV, p. 161)[25]

Having stressed Boyle's acceptance of the causal efficacy of matter, Jacobs claims (1994, p. 381) that 'Boyle's observation here (and elsewhere) that the production of events in the ordinary "course of nature" is by physical agents, makes it highly unlikely that he means by "concourse" a continuous, sustaining contribution by God'. But on the interpretation I am proposing the causal efficacy of matter is not incompatible with God's constant and all-pervasive active concourse. Boyle's view is that both are required. And again the context undermines Jacobs' interpretation. In section 3 of *Reason and Religion* (from which this quote is taken) Boyle is enlarging on the distinction between axioms being repugnant to reason and axioms in natural philosophy which might conflict with axioms, say, in natural theology. For example, it is an axiom that 'necessary causes always act as much as they are able', but this does not preclude God from performing miracles like saving Daniel's companions in the fiery furnace. It is in this context that Boyle says that God can withhold his concourse and therefore contradict the axiom in natural philosophy. There is nothing in the passage that forces us to understand 'concourse' as having the sense of potential to act. In fact, Boyle's point that God's 'general concourse is necessary to the conservation and efficacy of every particular physical agent' is quite naturally read as meaning active concurrence. The example of the fiery furnace where God withholds his concourse from the flames was a stock illustration amongst scholastics in their discussion of concourse as active concurrence in second causes.

A third passage cited by Jacobs, the one which he regards as the most 'refractory', is from *The Christian Virtuoso*. He quotes as follows,

> according to the Cartesians, all local motion (which is, under God, the grand principle of all actions among things corporeal) is adventitious to matter, and was at first produced in it, and is still every moment continued and preserved immediately by God: whence may be inferred, that he concurs to the actions of each particular agent (as they are physical) and consequently, that his providence reaches to all and every one of them . . .
>
> (*Works*, V, p. 520)[26]

Jacobs argues that Boyle's words 'motion . . . continued . . . by God' are ambiguous and that they could be interpreted in terms of God's active involvement or in terms of his (Jacobs') preferred passive detachment. The problematic words for his interpretation he regards as 'continued and preserved' which seem repetitious. Jacobs regards that the passage 'resists determination' and needs to be interpreted in the light of other relevant passages. But again there are several problems with Jacobs' discussion. First, the context is a defence of divine providence. Boyle deploys two arguments for providence 'from Cartesian principles'. Whether he accepts those principles or not is beside the point, for this is a common rhetorical ploy of Boyle's. The crucial point is that he is arguing from *Cartesian* principles, and, more specifically, he is arguing from the Cartesian doctrine of concurrence or conservation of matter. It is this which Jacobs seeks to interpret according to his 'detached consenter' view. But it can hardly be claimed that the Cartesian view of concurrence involves a God who is a passive onlooker! It is certain that in this instance the way God 'concurs to the actions of each particular agent' is actively and immanently, otherwise Boyle is seriously misrepresenting the Cartesian view. This brings us to the 'problematic' phrase 'preserved and conserved'. This redundant conjunction is typical of Boyle's style and the pairing of these words and their cognates is common amongst the mechanists.[27] Surely the difficult word in the passage for Jacobs' view is the term 'immediately' which in this context means not mediated. The use of this adverb is decisive in determining that 'concurs' is referring to active participation in the material realm and not passive disengagement.

But the passage itself provides only indirect evidence against Jacobs' view because it is referring to the Cartesian view of concurrence in the conservation of matter and motion and not to Boyle's view of the concurrence of God in the maintenance of the laws of motion.[28] Yet, in continuing his arguments for providence Boyle says,

> Nor will the force of all that has been said for God's special providence, be eluded, by saying, with some deists, that after the first formation of the universe, all things are brought to pass by the settled laws of nature.
>
> (*Christian Virtuoso, I, Works*, V, pp. 520–521)

This passage appears to preclude the type of view that Jacobs (and Du Hamel) is espousing, especially since it leads into the claim quoted above that the laws of motion do not arise from the nature of matter, but depend upon the divine will. The picture of matter in motion left to its own lawful devices is not, according to Boyle, an argument against God's special providence. This is because it rests on an inadequate conception of laws. And this brings us to the final argument against concurrence as consent.

The fourth argument is one from internal consistency. Jacobs' interpretation requires that we attribute to Boyle views that he did not hold. This is no more evident than in the account of the powers of matter that his view requires. He argues that for Boyle the propensities of matter 'exist *immanently* in, and are not divinely imposed on bodies' (1994, p. 375). This is important to his view because for him, the propensities of bodies to behave in certain ways when manifested are instantiations of laws of nature. Matter obeys laws of motion when its powers are manifested, and moreover, this is just what the doctrine of the causal efficacy of matter is. Matter is causally efficacious in so far as it has immanent propensities to behave in certain law-like ways once it is set in motion by God. Yet this view of propensities or powers is incompatible with what has been argued above. It is clear from Boyle's conception of laws that matter is incapable of obeying them because it is insentient. To attribute to matter the power to obey laws is, on Boyle's view, tantamount to attributing sentience to it. This is precisely why Boyle claims that 'the laws of motion . . . did not necessarily spring from the nature of matter, but depended upon the *will* of the divine author of things'. Instead, the powers or faculties of matter result from God's nomic intervention. Boyle tells us that even the so-called occult qualities are produced 'by the very same Catholique affections of matter and Laws of motion whence the more common Phenomena proceed' (*BP*, vol. 22, fol. 116r, M. B. Hall 1987, p. 137). I conclude therefore that Boyle's notion of the concurrence of God in natural phenomena is one of immediate active involvement at the same location and time as the second cause and not one of detached consent. His contribution is to impose the laws of motion on matter. As he says in *High Veneration*, all bodies

> are every moment sustained, guided and governed, according to their respective natures, and with an exact regard to the catholic laws of the universe; . . . [and] that there is a Being, that doth this every where, and every moment, and that manages all things, without either aberration or intermission . . .
>
> (*Works*, V, pp. 140–141)

5 Causes and laws

It is important to stress that Boyle's affirming of the causal efficacy of matter does not preclude the need for God's nomic intervention. Thus, for Boyle, it would seem that causes are not a species of law-like relation. The causal power of matter would be present even if God suspended or changed the laws of nature. So causes and laws come apart. To be sure, causal powers are imparted to matter by God just as is the motion of matter. But once matter has the power to transmit motion from one corpuscle to another, it retains this power irrespective of what the laws happen to be. The same holds for the other causal powers of matter. Thus Boyle can say,

> when a man shoots an arrow at a mark, so as to hit it, though the arrow moves towards the mark as it would if it could and did design to strike it, yet none will say that this arrow moves by a law, but by an external though well-directed impulse.
>
> (*Notion of Nature, Works*, V, p. 171, *S*. p. 182)

It is not the law that 'causes' the arrow to continue in motion even though the motion is law-like. Rather, as Boyle says earlier in the same work, it moves by an 'inward principle' that we have denominated a power of perseverance. There is nothing about the nature of matter, including its causal power to transmit motion, that determines how matter behaves. This is also implied by Boyle's discussions of chance. For instance, he claims that 'I think it utterly improbable that *brute* and *unguided*, though *moving*, matter should ever convene into such admirable structures as the bodies of perfect animals' (*Forms and Qualities, Works*, III, p. 48, *S*. p. 70). The point is that matter can interact causally with matter, but without the imposing on it of laws of nature by God, there is little, if any, chance of it forming the present marvellous arrangement.

Now if this ontological independence of causes and laws is the correct interpretation of Boyle, then there are two significant consequences. First,

Boyle is what we would call a singularist about causation. That is, he accounts for the regularities in nature in terms of the laws of nature only. No regularities are implied by the causal interaction of corpuscles colliding, for causal connections are not species of law-like connection. And second, Boyle's laws can be characterised as *kinematic* laws in so far as they entail no ontological commitments to powers or forces, but merely appeal to space, time, motion and the bulk of bodies.[29] Thus, not surprisingly, Boyle's corpuscular philosophy is not a 'dynamics' in the sense commonly attributed to Newton's physics. But neither is it a strict mechanism like that of Hobbes. Rather it can be broadly described as a theologico-physical mechanism.[30]

Yet Boyle did not see the issues as clearly as this interpretation suggests. For, he does not always distinguish between causes and laws. At one point in the 'Requisite Digression', Boyle mentions the possibility that it might ultimately be discovered that the most fundamental causes of natural phenomena are laws of nature. The passage reads thus:

> there are divers effects in nature, of which, though the immediate cause may be plausibly assigned, yet if we further enquire into the causes of those causes, and desist not from ascending in the scale of causes till we are arrived at the top of it, we shall perhaps find the more catholic and primary causes of things to be either certain primitive, general, and fixed laws of nature (or rules of action and passion among the parcels of the universal matter); or else the shape, size, motion, and other primary affections of the smallest parts of matter . . .
>
> (*Works*, II, p. 37, *S*. pp. 156–157)

Similarly in the *Cosmical Qualities* he says that 'under the name of catholick and unminded causes or agents, I comprehend not only divers invisible portions of matter, but also the established laws of the universe' (*Works*, III, p. 307).[31] Now, it is best to understand this not as a slip on Boyle's part, but rather as a lack of clarity on the relation between laws and causes. When he considers the connection between the nature of matter and its behaviour, Boyle sees their independence. But when considering the functions of laws, such as the arranging of the present world system, Boyle thinks of them as causes. Perhaps a terminological distinction might clarify things here. We might call the power of matter in impacts an *efficient* cause of the subsequent motion and the role of laws in the behaviour of corpuscles before, during and after impact as the (rather clumsy) *nomological* cause of their motion, taking 'cause' in a broad sense. The former accounts for the fact of the transference of motion, the latter for the various properties of that motion. The one is grounded in the power of matter to transmit motion, the other in the concourse of God. But this is to take us into the function of laws, a subject that awaits more detailed treatment below. And before that we must address another important feature of Boyle's conception of laws, their contingency.

6 The contingency of laws

For Boyle, the laws of nature are contingent. And this notion of nomic contingency plays a crucial role in wedding his corpuscular philosophy to his natural theology. The first step in establishing the contingency of laws has been outlined above. It is breaking the nexus between the nature of matter and its behaviour. Boyle denies that the behaviour of corpuscles arises from their nature: 'the laws of motion . . . did not necessarily spring from the nature of matter'. This allows him to break from an immanent[32] conception of laws. It also reveals just how far Boyle was from any form of dispositionalism about properties. For on the dispositionalist account, laws of nature are identical to the manifestations of dispositions of matter to behave in certain ways and uninstantiated laws are unmanifested dispositions. Moreover, a corollary of his denial of the matter/behaviour nexus is that it commits Boyle to a thesis akin to Humean independence. No particular corpuscular arrangement implies or excludes the existence of any other corpuscular arrangement. For example, one cannot deduce (in the strict sense) from the natures of iron and water that when the former is placed in the latter it will sink.[33]

But the thesis also leaves him with a number of pressing problems. First, there is a problem of epistemic access to laws. How do we know how things behave if their behaviour is not necessarily related to their natures? The danger here seems to be that the denial of the nexus will lead to a denial of what can be broadly construed as an empirical approach to the epistemology of laws and to the acceptance of a more rationalistic account akin to Descartes'. Second, and more pressing, is the problem of explaining what laws are. This brings us to the next step in Boyle's account of the contingency of laws, his voluntarism. Rather than being immanent, laws of nature are imposed upon matter by God. God is the 'ontological ground' of the laws of nature.[34] But this still does not guarantee their contingency. For it is open to Boyle to claim that God was compelled by his own nature to impose the determinate laws that actually are in nature, which has the 'Spinozan' consequence that God could not break those laws. The line of thought undergirding such a view would be that, as this is the best of all possible worlds (something Boyle explicitly denies[35]), its creator is compelled by his own goodness to fashion and maintain it by those laws that actually do obtain. Another set of laws would give rise to a different, less perfect world.

Yet Boyle, in spite of his acceptance of the teleology implied in such a view, instead chose to emphasise God's free and arbitrary will in determining the laws of nature. Laws of nature, for Boyle, are contingent in virtue of being expressions of the divine will. That is, they are contingent because the divine will is subject to change. To put it in his words, 'all the laws of motion were at first *arbitrary* to *him* and depended upon his free will' (*BP*, vol. 7, fols 113–114, in R. Colie 1963, p. 213).[36] One can see here the extent to which Boyle's conception of laws is grounded in his doctrine of God. But Boyle is not to be accused here of proffering an *ad hoc* solution, a 'God of the gaps' as one might regard More's *spirit of nature*.[37] For this conception had had a long history, perhaps even arising from the new freedom in speculative natural theology after the Condemnation of 1277. The doctrine can be traced at least as far back as Ockham.[38]

The final step in Boyle's account of the contingency of laws is his 're-establishing' of a connection between the natures of things and their behaviour. Boyle's conception of nomic contingency does not imply that the nature of particular corpuscles is completely independent of their law-like behaviour. Rather there is a connection between natures and laws. In particular there is a connection between the mechanical affections of bodies and the laws of motion. Which law is impressed upon a particular corpuscle is in part determined by its nature. For, Boyle says of the various parts of the mundane matter that they are

> every moment sustained, guided and governed, *according to their respective natures*, and with an exact regard to the catholic laws of the universe. . . .
> (*High Veneration*, *Works*, V, p. 140, italics added)[39]

He is not here specifying two conditions for God's governance of the world, but rather is implicitly assuming the distinction between determinate and determinable laws. The determinate law is that which God imposes 'according to [its] respective nature' and the determinable law is that catholic law of the universe considered in abstraction from any particular nature. God's will determines which laws apply and when and it is almost always determined by the nature of the corpuscles involved. Thus we sometimes find Boyle speaking of bodies *necessarily* acting according to them.[40] But this necessity is a derivative, 'theological' necessity. Once God has settled which laws will be imposed on corporeal objects, they necessarily conform to those laws unless he sees fit to suspend them for some higher purpose.

Now, perhaps the best way to gain a clear understanding of Boyle's doctrine of nomic contingency, is to see it in use in his writings. Thus we will focus on three examples, the first which focuses on a particular law, a second which emphasises the connections with his natural theology and a third which bears an interesting parallel with contemporary considerations for the cogency of the doctrine of nomic contingency. Let us turn then to the law of transmission of motion. In *High Veneration*, Boyle engages in an extended thought experiment concerning the nature of other worlds. Two sections of this involve a discussion of the contingency of laws as it relates to the doctrine of the plurality of worlds. It is here that Boyle speculates that there might be a world the same as ours, but where

> the laws of this propagation of motion among bodies may not be the same with those, that are established in our world; so that but one half, or some lesser part, (as a third) of the motion, that is here communicated from a body of such a bulk and velocity, to another it finds at rest, or slowlier

moved than itself, shall there pass from a movent to the body it impels, though all circumstances, except the laws of motion, be supposed to be the same.

(*Works*, V, p. 140)[41]

So here we have Boyle speculating that God, all other things being equal, could have imposed a different law of the transmission of motion on another world. Perhaps, suggests Boyle, the proportion of the motion transferred on collision is one half or one third of what happens in collisions in our world. To be sure, matter still has the power to transmit motion, but God may alter the proportion of motion transmitted because the proportion is determined by a divinely imposed law and not the 'bulk' or velocity of the bodies involved.

It is interesting here to contrast Boyle's speculation with that of Newton in the thirty-first query in the *Opticks*. There Newton tentatively argues that since space is infinitely divisible and matter is not everywhere, God could create atoms of matter that vary in size, density and forces

and thereby to vary the Laws of Nature, and make Worlds of several sorts in several Parts of the Universe. At least I see nothing of Contradiction in all this.

(Newton 1730, p. 404)

The point of comparison with Boyle is that for Newton the laws arise from the nature of matter, whereas for Boyle they are expressions of God's will. For Newton, matter has powers and the laws of nature are manifestations of those powers.[42] Vary the nature of the matter and the laws vary. But for Boyle, the laws can change in some other world simply if God so wills it.

A second use of the doctrine of nomic contingency is found in Boyle's notion of miracles. The fact that the laws of nature are contingent gives Boyle a ready explanation of miracles. Miracles are instances of God suspending or altering laws of nature. So, for instance, when God preserved Daniel's three companions in the fiery furnace of Nebuchadnezzar,[43] he did so by 'suspending the natural actions of bodies upon one another'. And, claimed Boyle, it should not be surprising that 'the most free and powerful Author of those laws of nature, according to which all the phenomena of qualities are regulated, may (as he thinks fit) introduce, establish or change them in any assigned portion of matter . . .' ('Possibility of the Resurrection', *Works*, IV, p. 201, *S*. p. 207).[44]

The third example of the doctrine of nomic contingency in Boyle is his suspicion that certain laws of nature may be restricted to particular regions of the universe. In the 'Cosmical Suspicions' he speculates that there may be some laws that are

not so much to be general rules or laws, as the customs of nature in this or that particular part of the world; of which there may be a greater number, and those may have a greater influence on many phænomena of nature, than we are wont to imagine.

(*Works*, III, p. 318)

For the contemporary metaphysician this might bring to mind Michael Tooley's Smith's garden argument (1977, pp. 686–687) for the claim that particulars rather than universals may have nomic powers. Boyle has no such metaphysical motive in his 'suspicion'. Nor does he introduce his suspicion as having any relation to the contingency of laws. His suspicion about the restricted domain of certain laws is posited to account for certain cosmical qualities. Yet the very unselfconscious manner in which it is introduced, reveals just how integral is the doctrine of nomic contingency to his corpuscular philosophy. He sees no philosophical objection to this delimiting of certain laws; and of course, the suspicion is entirely consonant with the doctrine of miracles outlined above.

So we have seen that the doctrine of nomic contingency has a range of applications in Boyle's corpuscular hypothesis. It is predicated both on his denial of the nexus between the nature of matter and the behaviour of matter and on his voluntarism. It is the latter feature that weds it to his natural theology and gives him a ready explanation of miracles. Laws of nature are expressions of the divine will which God can and does suspend from time to time.

7 The teleology of laws

According to Boyle, the primary function of laws of nature is the establishment and maintenance of the created order. That is, the laws of nature are directed to some purpose. They are teleological in that when a law is imposed by God on a corpuscle, it is with some end in mind. The teleology of laws is emphasised in most, if not all, of Boyle's summaries and detailed explications of the corpuscular hypothesis, as well as in his physico-theological works such as *The Christian Virtuoso* and *Final Causes*. There is a typical summary of his view early in the *Forms and Qualities* where Boyle says,

> the origin of motion in matter is from God; and not only so, but that thinking it very unfit to be believed that matter, barely put into motion and then left to itself, should casually constitute this beautiful and orderly world, I think also further that the wise Author of things did, by establishing the laws of motion among bodies, and by guiding the first motions of the small parts of matter, bring them to convene after the matter requisite to compose the world . . .

(*Works*, III, p. 15, *S*. p. 19)[45]

Now it is important to emphasise, as Boyle frequently does, the polemical context in which such a view is posited. In claiming that 'the origin of motion in matter is God', Boyle is consciously distancing himself from the Epicurean view of matter and likewise in denying that matter 'should casually constitute this beautiful and orderly world' he is rejecting the Epicurean notion of chance. But Boyle does not only define his view in contradistinction to Epicurus, he also explicitly rejects what he took to be a central tenet of Descartes' mechanism. It is the view that,

> God, having once put matter into motion and established the laws of that motion, needed not more particularly interpose for the production of things corporeal, nor even of plants or animals, which according to him are but engines . . .
>
> (*Forms and Qualities, Works*, III, p. 48, *S*. p. 70)[46]

For Boyle says,

> I do not at all believe that either these *Cartesian laws of motion*, or the *Epicurean casual concourse* of atoms, could bring mere matter into so orderly and well contrived a fabric as this world.
>
> (*Ibid.*)

And he goes on to tells positively what he does believe.

> And therefore I think that the wise Author of nature did not only *put matter into motion*, but, when he resolved to make the world, did so regulate and *guide the motions* of the small parts of the universal matter as to reduce the greater systems of them into the order they were to continue in, and did more particularly contrive some portions of that matter into seminal rudiments or principles . . .
>
> (*Ibid.*)

Underlying this view is his doctrine of insensible matter and his voluntarism. And so we find in his *Final Causes*, that Boyle tells us 'there are two accounts, on which the actions of natural agents may be said to tend to a certain end'. First, there is the case in which 'the agent has a knowledge of that end, and acts with an intention to obtain it', and second, there is the case in which a proximate agent is 'so directed, as it ought to be to obtain an end, and yet that end is neither known nor intended by the proximate agent' (*Works*, V, p. 413). It is only in this latter sense that inanimate objects can be said to work for an end. He admits that this second sense is difficult to explain. But in telling us how it is best conceived he relates the familiar explanation of the formation of the world, only this time the teleology is even more explicit. God was able

> to foresee all the effects, that particular bodies so and so qualified, and acting according to the laws of motion by Him established, could in such and such circumstances have on one another; so, by the same omniscient

power, He was able to contrive the whole fabric, and all the parts of it, in such a manner, that, whilst his general concourse maintained the order of nature, each part of this great engine, the world, should, without either intention or knowledge, as regularly and constantly act towards the attainment of the respective ends which He designed them for . . .

(*Ibid.*)

Once again it is instructive to contrast Boyle with Newton, this time with the Newton of the *Principia*. We have seen how Boyle rejected the view he attributed to Descartes, viz. that matter could be left to itself to form the ordered world as we know it. Newton entirely concurred. In the 'General Scholium' at the end of the second edition of the *Principia* he tells us that while the celestial bodies

continue in their orbits by the mere laws of gravity, yet they could by no means have at first derived the regular position of the orbits themselves from those laws.

(Newton 1729, p. 543)[47]

The difference is that for Newton, once the arrangement is set, the motions of the various bodies naturally flow out of the nature of the matter by which they are constituted. God intervenes only to perform certain fine tunings.[48] Whereas for Boyle, God not only uses the laws to establish the arrangement, but he also sustains the order of the cosmos by upholding those very laws.

8   Laws and God's omnipotence

From the foregoing discussion it is possible to reconstruct the internal logic of Boyle's position. The reconstruction offered below arises from the various emphases and the flow of the argument in numerous passages in Boyle's works.

The starting point for Boyle's view is the doctrine of insensible matter. In *Notion of Nature*, *Final Causes* and to a lesser extent in the 'Requisite Digression', Boyle introduces his discussion of laws of nature by drawing the distinction between those laws obeyed by intelligent agents and those to which inanimate objects are said to conform. The distinction between moral and physical laws is predicated on that between beings which are sentient and brute matter. The second premise of Boyle's view is that the behaviour of inanimate objects is directional and manifests regularities; it is (almost) always aimed at some end and matter in similar contexts will always behave in the same way. So, given that matter is insensible, how do we account for these features of its behaviour?

The first step is to break the nexus between the nature of matter and its behaviour. It is not that Boyle denies Descartes' acceptance of the sufficiency of laws to bring about the formation of the world. Rather it is that he denies that laws are in any sense immanent in matter. Even though it appears that matter in motion is directing itself, it cannot be because it is insensible. It only has the power to transmit motion from one corpuscle to another and to persevere in motion. Something external to the matter is required to impose, or determine the path of the motion or the result of the collision, etc. That something external is God, who imposes laws on insensible matter. But it is not as if once the laws are imposed, God's intervention is no longer needed, for, since the power to act does not reside in matter, God's incessant concourse is required to maintain the laws. So, it is not the case that the imposed laws require God's concourse, but that laws *are* a manifestation of God's concourse.

Furthermore, since the behaviour of matter is so obviously directed toward the specific end of creating the sorts of objects that there are in the world, it is clear that these manifestations of God's concurrence are expressions of his will. God wills that the earth should rotate around the sun and therefore he so directs its motion, or sets the lines of motion, to achieve that end. And finally, since laws are expressions of God's *free* will and are manifestations of his concurrence, he can suspend them when he sees fit. The laws are contingent. Thus,

> [i]t is true, that it is not easy to conceive, how one agent should, by so simple an instrument as local motion, be able to direct a multitude of agents, as numerous as the bodies that make up a world, to act as regularly, as if each of them acted upon its own particular design, and yet all of them conspired to obey the laws of nature. But if we consider, that it is to God, that is an omniscient and almighty Agent, that this great work is ascribed, we shall not think it incredible . . .
>
> (*Final Causes, Works*, V, p. 414)

Having established this, Boyle then claims that 'this doctrine is not inconsistent with the belief of any true miracle'. That is, the doctrine of miracles is a natural corollary of his voluntarism.

Now there is another seam to the dialectic of Boyle's corpuscular hypothesis which nicely brings out the intimate relation between his natural philosophy and his natural theology. It is the role of the doctrine of the omnipotence of God in the formation of Boyle's mechanism. Francis Oakley has argued in very general terms, that the defence of God's omnipotence is a major motive in the formation of Boyle's voluntarism. Oakley rightly argues that Boyle is not to be interpreted in the light of eighteenth-century deism where God was relegated to the post of First Cause only. His project in natural philosophy should not be characterised as a struggle to reconcile his theology with his corpuscular hypothesis. Rather, Boyle is to be interpreted in the light of a theological tradition that stretches back at least to Ockham; a tradition that denied the necessitarian tendencies of Aquinas (who seemed to bind God to his own eternal laws), seeing it as a threat to God's omnipotence. Oakley believes that the issue that fuelled the medieval dispute was at the forefront of Boyle's motives in the formation of his voluntarism. He speaks of 'Boyle's preoccupation with the divine omnipotence' (Oakley 1984, p. 85).

Yet it is important not to overemphasise the role of God's omnipotence here. For, it is not actually the doctrine of omnipotence that Boyle is keen to defend in his articulation of nomic contingency, but rather the related doctrine of divine providence. This is clear both from the immediate context of the discussion of nomic contingency in *The Christian Virtuoso*, which comes at the end of a series of arguments for divine providence, and also in the first section of *Notion of Nature*, where Boyle is setting up the rationale and scope of the enquiry. There Boyle tells us that

> I shall add, that the doctrine I plead for does much better, than its rival, comply with what religion teaches us about the extraordinary and super-natural interpositions of divine providence. For when it pleases God to over-rule, or controul, the established course of things in the world, by his own omnipotent hand, what is thus performed may be much easier discerned and acknowledged to be miraculous by them, that admit, in the ordinary course of corporeal things, nothing but matter and motion . . .
>
> (*Works*, V, p. 164)[49]

Moreover, it is not easy to pinpoint the precise direction of explanation here. That is, it is not clear to what extent the doctrines of providence and omnipotence are driving the dialectic or are a happy consequence of it. Having said this, however, Oakley has rightly highlighted the close interweaving of Boyle's theology and his natural philosophy. John Henry has taken up Oakley's point with the more specific claim that 'Boyle went so far as to deny the accuracy and universal applicability of natural laws on the grounds that to affirm either might imply that God too must obey these laws.'[50] Again, it is not clear here whether the theological motive resulted in the doctrine of nomic contingency, but Boyle certainly draws the connection between omnipotence and laws. He tells us that God by

> the laws of nature determin'd and bound up other Beings to act according to them, yet he has not bound up his own hands by them, but can envigorate, suspend, over-rule; and reverse any of them as he thinks fit.
>
> (*BP*, vol. 7, fol. 113)[51]

9   Problems of nomenclature

We are now in a position to draw together the threads that make up Boyle's account of the interactions of corporeal bodies. Having rejected the Aristotelian distinctions between natural and violent motions and natural and violent states and instead giving primacy to the local motion of material corpuscles in absolute space, Boyle furnishes us with an account of the dual contributions that matter and God make to the manifestation of all natural phenomena. Matter is causally efficacious in so far as it has the power to transmit motion on collision, to persevere in motion and to change the direction of the motion of bodies on collision. However, the nomic intervention of the author of things is required in order to guarantee that the behaviour of matter is law-like and oriented to the specific ends that God has in the formation and preservation of the world. This concurrence of God is constant, immediate and active; he contributes to the 'efficacy of every particular physical agent'. To be sure, his nomic contribution is contingent. He can alter the laws of nature if he so desires. But the regular and orderly arrangement of things rarely requires such an extraordinary intervention on God's part. Thus, Boyle's mechanical philosophy and his natural theology can be seen to form a seamless whole, the origin, purpose and behaviour of matter in motion being inexplicable without God. Moreover, this philosophy appears to have developed from a complex interplay of factors, both theological and metaphysical.

How then are we to sum up Boyle's position? What is the most informative way of categorising Boyle's natural philosophy in the light of the picture that has emerged in the foregoing chapters? Can we go beyond 'corpuscularian' or 'mechanist' as general descriptive terms by which to describe the philosophy that results when the various components of Boyle's world-view fit together? We have seen that in the history of interpretation Boyle has been variously described as a deist, an occasionalist and a voluntarist. Moreover, we have seen that the interpretation of Boyle's natural philosophy was significantly advanced with Timothy Shanahan's characterising of Boyle as what he dubs a 'concurrentist'. Yet there are grounds for questioning the suitability of Shanahan's term as a description of Boyle that differentiates his mechanism from that of others in the period.

A whole host of philosophers including Aquinas, Molina, many late scholastics and Descartes, held some doctrine of concurrence and might all be described as concurrentists. Yet there are many respects in which one would want to point out the dissimilarities between these philosophers and Robert Boyle. To call Boyle a concurrentist is helpful in so far as it highlights a certain family resemblance and differentiates him from deists and occasionalists. However, some of the discontinuities between Boyle and the concurrentists are just as important in understanding his natural philosophy, as the differences with the deists, etc. Boyle was a mechanical philosopher and an anti-Aristotelian who also resisted being grouped with the Cartesians and is often at pains to demonstrate the ways in which his philosophy differs from that of Descartes. In particular, a crucial difference is to be found in their respective doctrines of concurrence. Descartes' doctrine of concurrence centred around his law of conservation of matter and motion, whereas Boyle was at best ambivalent about the conservation law (see chapter 8, §3 below). By contrast, Boyle's account of concurrence seems to have arisen from his attempt to reconcile the law-like behaviour of matter with his insistence on the insentience of matter. The result was the view that the causal interaction of bodies is the occasion of God's nomic intervention in the world. I suggest then, that a more apt description of Boyle's view is 'nomic occasionalism' rather than concurrentism. For this captures both the causal efficacy of matter and the nomic intervention of God. The causal efficacy of matter in collisions is the 'occasion' of God's nomic intervention.

Moreover, having cited the weight of scholarship against the interpretation of J. E. McGuire and having stressed the doctrine of the causal efficacy of matter in Boyle's published works, it must be pointed out that there is some very strong manuscript evidence that Boyle was, in fact, attracted by the occasionalism of certain neo-Cartesians. In three extant folios among the *Boyle Papers*, Boyle, while not fully endorsing it, lists a number of arguments for occasionalism and in so doing presents a favourable defence of the doctrine (see Appendix 2). Further, he seems to have considered these occasionalist reflections of enough significance to warrant circulation amongst non-English speaking acquaintances, for a Latin translation of these folios is also extant in the *Boyle Papers*.[52] Here is not the place to attempt to account for, or to reconcile Boyle's favourable attitude to occasionalism, suffice to say that the description of Boyle as a nomic occasionalist hints at not only those concurrentist family resemblances mentioned above, but also those resemblances he shares with those later Cartesians whose views are incompatible with the late scholastic concurrentists. Boyle's natural philosophy was truly a *via media* in more ways than has commonly been appreciated.

Notes

1　See *Notion of Nature*, *Works*, V, p. 170, *S.* p. 181. See also 'Excellency of the Mechanical Hypothesis', *Works*, IV, p. 68, *S.* p. 139. Boyle does occasionally speak of 'those Catholic rules of motion, and other grand laws, which he at first established among the portions of the mundane matter', *Notion of Nature*, *Works*, V, p. 199. Compare the *Discourse on Method* where Descartes speaks of 'the laws of mechanics, which are identical with the laws of nature', *CSM*, I, p. 139.

2　See 'Excellency of the Mechanical Hypothesis', *Works*, IV, p. 71, *S.* p. 143.

3　Thus Boyle's view is impervious to the Millian criticism of natural law theories that they conflate two distinct senses of the term 'law'. See Mill's 'Essay on Nature' in his 1874, pp. 14ff.

4　Boyle here sees himself as departing from van Helmont's doctrine of laws; *pace* S. Shapin 1994, p. 330 who seems to miss the dialectic entirely, claiming that Boyle is rejecting what Shapin calls the 'vulgar' view of laws as notional rules of acting.

5　See also *Notion of Nature*, *Works*, V, p. 243, *High Veneration*, *Works*, V, pp. 139–140, §22–§23.

6　See J. E. McGuire 1972, p. 536. McGuire denies that his interpretation of Boyle is occasionalist (p. 532), but see T. Shanahan 1988, p. 556.

7　See J. Milton 1982, pp. 119–129, T. Shanahan 1988, pp. 554–559, E. McCann 1985b and S. Jacobs 1994.

8　See P. Anstey 1999.

9　One strength of this interpretation is that it enables us to account for the various deist and occasionalist interpretations of Boyle's natural philosophy that have flourished since the 1650s. See T. Shanahan 1988, p. 568.

10　See also *Works*, V, p. 210. See T. Shanahan 1988, p. 559. Of course the problems that Descartes faced in harmonising this thesis with the doctrine of modes applies equally to Boyle, see chapter 6, §4 above.

11 For the contingency of this power of matter see also *High Veneration*, *Works*, V, p. 140. Boyle may be alluding to this power in *Notion of Nature*, *Works*, V, p. 243. For the Cartesian view which is only superficially similar see *Principles*, II, §42, 'effecisse, ut unæ alias impellerent motusque suos in illas transferrent', '[God] brought it about that some [parts of matter] should impel others and transfer their motion to them' (*AT*, VIII, p. 66). The translation in *CSM*, I, p. 243 is misleading.

12 Boyle says there is 'an inward principle, by which they are moved, till they have attained their position' (*ibid.*) Elsewhere Boyle speaks of bodies 'which can neither excite themselves into motion, nor regulate and stop the motion once they are in' (*High Veneration*, *Works*, V, p. 141). For further discussion of perseverance see chapter 5, §8.

13 For further discussion of determination see chapter 8, §3.

14 This conception of the powers of matter is consistent with Boyle's conception of motion as a successive being. However, in keeping with his ambivalence on the ontological status of motion, he sometimes speaks of the motive power of matter, not as its ability to transfer motion, but as if it is the power of one body to initiate motion anew in another body; that is, to enable another body to acquire the mode of motion. So in *High Veneration* we find Boyle speculating that matter might have the power of 'exciting motion in another body, without the movent's losing its own [motion]' (*Works*, V, p. 139).

15 See for instance *Notion of Nature*, *Works*, V, p. 243, *Reason and Religion*, *Works*, IV, p. 163 and *Christian Virtuoso*, *I*, *Works*, V, p. 532.

16 See also *Notion of Nature*, *Works*, V, p. 170, *S.* p. 181. I use the term 'voluntarism' advisedly, taking the central notion in any 'theological voluntarist' view to be a necessary connection between natural laws (which include laws of nature!) and the divine will. As yet there is no definitive study of voluntarism in the seventeenth century, nor in Boyle's thought. For some preliminary soundings see J. E. McGuire 1972, E. B. Davis 1984 and M. J. Osler 1992. McGuire (1977, p. 108) has suggested, and the view has been endorsed by C. Webster (1986, p. 204), that theological voluntarism gained new impetus through the Reformation and that Reformation thinkers such as Calvin and his followers influenced the voluntarism of Boyle and Newton. However, I can find no textual or archival evidence for either claim and neither McGuire nor Webster provide any. Since the central tenets of Boyle's voluntarism were certainly all present in late scholasticism and his forebears in the 'mechanical' tradition such as Gassendi (as M. Osler has pointed out), and there are explicit references to them in Boyle's texts, it seems far more natural to regard them as the immediate influences on Boyle's views.

17 See also *Notion of Nature*, *Works*, V, p. 180, *S.* p. 191, *High Veneration*, *Works*, V, p. 140 and 'Requisite Digression', *Works*, II, p. 39, *S.* p. 160.

18 See also 'Cosmical Suspicions', *Works*, III, p. 322 and *Final Causes*, *Works*, V, p. 424.

19 For scholastic precedents see D. Des Chene 1996, pp. 321–322, from whom I have borrowed the term 'indetermination'. Des Chene offers an interpretation of Descartes along these lines (see *ibid.*, pp. 335–336).

20 See for example the Latin version of Descartes' *Discourse on Method*, *AT*, VI, p. 564.

21

> However this most learned man [Boyle], the living creatures having been equipped with organs (which indeed without the excellent and admirable wisdom of the author would not be able to become so) and the laws of motion having been established in nature, the origin and growth of living things he considers to be comprised by what we often call the affections of matter, figure, size, contexture of parts, motion and rest apart from the new concourse of the author, besides him, to whom he appeals for the preservation of things.
>
> (J. B. Du Hamel 1670, p. 57)

22 J. E. McGuire has pointed out that the 1950s and 1960s saw a number of deist interpretations of Boyle's corpuscular hypothesis. See his 1972, p. 524. There is a sufficient lack of clarity in some of Boyle's writings to lead interpreters astray.

23 See for example Suárez's *Disputationes Metaphysicæ*, 22. For a stimulating discussion of the late scholastic doctrine of concurrence and its relation to Descartes see D. Des Chene 1996, pp. 314–341.

24 See also §42, p. 243 and *Letter to More*, August 1649, *CSMK*, p. 381.

25 Wrongly cited in Jacobs 1994 as p. 163 as are the two references that follow. These are not from *Reason and Religion*, but 'Possibility of the Resurrection', a separate essay which was originally published with the former.

26 See also *Excellency of Theology, Works*, IV, p. 43.

27 See for example Descartes' *Principles*, II, §42, *CSM*, I, p. 243.

28 There is good evidence that Boyle believed in the Cartesian notion of concurrence: see for example *Forms and Qualities, Works*, III, p. 48, *S*. pp. 70–71.

29 Strictly speaking they are not all kinematic laws as originally defined by Ampère, for some at least involve reference to the bulk of bodies (e.g. see *High Veneration, Works*, V, p. 140). For a useful discussion of the taxonomy of laws, see J. Barbour 1989, pp. 52–54.

30 For a discussion of the taxonomical issues involved here see the Introduction and A. Gabbey 1980 and 1992.

31 Compare Descartes' *Principles*, II, §37, 'we can also know certain rules or laws of nature, which are secondary and particular causes of the various motions we see in particular bodies' (*CSM*, I, p. 240).

32 Here I am following F. Oakley (1961, p. 435) in adopting A. N. Whitehead's (1933) useful classification of conceptions of laws of nature as immanent or imposed.

33 See *Reason and Religion*, section III, *Works*, IV, pp. 161ff.

34 *Pace* J. E. McGuire 1972, p. 536, Boyle does not hold a naive regularity view of laws. He admits the presence of regularities, but finds their explanation, or better, their ontological ground, in the immanent activity of God.

35 See Boyle's discussion of this issue in *Notion of Nature, Works*, V, p. 195f.

36 See also *Christian Virtuoso, I, Appendix, Works*, VI, p. 679 and p. 714.

37 See A. Gabbey 1990, p. 24.

38 See F. Oakley 1961 and 1984 chapter 3, E. Grant 1981c and D. Des Chene 1996, p. 322.

39 See also *Notion of Nature, Works*, V, p. 164, though in this section Boyle, in distancing himself from the vulgar notion of nature, casts his mechanism in more deistic terms than is usual, see especially p. 163.

40 '[T]he known laws of the *hydrostatics* make it necessary that the gold should sink

in it (quicksilver) and all lighter bodies swim on it', 'Requisite Digression', *Works*, II, p. 36, *S.* p. 156. See also p. 39, *S.* p. 160.

41 For a parallel passage in the *Boyle Papers* see vol. 3, fol. 113, in R. Colie 1963, p. 214.

42 See Newton 1730, p. 401.

43 *Daniel*, chapter 3.

44 See also *Final Causes*, *Works*, V, p. 412 and p. 414, *Reason and Religion*, *Works*, IV, p. 161 and p. 163, *Notion of Nature*, *Works*, V, 197, *Christian Virtuoso, I, Appendix*, *Works*, VI, p. 679. On the connection between laws and miracles see also S. Shapin 1994, pp. 330–333.

45 See also

> [God] put them [corporeal things] into such motions, *that*, by the assistance of his ordinary preserving concourse, *the phenomena which he intended should appear in the universe must as orderly follow*, and be exhibited by the bodies necessarily acting according to those impressions or *laws*, though they understand them not at all.
>
> ('Requisite Digression', *Works*, II, p. 39, *S.* p. 160, italics added)

46 Descartes says,

> I therefore supposed that God now created . . . enough matter to compose such a world; that he variously and randomly agitated the different parts of this matter so as to form a chaos as confused as any of the poets could invent; and that he then did nothing but lend his regular concurrence to nature, leaving it to act according to the laws he established
>
> (*Discourse on Method*, V, §42, *CSM*, I, p. 132)

In *The World*, a work Boyle may not have read, Descartes says that 'the laws of nature are sufficient to cause' the formation of 'a quite perfect world' (*CSM*, I, p. 91).

47 See also Query 31, *Opticks*, p. 402.

48 But see the cautionary note of R. S. Westfall in his 1986, p. 233.

49 See also section III of *Reason and Religion*, *Works*, IV, pp. 161–164.

50 J. Henry 1990, p. 75, n. 59. Henry provides no textual evidence for his claim but refers us to S. Shapin. But all that Shapin says is that, for Boyle, there are 'two dangers implicated in writing down natural laws as part of experimental practice'. The first is it would intimate that they held 'universally and precisely' and the second that

> we would be making a move potentially damaging to right religion, for we would be utilising a resource contingently associated with those deists and free-thinkers who conceived God to be bound by the laws of which he himself was the author.
>
> (1988, p. 38)

51 Quoted from R. Colie 1963, p. 214, who wrongly attributes them to vol. 3. See also *ibid.*, p. 198. It seems that Boyle's concerns about divine omnipotence as it relates to the contingency of laws were heightened after he became familiar with

the philosophy of Spinoza. It is possible that Boyle did not know that Spinoza was the author of the *Theologico-Politicus* until late in 1671, for More tells him that he himself had only just learnt who the author was on 4 December 1671, *Works*, VI, p. 514.

52 The Latin translation found in *BP*, vol. 29, fols 77–82v was kindly pointed out to me by Michael Hunter.

8 Mind/body interaction

It has been argued above that Boyle is aptly dubbed a 'nomic occasionalist' with regard to body/body interactions.[1] That is, matter has causal efficacy in so far as it can transfer motion from one corpuscle to another, and has the power to change the direction of motion and to persevere in motion. However, God ensures that the persevering motion of corpuscles after a collision is uniform and rectilinear (or circular) and that a predetermined quantity of motion is transferred on collision. So the collisions of corpuscles are the occasion of God's nomic intervention in the world. And in addition to being a nomic occasionalist, Boyle was a substance dualist.[2] He believed that there are two fundamentally different types of created substance: spiritual and material. Boyle's is a classical Cartesian dualism, the rudiments of his view being borrowed straight from Descartes himself.[3] And this dualism is integral to both his anthropology and his natural theology. Needless to say then, that his writings are replete with discussions of spiritual substances and in particular the incorporeal soul. Even in the *Notion of Nature* where he explicitly says that he will not deal with the subject of the soul, we find it intruding.[4]

The pertinent question then, given both his dualism and his nomic occasionalism, is just how thorough was Boyle's nomic occasionalism. Is it a global nomic occasionalism applying not only to relations between bodies, but also to relations between bodies and spiritual substances and between spiritual substances themselves? Or is it a mitigated nomic occasionalism, restricted to body/body interactions only? That is, does Boyle account for mind/body relations by appealing to God's nomic intervention in the same way as for body/body relations? Or does he give another account of mind/body relations? This chapter aims to answer these questions.

The attempt to answer such questions on Boyle's behalf may appear to impose a degree of systematicity on his thought that is foreign to his texts. For instance, there is no clear evidence that Boyle intentionally set out to give an account of mind/body relations that was consistent with his account of body/body relations. But the answers to these questions are extremely enlightening for the modern commentator who is attempting to understand the contours of his thought and his place within his broader intellectual milieu. This chapter then, aims to sketch Boyle's account of the mind and of mind/body interaction and to discuss its compatibility with his nomic occasionalism.

However, before we proceed there is an important caveat about epistemic access to, and the intelligibility of, relations between the soul and the body. Many of Boyle's discussions of the relations between the body and mind are presented as examples of things above reason. That is, examples of events that we know occur, but for which we do not have adequate explanatory categories. Boyle would have heartily concurred with Descartes' claim to Arnauld '[t]hat the mind, which is incorporeal, can set the body in motion is something which is shown to us not by any reasoning or comparison with other matters, but by the surest and plainest everyday experience' (*CSMK*, p. 358). But at the same time, for Boyle, these were the most inexplicable of events, as he puts it in *The Second Part of the Christian Virtuoso*, '[t]he operations of spirits upon bodies and vehicles, and much more upon one another, we are in the dark about' (*Works*, VI, p. 752).[5] This nescience about mind/body relations, according to Boyle, renders all accounts of such interaction as hypothetical at best.

1 The nature of mind

In order to clarify Boyle's account of mind/body relations, a more detailed presentation of Boyle's doctrine of the mind is called for. His view of the mind is heavily indebted to Descartes.[6] It is set within a Cartesian substance dualism, 'there being but two sorts of substances – material and immaterial' (*Forms and Qualities*, *Works*, III, p. 40, *S*. 57). The soul is an immaterial substance. Of course, souls are not the only immaterial beings; there are also angels, demons and God. And the soul has some affinity with these other incorporeal beings.[7] And like Descartes, Boyle believes that the soul is rational, that is, it thinks.[8] Boyle claimed in the *Excellency of Theology* that this was one of only two theses that 'mere reason can demonstrate' about the mind (*Works*, IV, p. 13).[9]

The second thesis that unassisted reason can establish about the soul is that 'being an incorporeal substance, there is no necessity, that it should perish with the body' (*ibid*.). This, claims Boyle, and here he is following Descartes, does not entail that the soul is immortal by nature, but merely that, in virtue of its being different from material bodies, it can exist apart from them, and that it retains its power of thinking even when divorced from the body. We require another source of knowledge about the soul, over and above natural reason, if we are to establish its immortality. And Boyle believes that this source is Scripture. He tells us in the *Excellency of Theology* that 'we are yet much beholden to divine revelation for assuring us, that its duration shall be endless' (*ibid*.). Yet later in the same work (p. 20), and elsewhere, he seems to accept that the soul's immortality follows from its immateriality. Boyle spells this out in *The Christian Virtuoso*. There, while arguing that the immortality of the soul is one of the grand principles of natural religion, he tells us that the soul, 'being an immaterial spirit, and consequently a substance not really divisible, can have no parts expelled or transposed, and so being exempted from the physical causes of corruption that destroys bodies, she ought to last always' (*Works*, V, p. 518).

It appears from this passage that from the mere fact of the soul's immateriality, Boyle derives its indivisibility, its immortality and even its penetrability.[10] But in his *Final Causes* Boyle goes further and claims of the soul that '*not having extension*, it is not divisible; which is the prerogative of substances, which, for that reason, are immaterial and immortal' (*Works*, V, p. 416, italics added).[11] Here he is siding with Descartes against More that the soul is not extended, and he deduces its indivisibility, immateriality and immortality from this lack of extension. And, as M. A. Stewart has pointed out (*S.*, p. xxiii), Boyle takes it for granted that souls themselves are individuated; the Averroist heresy of the universal mind is not even alluded to. Therefore, given that the soul is immortal, as Boyle thinks Scripture affirms, it would seem that he now has a ready-made criterion for personal identity over time. However, in his 'Possibility of the Resurrection' he argues that, while it would be easy to appeal to the soul alone as such a criterion, some degree of partial identity of the relevant material body is also required for there to be the same person at the resurrection (*Works*, IV, pp. 200–201, *S.* p. 206).[12]

As for the origin of the soul, Boyle claims that it is fashioned by God. For,

> there being no proof, but a great improbability, that it has been from all eternity; it must have had a beginning of existence, which being incorporeal, it cannot have received from any thing that is a body; and therefore must have been created by some spirit.
>
> (*Christian Virtuoso, II, Works*, VI, p. 753)

And since it was created by God, it bears his image, thus setting humans apart from animals, for it is only humans who have souls.[13] So Boyle, in spite of early reservations,[14] was committed to the Cartesian doctrine of the *bête machine*. Moreover, it is the uniqueness of the possession of an incorporeal substance that makes humans incomparably more valuable than any other material beings, the soul itself being of inestimable worth and more worthy a subject of reflection than any corporeal entity. This is quite an admission from a natural philosopher. He says,

> when I consider the rational soul as an immaterial and immortal being, that bears the image of its divine maker, being endowed with a capacious intellect, and a will, that no creature can force: I am by these considerations disposed to think the soul of man a nobler and more valuable being, than the whole corporeal world . . .
>
> (*Excellency of Theology, Works*, IV, p. 19)[15]

Once fashioned by God the soul is implanted into the human foetus. This takes place, 'if we will admit the general opinion of philosophers, physicians, divines and lawyers', at about the end of the sixth week of the formation of the embryo, when the embryo has developed to the point where it is able to receive the soul. Thus, the embryo does not need the soul in order to develop, at least in the early stages.[16] When the young foetus is ready the soul is implanted somewhere in the brain. Normally Boyle speaks 'conditionally', as he puts it, as if it is located in the *conarion* or pineal gland, where it interacts with the body. However, he was aware of dissenting opinions.[17]

Having been housed the soul can now perform its functions. Its primary functions when united to the body are understanding, volition and action and the response to external stimuli by the production of sensations.[18] But the soul can also function independently from the body. It has powers of inference and the forming of clear and distinct ideas, the ability to reflect upon its own operations and of knowing its own limits that in no way depend upon its union with the body.[19] And of course, unlike any corporeal entity, it is fitted to ponder and appreciate the excellencies of God.[20] However, not all mental functions are to be attributed to the soul. For it is to be distinguished from the sensitive or corporeal soul which includes memory, common sense and imagination.[21] These are purely corporeal functions of the brain. Finally, Boyle tells us that while God can act immediately on souls, souls cannot act immediately upon one another. He says, 'he [God] can immediately act upon human souls, as having created them; but they are not able so to act upon another' (*Notion of Nature*, *Works*, V, p. 242). Thus Boyle has no account of mind/mind interaction.

2 Mind/body union

Having established the nature of the mind, it is now incumbent on us to spell out the nature of the union between the mind and the body as Boyle conceives it. For any causal traffic between body and mind arises only as a result of this union. As for sources, there is an extended treatment of mind/body union in the posthumously published *The Second Part of the Christian Virtuoso*, section II sub-section 3, and numerous discussions and miscellaneous comments on mind/body union are found elsewhere in Boyle's writings. At times we find Boyle speaking in scholastic terms, even if hesitatingly, of the soul as the *form* of the body.[22] Yet the analysis he attempts to give of this union and the problems that an explication of it gives rise to, arise directly from the constraints of his mechanism. The really pressing problem arising from their union is the articulation of how two such distinct substances can causally interact, especially in the light of the central tenets of mechanism. Given that all natural phenomena are the result of matter in motion, and that the soul is by definition immaterial, how is it that one can affect the other?

On Descartes' view, there is a substantial union between the body and the mind that renders the capabilities and characteristics of such mental faculties as the imagination and sensation different from the same faculties in animals or mere automata.[23] For Descartes, the union is not a third substance, not a scholastic substantial form, but rather a relation that augments or, better, transforms the powers of both the corporeal functions of the brain and those of the mind. Just how this is to be spelled out in detail is, of course, a notorious problem for Descartes. It is not at all clear just how the imagination is modified, nor what role the incorporeal memory has. But since Descartes furnishes us with no detailed account of mind/body union there is little more one can say.

When we turn to Boyle we find that he has appropriated the fundamentals of the Cartesian view, though he has clothed it in different terminology and, importantly, that he makes a significant new development. In *The Second Part of the Christian Virtuoso* Boyle opens his section II sub-section 3 with a restatement of his aim 'to find, by a heedful inspection into the works of God, just motives to admire; to praise, and to thank him for them' (*Works*, VI, 753). And to this end he intends to discuss the union between body and mind. Thus, the context of the discussion of mind/body union is theological rather than polemical or aimed at systematic exposition. He then introduces what he takes to be a new tripartite distinction, one 'that appears not to have yet occurred to philosophers, or divines'. He goes on,

> [f]or instead of dividing the operations of God, here below, into two sorts only, natural and supernatural; I think we may take in a third sort, and divide the same operations into supernatural, natural in a stricter sense, that is mechanical, and natural in a larger sense, which I call supra-mechanical.
>
> (*Ibid.*, p. 754)

This third category arises because the relations between the soul and body are neither supernatural, because they are 'produced according to the course of nature', nor mechanical, 'because they cannot be mechanically explicated or produced' (*ibid.*).[24] And he goes on in Aphorism IV of this sub-section to give us an example of such a supra-mechanical operation. It is the case of a man lifting a heavy book with his arm. He says,

> when he raises the book to his eyes, and sustains it there, notwithstanding its gravitation on his hand, the motion upward, and the *conatus* that keeps the body from falling, is the effect of the arbitrary power of his will, and not derivable from the merely mechanical laws of motion . . .
>
> (*Ibid.*, p. 756)

It is the 'supra-mechanical' then that needs to be explained and Boyle lists for us the headings of the topics that would constitute such an explanation. They include, *inter alia*, the power of the mind on the body, the passions and what he calls the 'laws and *phænomena* of the union and intercourse of the soul and body' (*ibid.*, p. 754). It is this last subject that is the significant development in Boyle's treatment of body/mind union.

According to Boyle, God has determined that the mind and body will interact according to a set of arbitrarily established laws that have no parallel in nature.[25] These laws pertain (at least) to the domain of interaction between the two substances. That is, God has subjected only certain parts of the body to the operations of the mind. For mind→body relations these include the animal spirits and 'some muscles, and other instruments of voluntary motion'. But they do not include 'many other parts of the same body, such as the stomach, spleen, liver, kidneys, &c' (*Christian Virtuoso*, *II*, *Works*, VI, p. 755).[26] And for body→mind relations it appears that only the animal spirits and the pineal gland can act upon the mind.[27] The laws are arbitrary in that God could have linked other parts of the body to the mind, but has chosen not to.[28] But these laws serve only to delimit the sphere within which the interaction can take place. They do not specify what the nature of that interaction is, a subject to which we will turn in the next section. Moreover, consonant with Boyle's broad conception of law, he makes no explicit distinction between the laws of mind/body interaction and such natural laws as the laws of motion.

Finally, there are three other features of Boyle's discussion of the union of mind and body that call for our attention. First, like Descartes, Boyle believes that, as a result of the union between these two substances, each substance receives new powers. With regard to their union Boyle tells us that it is 'by divine appointment [that] a soul and a body have each of them a power transcending that which belongs to it, on the account of its own nature . . .' (*Christian Virtuoso*, *I*, *Appendix*, *Works*, VI, p. 681).[29] The power that the soul receives is that of acting on the body and the power that the body receives is that of creating impressions on the soul. And the product of these new powers is action in the body and sensations and passions in the soul.[30] Second, Boyle regards it as a strange consequence of the union of body and mind that the mind cannot quit the body when it so desires, even though there are no 'strings or chains, that can tie, or fasten to it that, which has no body, on which they may take hold' (*Reason and Religion*, *Works*, IV, p. 170). And third, the particular disposition or corpuscular arrangement of the relevant parts of the body is crucial to the establishment and maintenance of the union. We have already seen that the soul cannot be housed in the body until the foetus is sufficiently formed to receive it. And likewise, 'when the necessary parts [for the union] have lost their vital dispositions, without which, they must be unfit to obey the mind, there ensues a total separation of the two differing substances, in which divorce consists, what we call death' (*Christian Virtuoso*, *II*, *Works*, VI, p. 756).[31]

The union of body and mind then, is of the utmost importance for Boyle. It is a union established by God according to certain laws that demarcate the scope of interaction and it furnishes both the body and mind with new powers. Boyle styles the interaction that results from this union as 'supra-mechanical' and interestingly, he takes this to be the third in a tripartite division of the 'operations of God' in nature. Ostensibly this implies that God is integral to supra-mechanical interactions. And if so, is Boyle's account of such interaction occasionalist? In order to answer this question we need to turn to Boyle's account of mind/body interaction.

3 Mind/body interaction and determination

Most of the discussions in Boyle's writings that pertain to mind/body relations concern the mind's effect on the body. The few discussions of the reverse relation are those that concern perception and have been discussed in chapter 3 above. When we turn to Boyle's discussions of the mind's action on corporeal bodies we find the same thesis recurring, viz. that the mind cannot initiate new motion in bodies, but can only change the determination of the motion that they already possess (the determination thesis). Here is a selection of passages:

> the rational soul . . . though vitally united to it [the body], can only determine the motion of some of the parts, but not give motion to any, or so much as regulate it in most.
>
> *(Notion of Nature*, V, p. 242)

> the reasonable soul in man is able to produce what changes it pleases in the body, but is confined to such as it may produce by determining or guiding the motions of the spirits, and other parts of the body subservient to voluntary motion.
>
> ('Excellency of the Mechanical Hypothesis', II, p. 78,
> *S*. pp. 153–154)

> it does not appear, that the rational soul doth give any motion to the parts of the body, but only *guide* or *regulate* that, which she finds in them already.
>
> *(Things Above Reason*, IV, p. 416, *S*. p. 224)[32]

What is the origin of the determination thesis? It is certainly Cartesian and may even originate with Descartes himself.[33] For, central to Descartes' physics was the conservation law that God maintains the same quantity of motion in the universe from moment to moment. Bodies can speed up or slow down, but the total quantity of motion within the system remains constant. The conservation law, on Descartes' account, pertains only to body/body interactions and bodies themselves do not have the power to initiate new motions. But what of minds? If immaterial substances, such as human souls, have the power to introduce new motion among bodies, the law would be violated. Yet Descartes was adamant that minds and bodies could interact. So how can they interact without the mind introducing more motion? The solution, at least as Descartes' followers and early interpreters saw it, was to claim that minds do not have the power to *initiate* motion in bodies, but that they do have the power to *change the determination* of the pre-existing motion of bodies.

This is certainly how Leibniz interpreted Descartes; it is the traditional reading of Descartes; and was the view of the later Cartesians Clerselier and La Forge.[34] And it was also Boyle's understanding of Descartes' position. In *Final Causes* he tells us that human souls are 'according to *Des Cartes*, endowed with a power to determine and regulate the motions of the spirits and the conarion, which are things clearly corporeal' (*Works*, V, p. 397). And Boyle knew that it was the position of the later Cartesians as well.[35] These facts are of historical significance in tracing the infiltration of Cartesian ideas in Britain in the mid-seventeenth century, and mark yet another point of influence of Descartes on Boyle's anthropology and his mechanism. But it is not at all clear why Boyle embraced the determination thesis, for in some places Boyle expresses reservations about Descartes' conservation law. Therefore it is pertinent to ask whether it was a wholesale borrowing on Boyle's part, or whether Boyle took over a Cartesian thesis that was motivated by the conservation law, but rejected the law itself. And is Boyle's conception of determination equivalent to that of Descartes? In order to answer these questions we need first to grasp Boyle's attitude to Descartes' conservation law, and then to ascertain Boyle's understanding of the nature of determination.

Descartes' conservation law in the *Principles* (II, §36) states that 'God is the primary cause of motion; and he always preserves the same quantity of motion in the universe'. In elaborating the law Descartes tells us that

> motion is simply a mode of the matter which is moved. But nevertheless it has a certain determinate quantity; and this, we easily understand, may be constant in the universe as a whole while varying in any given part. . . . For we understand that God's perfection involves not only his being immutable in himself, but also his operating in a manner that is always utterly constant and immutable.
>
> (*CSM*, I, p. 240)[36]

Boyle discusses this law and its apparent derivation from the immutability of God in a number of places, including *Final Causes* and the *Notion of Nature*. The treatment of the conservation of motion in *Final Causes* is part of a longer, sustained attack on the Cartesian rejection of final causes in nature. It is worth quoting his first point in full.

> It is a known principle of the Cartesian philosophy, that there is always just the same quantity of motion in the world at one time that there is at another: of which assertion this reason is given, that there is no cause, why God, who is immutable, should at the beginning of things, when He first put matter into motion, have given it such a quantity of motion, as would need to be afterwards augmented or lessened. But I see not how, by this negative way of arguing, those, that employ it, do not (implicitly at least) take upon them to judge of the ends, that God may have proposed to Himself in natural things. For, without a supposition, that they know what God designed in setting matter a-moving, it is hard for them to shew, that his design could not be such, as might be best accomplished by sometimes adding to, and sometimes taking from, the quantity of motion He communicated to matter at first.
>
> (*Works*, V, p. 396)

Boyle's initial point against the Cartesians is that the conservation law itself implies that God has ends for the creation which will only be achieved by maintaining this law. Now, since Boyle is arguing for the existence of final causes, one might think that this would constitute a reason for Boyle to accept the conservation law. But Boyle goes on to ask why it could not be the case that to achieve his ends, God may not occasionally add or subtract a little from the sum of the motion in the world. So, while the conservation law might imply that God has ends, it is certainly not a necessary condition of him having such ends. In fact, Boyle claims that

> to me it is not evident, why God's having particular ends, though some of them seem to require a change in his way of acting in natural things, must be more inconsistent with his immutability, than his causing many things to be brought to pass, which though *ab æterno* he decreed to do, are yet not actually done, unless in process of time. And particularly it seems not clear, why God may not as well be immutable, though He should sometimes vary the quantity of motion, that He has put into the world . . .

especially, argues Boyle, since he is constantly creating new souls and joining them to human bodies and these souls have the 'power to determine and regulate the motions of the spirits and the conarion' (*Works*, V, p. 397).

But Boyle, with his typical caution, stresses that he is not to be taken as rejecting Descartes' conservation law, 'for, whether or no it be a truth, I think it no unuseful nor improbable hypothesis; and I have not so much argued against it, as upon the grounds on which they argue for it' (*ibid.*).[37] Boyle's reservations about the derivation of the law are that the Cartesians proceed from metaphysical premises rather than physical ones when, at the same time, they claim that in physics one should start from physical premises.[38] That he considered the law not 'unuseful' is evidenced in the way he deploys it in the *Notion of Nature* against the conception of nature as a corporeal substance. Boyle argues there that if nature is corporeal, and it can impart motion to matter, then ever since the creation of matter the quantity of motion in the universe would have continually increased and will do so in the future. He considers this to be 'a concession, that would much disorder the whole theory of local motion' (*ibid.*, p. 244). But even here he is non-committal as to whether he accepts the law.

Having witnessed Boyle's non-committal attitude to Descartes' conservation law, we turn now to the notion of *determination* in Boyle's natural philosophy. Here we find from an assessment of the numerous references to it, that his conception is far simpler than that of Descartes. For Descartes, determination is a physical concept that is integral to his sophisticated physics and (in the *Principles*) is explicated in terms of his substance/mode ontology. Alan Gabbey (1980, p. 258) ends his very detailed and technical discussion of it by defining it as *the directional mode of motive force*. Whereas for Boyle, like many of his contemporaries, determination appears to be equivalent simply to *direction of motion*. Here a passage from his 'Advices' will suffice to bring home the point:

> whereas men think they have sufficiently enumerated the ways of determining the motion of a body, by saying, that the determination must be made, either in *the line*, wherein the impellent, that put it into motion, made it move, or in *the line*, wherein it was determined to move by the situation of the resisting body, that it met with in its way; the motions of the animal spirits, if not also some other internal parts of the body, may, the body being duly disposed, be determined by the human will; which is a way quite differing from the other. And how this attribute, I mean the power of determining the motion of a body, without any power to impart motion to that body, should belong to an immaterial creature, which has no corporeal parts to resist the free passage of a body, and thereby change *the line of its motion*, is not yet, nor perhaps ever will be in this life, clearly conceived by us men . . .
>
> (*Works*, IV, p. 457, italics added)

In speaking of the *line* of motion Boyle here is revealing that it is really the direction that he has in mind in discussing determination. There is no talk of modes and Boyle rarely speaks of forces. However, the basic Cartesian point, that change of determination implies no change in quantity of motion, is implicit throughout. The world is a closed system so far as quantity of motion is concerned, even if the direction of the corpuscles in motion is subject to change.

It is clear then that while Boyle holds to the determination thesis in a more explicit way than Descartes, it is not motivated by the conservation law, about which he was ambivalent. And it remains now for us to specify just how he conceived of this power of the mind to determine the motions of bodies. First, we should notice that it is the motion of the animal spirits and those parts of the body that are subject to the will that the mind can determine. This limited scope of mind/body interaction, as we have seen, is in accordance with the laws of mind/body union arbitrarily established by God. Second, the power that the mind has to determine the motions of the spirits, etc. is a supra-mechanical operation. It differs from efficient causation even though it also involves God's immediate action in the world. Boyle speaks of the mind putting

> a check, at pleasure, to the motion of a body, that does already actually move in one line, and determine its motions to continue in another, that is perhaps differing from it, or even opposite to it; to do this, I say, without opposing to the moving body, some other body, which by its resistance and situation may change its former course, is not a mechanical operation.
>
> (*Christian Virtuoso*, II, *Works*, VI, p. 756)

In a number of places Boyle claims that one of the key differences between mind/body interaction and body/body interaction is that in the former case the mind lacks impenetrability. In fact, a passage from the *Boyle Papers* gives us an interesting insight into Boyle's understanding of the necessity of impenetrability in mechanical operations. He says that,

> neither the Conarion, nor the Animall spirits, nor any part, whether gross or subtill of the Body, can mechanically act, upon the incorporeal soul; which wants Impenetrabillity, on whose account, in the subject that receives it, Local motion can be produced by the action, or motion of a Body.
>
> (*BP*, vol. 2, fol. 105)

Moreover, when Boyle speaks of the mind's influence on the animal spirits, etc. he sometimes speaks loosely of it 'guiding' and 'regulating' motions.[39] Such imprecise language is indicative of the fact that Boyle does not have a worked-out theory of mind/body interaction, but has appropriated the Cartesian thesis as the most convincing explanation of a phenomenon that we are certain occurs, but that we do not really understand. If pressed to furnish us with a more detailed account, he would undoubtedly repeat his claims about our lack of epistemic access to the true causes of this phenomenon. However, this is not to say that we cannot classify the sort of interaction that the determination thesis involves. It is clearly not mechanical causation. But is it a species of occasional causation? And how does it compare with Boyle's account of body/body interaction?

4 Nomic occasionalism again

Following the work of Steven Nadler, it is helpful to construe the relation of occasional causation as a genus of which classical occasionalism is a species. Nadler's analysis of the relation (1994, pp. 35–54) is that the state of affairs A is the occasional cause of effect *e*, if and only if, A occasions B to efficiently cause *e*. Schematically,

$$A \overset{o}{\rightarrow} B \overset{e}{\rightarrow} e$$

where '$\overset{o}{\rightarrow}$' means occasional cause and '$\overset{e}{\rightarrow}$' means efficient transeunt cause. Efficient transeunt causation occurs when a state of affairs A is the primary and immediate agent responsible for bringing about a state of affairs B (where B is a different particular from A). On this construal of occasional causation, occasionalism is the thesis that: (1) the state of affairs A has no causal powers; (2) B is God who, as a result of A obtaining, efficiently causes the effect e; and (3) efficient causation is a species of law-like relation; that is, there is a nomological relation between the obtaining of the state of affairs A and God causing *e*. This nomological relation is an expression of God's general will, and is instantiated by specific volitional acts on God's part. Moreover, it is important to emphasise that A is the *occasional* cause of e, while God is the *efficient* cause of e.

By contrast, Boyle's nomic occasionalism has the following schema,

where '$^{o}\!\!\rightarrow$' means occasional cause, '$^{e}\!\!\rightarrow$' is the efficient causal relation that guarantees the instantiation of the salient law and '$^{n}\!\!\rightarrow$' is the 'nomological' cause. Hence, the effect e is the combined result of: (1) the efficient cause A; and (2) the 'nomological' cause G, where G is God. This schema is, like that of the occasionalists, to be augmented by the thesis that there is a nomological connection between the obtaining of the state of affairs A and the effect e. This nomological relation is an expression of God's general will, but the actual instantiation of $^{n}\!\!\rightarrow$ is contingent upon specific volitional acts of God. Moreover, it is important to emphasise why 'A $^{e}\!\!\rightarrow$ e' is not the state of affairs which occasions God's nomic intervention. According to Boyle's corpuscularianism, it is not the transmission of motion on the collision of two corpuscles that is the occasion of God's directing the line of motion subsequent to the collision. For part of God's nomic contribution is that of determining what quantity of motion is transferred from one corpuscle to another. Rather, as on the analysis given by the occasionalists, it is the state of affairs immediately prior to the collision that is the occasional nomic cause of e.

The important differences between occasionalism and Boyle's nomic occasionalism are now clear. For Boyle, A is an efficient cause of e whereas the occasionalists deny this. They claim that A is the occasional cause of e, but for Boyle A is only the occasional cause of the law-like behaviour of e. Thus Boyle can be seen to drive a wedge between causes and laws. The fundamental conception of causation for Boyle is, speaking anachronistically, that of singular causation and the account of laws voluntaristic. Determinable laws of nature are general expressions of God's will that have their determinate instantiations in individual volitional acts that accompany the obtaining of certain states of affairs. Is Boyle's nomic occasionalism a species of the genus occasional cause? It would seem not on Nadler's construal of occasional causation. For his genus 'occasional cause' implicitly treats causation as a species of law-like connection, something which Boyle denies. However, it seems that the essential element in occasional causation, if we pare it down to its barest essentials, is the presence of the occasioning relation '$^{o}\!\!\rightarrow$'. If we make this the minimal requirement for membership of the genus 'occasional cause' then Boyle's understanding of body/body interaction is a species of occasional causation.

What then of his account of mind→body relations? Not all the details are as clear as we would like. What is clear is that God has given to the mind the power to determine some motions. The mind uses this power in accordance with certain arbitrarily established laws. For example, the will can act to change the determination of motion of some of the animal spirits according to a predetermined law. We can represent Boyle's view by the following schema:

where 'V' is an act of the will, '^{e}→' is the manifestation of the mind's power to change the determination of a body which Boyle styles 'supra-mechanical', 'e' is the effect of a body having its determination changed, '^{o}→' is an occasional cause, 'G' is God and '^{n}→' is God's maintenance of the laws of mind/body union and change of determination. Thus '^{e}→' is efficient causation because the mind is the immediate cause of the change of determination. But Boyle is at pains to stress that it is not mechanical causation, and this is obvious when one compares it with body/body interaction. For in mind/body interaction no collision is involved because the mind lacks impenetrability.[40] Moreover, God does not need to guarantee that a determinate quantity of motion is transmitted, for there is no change in the quantity of motion in the body. Descartes' tennis ball analogy for the reflection of light in the *Optics* seems to capture part of what Boyle understands here about the mind acting to change the determination of matter. He says,

> the power, whatever it may be, which causes the ball to continue moving is different from that which determines it to move in one direction rather than another. It is very easy to recognise this from the fact that the movement of the ball depends upon the force with which it has been impelled by the racquet, and this same force could have made it move in any other direction as easily as towards B [a point on the ground]; whereas the ball's tending towards B is determined by the position of the racquet, which could have determined the ball in the same way even if a different force had moved it.
>
> (*CSM*, I, p. 157)

Boyle shares with Descartes the view that speed rather than velocity is the fundamental notion of motion and that change of direction does not imply change in motion.

As for the role of God, his immediate nomic intervention is required to guarantee both that the laws of change of determination and of mind/body union are 'obeyed'. And this is the sense in which mind→body relations are 'operations of God'. God guarantees that the regularity between a particular type of volition and a particular type of change in the determination of a corpuscle obtains.[41] The mind's role in determining the animal spirits parallels one aspect of God's role in collisions between bodies, viz. guaranteeing the specific determinations. For example, when I have a token volition of the type 'choosing to raise my arm', God guarantees that it is followed by the appropriate change of determination of the animal spirits but it is the mind that (supra-mechanically) causes the change of determination and consequently the raising of my arm. But God's role remains integral as Boyle puts it in an unpublished remark:

> If it bee said, that God hath been pleas'd to make an union of 2 such differing substances, according to certaine Laws, by vertue of which they are enabled to act upon one another; I readily grant it: but stil I say this is not to give a Mechanical or Physical account of this affaire, but to have recourse to the arbitrary & immediate agency of the first cause.
>
> (*BP*, vol. 2, fol. 105)

So was Boyle an occasionalist with regard to mind/body relations? On the definition of occasionalism given above the answer is no, because on Boyle's account the mind has the power to redirect the animal spirits. But it is important not to engage in hair-splitting here, for on Boyle's account God *is* immediately involved in mind/body interaction even though the mind is not causally impotent. Perhaps it is best to regard it as an impure form of occasionalism, a variant on his nomic occasionalism for body/body relations.

What can be gleaned from the foregoing discussion of Boyle's conception of the soul and the interpretation presented with regard to the soul's interaction with the body? It might be said that Boyle held a mitigated form of nomic occasionalism because his account of mind/body relations differs from that of his account of body/body relations. But the similarities between the two accounts are more striking than the differences. It seems that one could justly say that Boyle's account of mind/body interaction is the same as his account of body/body interaction except that he has granted the mind the power of determining motion which on the body/body account is restricted to God.

Notes

1 Throughout this chapter the words 'mind' and 'soul' are used interchangeably as Boyle himself used them. Further, relations represented by a '/' imply no direction, whereas relations represented by an '→' are directional. Thus 'mind/body relations' includes both 'mind→body' and 'body→mind' relations.

2 That Boyle was a dualist hardly needs to be established. However, remarkably, this is effectively denied by Thomas S. Hall who seems to fail to distinguish between Boyle's use of 'vital soul' and 'rational soul' and who speaks of the tendency in Boyle for the soul 'to be given a material aspect'. See Hall 1969, I, p. 284 and p. 294. Hall's view is endorsed by Barbara Kaplan. See her 1993, pp. 64–65.

3 In almost every significant discussion of the soul in his writings Boyle mentions Descartes or the Cartesians.

4 See *Notion of Nature, Works*, V, p. 166 where Boyle tells us that he will 'set aside the considerations of it in the present treatise' and yet this work contains perhaps his most interesting discussion of the origin of the soul and its implantation into the foetus, pp. 241–242 and p. 244. See also p. 216.

5 See also *Things Above Reason, Works*, IV, p. 416, *S*. p. 224, 'Requisite Digression', *Works*, II, p. 38, *S*. p. 159 and 'Excellency of the Mechanical Hypothesis', *Works*, IV, p. 76, *S*. p. 150. Note that in *Notion of Nature, Works*, V, p. 242 Boyle categorically denies that souls can act immediately on one another.

6 With regard to Boyle's adoption of Cartesian body/mind dualism, it is clear that he had encountered it by the late 1650s as he alludes to it in his 'Requisite Digression'. But there is no evidence that at this time dualism had as prominent a role in his thought as it was later to acquire in the 1660s. For instance, although in Essay II of the first part of the *Usefulness of Natural Philosophy* (composed c.1649–1651, see R. Frank 1980, p. 316, n. 33), Boyle speaks of 'God, who hath composed us both of body and soul' (*Works*, II, p. 29), he makes little use of the distinction in his argument; see also Essay V, *ibid.*, p. 53. Whereas in later works such as *Christian Virtuoso, II* and *Final Causes*, which are otherwise similar in content and aim, the doctrine of the immaterial soul features prominently.

7 See *Final Causes, Works*, V, p. 415 and *Excellency of Theology, Works*, IV, p. 19.

8 In fact, in at least one place Boyle tells us, like Descartes, that the soul always thinks (*Excellency of Theology, Works*, IV, p. 14). For Descartes see for example his *Letter to Gibieuf*, 19 January 1642, *CSMK*, p. 203.

9 The long discussion of the nature and immortality of the soul in *Excellency of Theology*, (*Works*, IV, pp. 12–14) draws heavily on Descartes, quoting from his 'Replies to the Second set of Objections' and a letter to Princess Elizabeth.

10 In *BP*, vol. 17, fol. 167, Boyle speaks of the soul as 'an immateriall & consequently indivisible substance' (published in Conry 1980, p. 71).

11 Of course, all this is too swift on Boyle's part. Why cannot extended substances be immortal? What is it about immateriality that 'entails' immortality? These questions are all the more pressing when one considers that elsewhere Boyle insists on the indestructibility of matter. See for example *Forms and Qualities, Works*, III, p. 32, *S*. p. 46.

12 It is interesting to note on the question of personal identity that Boyle sees no requirement for continuity of memory or psychological states. For the notion of partial identity as applied to the problem of identity through time see D. K. Lewis 1993 and D. M. Armstrong 1993, pp. 39–40.

13 See *Forms and Qualities, Works*, III, p. 40, *S*. p. 58. This dichotomy between animals and humans furnishes Boyle with another platform from which to launch an attack on Aristotelian substantial forms. For, if animals have

> a being more noble than matter, that can actuate and inform it, and make itself the architect of its own mansion . . . if this being can in the body . . . perform all the functions of a vegetable soul; and besides those, see, hear, taste, smell, imagine, infer, remember, love, hate, fear, hope, expect, &c. and yet be a mortal thing, and perish with the body; it will not be difficult for those enemies of religion . . . to fancy, that human minds are but a somewhat more noble, but not for that less mortal kind of substantial forms . . .
>
> (*Christian Virtuoso, I, Works*, V, p. 518)

14 See *BP*, vol. 27, fols 166–167, published in Y. Conry 1980. According to M. Hunter the hands are E and G both of whom worked for Boyle in the 1660s (see Hunter 1992, pp. xxxvii–xxxviii). For Boyle's views on animal suffering see M. Oster 1989 and J. J. MacIntosh 1996.

15 See also *Christian Virtuoso, II, Works*, VI, p. 753, p. 775, Aphorisms V and VI and *Final Causes, Works*, V, p. 400.

16 *Notion of Nature, Works*, V, p. 241. Compare the parallel passage in *BP*, vol. 2, fol. 62.

17 See *Christian Virtuoso, II, Works*, VI, pp. 741–742 and *BP*, vol. 2, fol. 105 and vol. 1, fol. 20. The very act of God uniting the soul with the body is for Boyle, in *Christian Virtuoso, I*, the basis for an argument for divine providence: see *Works*, V, p. 520.

18 See *High Veneration, Works*, V, p. 141

19 See *Things Above Reason, Works*, IV, p. 419, *S.* p. 229 and pp. 233–234. In the *Christian Virtuoso, I* Boyle enumerates the functions of the soul as

> to understand, and that so, as to form conceptions of abstracted things, of universals, of immaterial spirits, and even of that infinitely perfect one, God himself: and also to conceive, and to demonstrate, that there are incommensurable lines, and surd numbers; to make ratiocinations, and both cogent and concatenated inferences, about these things; to express their intellectual notions, *pro re natâ*, by words or instituted signs to other men; to exercise free will about many things; and to make reflections on its own acts, both of intellect and will.
>
> (*Works*, V, p. 517)

20 See *Final Causes, Works*, V, p. 416.

21 See *Christian Virtuoso, II, Works*, VI, pp. 740–742, p. 748 and *Notion of Nature, Works*, V, p. 166. Boyle's Cartesian neuropsychology has been discussed in chapter 3, §1 above.

22 For example in the *Forms and Qualities* Boyle speaks of man as 'made up of an immaterial form and a human body' (*Works*, III, p. 40, *S.* p. 58). See also *ibid.*, p. 12, *S.* p. 15, and p. 38, *S.* p. 53. For a non-committal discussion of the Aristotelian view see *Forms and Qualities, Works*, III, pp. 116–117.

23 For discussion of this see S. Gaukroger 1995, pp. 388–394.

24 See also *Things Above Reason, Works*, IV, p. 424, *S.* p. 236.

25 See *High Veneration, Works*, V, p. 150. Boyle tells us here that he has treated of 'the very conditions of the union of the soul and body' in another paper entitled 'The Imperfection of Human knowledge manifest by its own light'. However, the surviving fragments of this work, *BP*, vol. 16, fols 72–85 do not deal with the subject.

26 See also *Notion of Nature, Works*, V, p. 232, p. 241 and p. 244 and 'Excellency of the Mechanical Hypothesis', *Works*, IV, p. 78, *S.* pp. 153–154.

27 See *BP*, vol. 2, fol. 105.

28 In Aphorism II Boyle says,

> if it should please the Divine Author of things, to furnish a human body whereto the soul is united, with a greater number of sensitive organs, or a greater tenderness of those that belong naturally to it; it [the soul] would be found

capable of modifications correspondent to the impressions, it were then disposed to receive, from bodies or actions that do not now affect it . . .

(*Christian Virtuoso*, II, *Works*, VI, p. 755)

See also *Christian Virtuoso*, I, *Appendix*, *Works*, VI, p. 681 and *BP*, vol. 2, fol. 62.

29 See also *Reason and Religion*, *Works*, IV, p. 170.

30 See *Christian Virtuoso*, II, *Works*, VI, p. 763.

31 *Contra* B. Kaplan who in failing to recognise Boyle's dualism and therefore his distinction between humans and other animate creatures claims that

Boyle does not see life and death as substantive opposites; his formulation is more a relativistic continuum leading from life to a number of diseased states to death. The degree of functional capability determines which label we give to each state.

(1993, p. 65)

Notice too that Boyle's view differs slightly from Descartes' in that Boyle considers death to occur with the separation of the two substances whereas for Descartes 'death never occurs through the absence of the soul, but only because one of the principal parts of the body decays' and because the heat of the body ceases, *Passions*, *CSM*, I, p. 329.

32 See also *Notion of Nature*, *Works*, V, p. 216 and p. 244, *Reason and Religion*, *Works*, IV, p. 170, 'Advices', *Works*, IV, p. 455 and p. 457 and *BP*, vol. 6, fol. 59. The thesis even turns up in Boyle's correspondence: see Boyle's *Letter to Glanvill*, 18 Sept 1677, *Works*, VI, p. 58.

33 For a lucid discussion in favour of attributing the view to Descartes see Peter McLaughlin 1993. For a discussion of the view that Descartes thought that minds could impart motion to matter see A. Gabbey 1985, pp. 14–28.

34 See Clerselier's *Letter to La Forge* (4 December 1660) reprinted in *Oeuvres de Descartes* vol. X, (ed.) V. Cousin, 1825, pp. 541–542 and La Forge's *Traité de L'Esprit de L'Homme*, 1666, (1974), pp. 245–246.

35 See 'Advices', *Works*, IV, p. 455. It is not clear whether Boyle interpreted Descartes through the later Cartesians. What we do know is that Boyle was introduced to Descartes' philosophy by Hooke c.1658–1660 and before this period he had not engaged with it in a serious way. See E. B. Davis, 1994, pp. 159–160. Davis points out Boyle's comment in the early or mid-1650s that Descartes' *Passions* is 'the only book of his which I remember my selfe to have read over', *BP*, vol. 28, fol. 270, quoted in Davis 1994, p. 160. And the allusion to the Cartesians in 'Requisite Digression', written in c.1659, indicates that Boyle had not yet attributed the determination thesis to Descartes or his followers. For there, Boyle speaks of 'others, that seem no less speculative, seriously and solemnly profess that they can conceive a clear and distinct notion of a spirit – which they believe the human soul, that regulates at least, if not produces, divers motions of the body . . .' (*Works*, II, p. 47, *S*. p. 172).

36 Charleton accepts the law: see *Physiologia*, p. 445.

37 See also *High Veneration*, *Works*, V, p. 140.

38 See *Final Causes*, *Works*, V, p. 399. See also *BP*, vol. 8, fol. 169.

39 See *Reason and Religion*, *Works*, IV, p. 170, *Things Above Reason*, *Works*, IV, p. 416, *S*. p. 224, 'Advices', *Works*, IV, p. 455, 'Excellency of the Mechanical Hypothesis', *Works*, IV, p. 78, *S*. p. 154.

40 Boyle says,

> since all Mechanical action is performed by Locall motion, or requires the Intervention of it: and for the same reason neither the Conarion, nor the Animall spirits, nor any part, whether gross or subtill of the Body, can mechanically act, upon the incorporeal soul; which wants Impenetrability, on whose account, in the subject that receives it, Local motion can be produced by the action, or motion of a Body.

(BP, vol. 2, fol. 105)

41 It should be added that body/body interactions are also divine operations for Boyle (see *Christian Virtuoso*, *II*, *Works*, VI, p. 754).

Conclusion

It is time now to draw the threads together and to assess the philosophy of Robert Boyle as presented in the preceding chapters. In the first place, we have seen that Boyle was a philosopher of the qualities. Of course this has long been known but we have, in Part I of this study, aimed to explore the dimensions of Boyle's theory of the qualities with a breadth and depth that sheds new light on his views. His particular taxonomy of the qualities has been explored in detail, revealing a natural philosopher who is really a transitional figure with certain natural ties to his immediate intellectual heritage, but with new innovations and exploring new terrain. Boyle accepts that there are occult qualities; he accepts the distinction between proper and common sensibles; he employs the Aristotelian terminology of first and second qualities. But Boyle was working with a more elaborate set of distinctions of the qualities than many of his forebears, one to which he was able to apply the various reductive and explanatory principles of his corpuscular mechanism. In particular, the distinction between the mechanical and non-mechanical qualities is of enormous significance in his articulation of his corpuscular hypothesis. For it is the mechanical affections of shape, size, motion and texture that provide the main explanatory categories of his mechanism. Furthermore, in one respect he is a pioneer, for he was the first of the mechanical philosophers to plumb the depths of the issue of the ontological status of the sensible qualities. And while it appears that there is no definitive Boylean view on the matter, it is clear that he set the issue up for Locke and his successors.

In Part II I have attempted to piece together Boyle's mechanism in general, exploring his discussions of motion, states, place and in particular to explicate his unique account of just how God and matter interact to bring about the phenomena that we see around us. It was argued that Boyle did not have a clear conception of inertial motion, but his rejection of the twin scholastic distinctions between natural and violent motions and natural and violent states was, in its own right, an important step in the extrication of natural philosophy from the traditional categories and conceptual confusions in which it was shrouded. By refuting the notion that a substance like water has the natural state of being liquid and by furnishing corpuscular explanations of fluidity and solidity, Boyle reveals that his polemic against the traditional views and for the mechanical philosophy extended well beyond his well-known critique of the theory of forms.

Furthermore, Boyle's treatment of the nature of the states of bodies is nicely illustrative of the dynamics of conceptual change. It is widely known that the idea of inertia did not emerge fully born from the mind of Descartes to be utilised, explored and refined by those who followed. But it is not always appreciated just how convoluted, laboured and protracted was the process by which this concept emerged. If birth is a useful analogy here, then Descartes' first law signalled only the onset of labour, the commencement of the birth pangs. For many conceptual accretions remained to be cleared away and, as we have seen from Boyle's minor contribution, not all of them had to do with the quantitative analysis of motion. Conceptual advances in science are normally hard won, their histories are usually messy and their dates of birth often indeterminate.

As has been stressed, Boyle's discussions of the states of bodies arise from that distinctive orientation of his natural philosophy, the theory of qualities, and are not developed with any view to exploring the newly emerging science of mechanics. He was aware of developments in this latter field and admired mechanical philosophers, like Descartes, who explored them, just as he knew of the deep conceptual issues involved in defining matter, space and motion. Yet unlike Descartes, Boyle never articulated any laws of motion, nor, as we have seen, did he have a fully developed theory of space, even though much of what he says about space is implicitly absolutist.

Where Boyle's mechanism is typical of other mechanists like Descartes is that he addressed the wider issue of just how God is related to the mechanical universe that he created. It was argued in chapter 7 that Boyle is best described as a nomic occasionalist, because he claims that matter does indeed have some minimal causal powers, but that every causal interaction of material bodies requires the nomic intervention of God. This divine concourse guarantees that matter behaves in a law-like manner, and at the same time situates Boyle between the extremes of deism and occasionalism. To be sure, things are a little more complicated when it comes to mind/body interaction, because there the mind has the power to change the determination of the motion of bodies. But overall the picture is one of mutual contributions of the material and the spiritual, one that minimises the chance of theological objections and preserves the central tenets of a mechanical approach to nature. Boyle's position can at the same time accommodate miracles and explain regularities without rendering matter completely inert or denying or overstating God's immanence.

It is this feature of Boyle's mechanism, his nomic occasionalism, that brings me, in conclusion, to explore some of the implications of this study for interpretative issues that pertain both to Boyle and the mechanical philosophy in general. First, it is common in the secondary literature on early modern mechanism, and on Locke in particular, to find judgments of individual natural philosophers in terms of the purity or impurity of their mechanism. Michael Ayers, Edwin McCann, Margaret Wilson and others have argued over just how pure Locke's mechanism was. Purity here is defined in terms of the extent to which a mechanist resorts only to matter and motion in their explications of natural phenomena. If a philosopher includes God, spiritual beings or a world soul, then their mechanism is regarded as impure. And of course purity comes in varying degrees. In the particular case of Locke, the purity or otherwise of his mechanism is thought to reside in the extent to which the powers or secondary qualities of bodies can be deduced from or have their ontological ground in the primary qualities of those bodies. Wilson (1979) and McCann (1985a) maintain that Locke was a decidedly impure mechanist, whereas Ayers (1991, II, 2: chapter 12) begs to differ.

Now if this way of characterising respective mechanical philosophies is accurate or expedient, and there is an historical precedent for it in the correspondence of Henry More (Gabbey 1990), then it is clear that Boyle was a very impure mechanist indeed. For as has been argued above, not only is God appealed to in explaining the relation between the mechanical and non-mechanical properties of bodies, but he has a role to play in every causal interaction of material bodies whatsoever. Yet would Boyle have accepted the suggestion that his was an impure mechanism? Would relative purity or impurity have been a standard by which he evaluated his own and other mechanical philosophies? I believe that the notion of an impure mechanism as discussed by contemporary scholars jars with the mechanism as found in the likes of Boyle, Descartes and Locke. After all, Boyle was perhaps the leading populariser of the term 'mechanical philosophy'. He used the term to describe his and Descartes' natural philosophy. So it must be that Boyle's corpuscular philosophy is constitutive of mechanism if anything is. Yet Boyle, like Descartes and perhaps Locke, openly admitted a crucial role for God in his explanations of natural phenomena. It seems wrong then to say that what mechanism really is is something *like* Boyle's or Descartes' view, but with no explanatory role for God and to imply therefore that Boyle was an impure mechanist. Boyle was a pure mechanist if anyone was. To argue otherwise is to impose terms of reference upon him that are of little explanatory value. To argue that Boyle's was a 'pure' mechanism and to use that as a standard by which to evaluate Locke, as for example Margaret Wilson does (Wilson 1979), is not only to misinterpret Boyle, but to set up a false contrast using unhelpful terms of reference.

A second issue arising from this study of Boyle is just how his writings on the corpuscular philosophy mesh with his other intellectual pursuits. Of particular interest here is Boyle's continued interest in alchemy which has been so ably documented by Lawrence Principe. Principe himself has some suggestions as to the respective roles of alchemy and mechanism in Boyle's thought. He sees Boyle's alchemy as functioning as a 'middle-term' effectively unifying Boyle's principal spheres of interest, the mechanical philosophy and theology. He claims that 'there was no escaping the fact that the mechanical philosophy which Boyle so successfully championed *did* distance God from His Creation' (Principe 1998, p. 209). For Principe Boyle's mechanical philosophy verged on deism, was tainted by atheistic associations of Epicurean atomism and faced the problem of determinism. Yet Boyle was fully committed to the existence of God, angels, spirits and incorporeal souls all of which could interact with the material realm. Principe claims that Boyle's version of alchemy helped to resolve the tension between his mechanism and his theology, the Philosopher's Stone being a tangible interface between the material realm of matter and its qualities on the one hand and the spirit world on the other.

The implication of the interpretation of Boyle offered here, however, is that there was in fact no tension between Boyle's corpuscular mechanism and his theology. Boyle's natural philosophy does not relegate God to the status of 'outsider' with regard to the material realm. It does not tend to a deism incompatible with his orthodox theology. So, rather than being a unifying middle-term, Boyle's alchemy can be seen as a natural concomitant of his nomic occasionalism. Boyle's belief that the Philosopher's Stone was an important link between the material and immaterial realms, which Principle has amply documented, can be viewed as in some sense analogous to Boyle's belief in mind/body interaction. Both are entirely consonant with his nomic occasionalism.

It has long been appreciated that Boyle was deeply interested in the qualities, that he was a mechanist and that he had some sort of account of how God interacts with matter. If the more nuanced and systematic exposition of this study of Boyle's philosophy is substantially correct, Boyle the philosopher of the qualities and Boyle the nomic occasionalist must now be set alongside Boyle the experimentalist, Boyle the alchemist and Boyle the Christian virtuoso.

Appendices

The following transcriptions from the *Boyle Papers* are from the microfilm edition by University Publications of America (Bethesda: MD, 1992). The editorial conventions I have employed in transcribing these folios are as follows.[1] All underlining in the original has been italicised. Interlineations are indicated by <angle brackets> and other corrections have been noted in the footnotes. The original spelling, punctuation and capitalisation have been retained, but gaps between words have been silently inserted. Contractions in the original using 'w' or the thorn have been expanded in order to render the text easier to read. And I have inserted the folio number before the first word of each new folio, omitting the catchwords that link these pages.

APPENDIX 1

1 *Boyle Papers* vol. 10, fols 29–31[2]

> Hand: E
> Date: 1660s
> Subject: sensation & the sensible qualities

I come now Pyrophilus to the 4th[3] sort of <those> observations I formerly <mentiond to>[4] you, & this[5] sort consists of those which perhaps will appear as the newest to you. And you will possibly not be displeasd to be entertaind with them since this sort of Instances as it will appear <much more to>[6] favour[7] the Corpuscularian[8] Doctrine about Sensation <then>[9] the Vu<l>gar, soe it will consist of <such> particulars[10] seeme[11] as I think you have not met with among the Writers of Philosophy who <seeme>[12] not to have knowne or at least taken notice of Examples of this kind except one mention'd by the Excellent Cartesius, which I shall presently have occasion to mention.

Whereas then Philosophers are wont to teach us, then that those Qualitys we call sensible are certaine reall Entitys residing in the objects & producing by their proper & peculiar Actions upon the outward Organs, it will appear by severall Examples that I am now about to alledge, that the same[13] sensations as are thought necessarily to depend upon such determinate Qualitys in sensible objects may be produc'd not only without the <agency>[14] of those Qualitys, but ev'n in the absence of the Objects by a <bare> locall motion of <some>[15] internall parts of the <sentient> Body itselfe. §[16] And the Examples I have heretofore been able to meet with of this kind are not soe few but that[17] it will be convenient to referr them to five distinct heads.[18]

And[19] I shall <recount>[20] in the first place those Instances, which have been afforded /30/ me by such persons either[21] by Enemys or Chyrurgions have had some of their Limbs Cut off. Of this sort is the story mentiond by[22] newly pointed at, as related by monsr. Des Cartes,[23] who tells us of a maide, whose hand[24] the Surgions that had long had it in cure were at length obleigd to cut off, but <fearing>[25] <to>[26] let the Patient know of it, least it should too much fright or trouble her, they kept her a Stranger to it, & pretended dayly to dresse her hand as they were wont, which deceit[27] was not very difficult fot them to continue, because they had been wont[28] to cover her Eyes when they dress'd her hand that the sight of it might not discompose her. But notwithstanding the losse of her hand she was wont at the times of dressing to complaine <as before> of paines, sometimes in one finger, or part of her hand sometimes in another. The Curious are obleigd to this Excellent Philosopher as <well>[29] for soe instructive a story, <as>[30] for the Ingenious Reflection he makes upon it. But because, when I read it I thought it might be suspected that the maides Imagination might have a share in her complaints since she believd her selfe to be still in the of her hand <as the Surgeons were tampering with it>, I will add 2 or 3 Instances not lyable to such a suspicion

I was once acquainted with a Woman who by a[31] Gangreene that invaded both her feet was reducd to have them both cut off, within the Compasse of /31/ 8 dayes. And though shee seemd otherwise of a healthy & robustous Constitution yet <when> I ask whether shee did not sometime fancy that she felt paines in <either>[32] of her feet; she told me that she often did,[33] in spight of her knowledge that shee had lost them, <that she>[34] could scarce perswade herselfe but that the paine she felt was really in this or that particular part of her foot, <&>[35] most commonly in her great toe, Only she[36] answerd me furthar that <in processe>[37] of time[38] these[39] Impressions were growne lesse frequent & vivid, & when I enquird how long it was since she had lost her feet, she told me punctually the time, which I found to be near 14 year before. [she furthar told me that she had severall times been like to breake her neck, when forgetting <her>[40] losse she went to step downe <as formerly,> from the bed[41] <or seat>[42] she usually sate <on>[43].,][44] I enquir'd[45]

APPENDIX 2

2 *Boyle Papers* vol. 10, fols 38–40[46]

Hand: A
Date: late 1670s to 1680s
Subject: occasionalism

As to your Question what I think of the new Paradox of some Cartesians, who will not allow that bodys can move one another; but thinke that of all Motions amongst things corporeal, *God* himself is the only proper and immediate[47] cause. As to this question, I say, <I> confesse,[48] I some what wonder, that you, to whom I have the honnour to be so well known should require my opinion, in a Physicall probleme as you thinke it, which cannot be clearly determined by any sensible experiment, nor perhaps by any physical reason. And your commands surprise me the more, because I have not converst with any assertor of th<is>[49] Paradox, to learn of him, upon what grounds they maintain it, but haveing, I remember, <found> the like opinion fatherd upon one or two of the Antienter School-men, I cannot say that I never had any thoughts about it: and therefore, I shal so far obey you, as to acquaint you with what came into my mind, as[50] I was thinking what might, <be said> not to prove this opinion true, but to keep it from appearing absurd.

First then I consider that 'tis an acknowledg'd *Axiome* that *entia non sunt multiplicanda absque necessitate*; and therefore since the action of God is sufficient to all the motions that occur among bodys, 'tis needless and superfluous,[51] to have recourse to any other cause; especially since (in the *second place*) it does not manifestly appear to us, that one body does really and truely move another, but only that upon a moved body's hitting another, there follows a motion in the body that is <shocked>[52], or hitt against, nay (in the *third place*) it may well be question'd, whither we can so much as *conceive*, how a body can communicate motion to another and loose it, its self.

But now I expect you will make weighty objections against the grounds of our *Paradox*: which I have thus briefly propos'd, because I would avoid tautologies[53] and foresaw there will be occasion to enlarge on them when I come to vindicate them.[54]

/39/ First then I know it may be said that the propos'd Paradox deprives all material[55] Agents of the honour of being true Causes, as hitherto Philosophers themselves, as well as the vulgar, have believed them to be, and <turns>[56] them into meer Instruments: since motion being the grand efficient in all the actions of one part of matter upon another; if these have no inherent motion and power to communicate it, they have really and properly no power to act, but only are Instruments acted and mov'd by the first cause. I will not now examine, whiter thô motion be granted to be the chief of second Causes, some other things, such as Bulk, figure, rest, Situation and Contexture, may not entitle Natural bodys to the name of Phisical Agents, especially according to *Cartesius*, who will have *rest* to be, not a privation, but a positive thing in Nature, as well as Motion. But whatever become of this question, in Answer to the Objection, I say, that we ought to be far more carefull that our Notions be agreeable[57] to the nature of things, than to the Opinions of Men, or Termes of Art. And if there be sufficient reason to believe, that all motion in Bodys is produc'd immediately by God, we are not to oppose, or refuse that truth, for fear it should be thence inferr'd, that men spoke not properly, when they conferr'd on bodys a title that is not due to them. And I thinke it may be considered, whiter it be not more safe, as well as pious, in a doubtful case, to Attribute a power that <must>[58] be lodg'd some where,[59] rather to an omnipotent Spirit, than to senseless Matter, it being a less dangerous error[60] to derogate from bodys, than from God.

I expect also to be told that 'tis very unphilosophicall to have recourse, without necessity, to the first Cause: And I allow the assertion; but think it misapplyd when urg'd against our Paradox; For it must be provd, not barly[61] presum'd, that in our present case, a recourse to the first cause is unnecessary; and the Cartesians that oppose our paradox must allow me, to put them in mind of what themselves doe, when they truely teach that motion does not att all belong to the nature of Matter; and consequently that all the motion that was put in to the Universall Matter at the beginning of things, was produc'd in it immediately by God himselfe; and this the *Epicureans* and many other Philosophers look upon as an unphilosophicall doctrine,[62] because the /40/ Assertors of it have recourse, not to a Phisical but a Supernatural cause. So that the maine difference between those Cartesians I plead for, and the rest of that sect, is only this, that the latter ascribe to God, all that quantity of Motion in gross, that others ascribe to him in parcelles.

Notes

1   The conventions employed largely follow those recommended in Michael Hunter 1995b.
2   Michael Hunter has kindly collated my transcription with the original folios of *BP*, vol. 10, fols 29–31 at the Royal Society.
3   Followed by *and last* deleted.
4   Replacing *promised* deleted.
5   Followed by *sort (indeterminate) place being reserved for* deleted.
6   Replacing *very* deleted.
7   Followed by *-able* deleted.
8   Followed by *Philosophy* deleted.
9   Replacing *about* deleted in pencil.
10 Followed by *that the (indeterminate) writers of Philosophy* deleted.
11 Followed by *to have been great strangers* deleted.
12 Replacing an indeterminate deleted.
13 Followed by *Effects* deleted.
14 Replacing *help* deleted.
15 Replacing thorn deleted.
16 Refers to marginal insertion §.
17 Followed by an indeterminate deleted.
18 Followed by *these* deleted.
19 Replacing *<The first sort of Examples>* deleted.
20 Replacing *next relate* deleted.
21 Followed by an indeterminate deleted.
22 Followed by an indeterminate deleted.
23 *Principles*, IV, §196, *CSM*, I, pp. 283–284.
24 Followed by *haveing* deleted.
25 Inserted in pencil, replacing *forbearing*.
26 Replacing thorn deleted.

27 Following an indeterminate deleted.
28 Underlined in pencil.
29 *well* in margin.
30 Replacing & *more* deleted.
31 Followed by *distemper that fell* and an indeterminate deleted.
32 Replacing *one or both* deleted.
33 Followed by & *could scarce persuade herselfe* deleted.
34 Replacing *but that shee* deleted, *that* added in pencil.
35 Added in pencil.
36 Followed by an indeterminate deleted.
37 Replacing *length* deleted.
38 Followed by an indeterminate deleted.
39 Followed by an indeterminate deleted.
40 Replacing *the* deleted.
41 Following *Bed* deleted.
42 *or seat* in margin.
43 Replacing <*on*> deleted and followed by . *as she had* deleted, <*been w*>replacing an indeterminate deleted.
44 Lines within brackets have been crossed through in ink.
45 Last two words are added catchwords indicating that the text continues.
46 Michael Hunter has kindly collated my transcription with the original folios of *BP*, vol. 10, fols 38–40 at the Royal Society and informed me that a Latin translation of these folios exists at *BP*, vol. 29, fols 77–82v. Variant readings in the Latin translation have been noted.
47 Latin *solam et immediatam*.
48 The Latin translation interpolates *et quidem non sine respectu huius quaestionis ego confiteor*.
49 Altered from *that*.
50 Followed by an indeterminate deletion.
51 For *'tis needless and superfluous* the Latin has only *supervacuum est*.
52 Replacing *shock'd* deleted (partly obscured by a blot).
53 Altered from *tautology*.
54 For *when I come to vindicate them* the Latin has *cum corrobanda et afferenda venerint*.
55 Followed by *causes* deleted.
56 Replacing *termes* deleted (i.e. misheard in dictation).
57 Following *aggre* deleted.
58 Replacing *may* deleted.
59 Followed by *and* deleted.
60 Followed by a small indeterminate deletion.
61 Altered from *bearly*.
62 For *look upon as an unphilosophicall doctrine* the Latin has *videtur a genio Philosophorum abhorrer, eo quo euis Assertores non ad Philosophicam* . . .

Bibliography

Agrippa, H. (1533) *De occulta philosophia libri tres*, Cologne.

Alexander, P. (1974) 'Curley on Locke and Boyle', *Philosophical Review*, 83, pp. 229–237.

—— (1977) 'The Names of Secondary Qualities', *Proceedings of the Aristotelian Society*, 77, pp. 203–220.

—— (1981) 'The case of the lonely corpuscle: reductive explanation and primitive expressions' in R. Healey, (ed.) *Reduction, Time and Reality: Studies in the Philosophy of the Natural Sciences*, Cambridge: Cambridge University Press, pp. 17–35.

—— (1985) *Ideas, Qualities and Corpuscles: Locke and Boyle on the External World*, Cambridge: Cambridge University Press.

Amerpoel, J. (1669) *Cartesius Mosaizans*, Leuwarden.

Anstey, P. (1999) 'Boyle on occasionalism: an unexamined source', *Journal of the History of Ideas*, 60, 57–81.

—— 'Robert Boyle and the heuristic value of mechanism', forthcoming.

Ariew, R. and Gabbey, A. (1998) 'The Scholastic Background' in *The Cambridge History of Seventeenth-Century Philosophy*, (eds) D. Garber and M. Ayers, Cambridge: Cambridge University Press, pp. 425–453.

Armstrong, D. M. (1987) 'Smart and the Secondary Qualities', in *Metaphysics and Morality: Essays in Honour of J. J. C. Smart*, (eds) P. Pettit, R. Sylvan and J. Norman, Oxford: Blackwell, pp. 1–15.

—— (1993) 'Reply to Lewis', in J. B. Bacon, K. K. Campbell and L. Reinhardt (eds) *Ontology, Causality and Mind: Essays in Honour of D. M. Armstrong*, Cambridge: Cambridge University Press, pp. 38–42.

Armstrong, D. M. and Martin, C. B. (eds) (1968) *Locke and Berkeley*, New York: Doubleday.

Averill, E. W. (1992) 'The Relational Nature of Colour', *The Philosophical Review*, 101, pp. 551–588.

Ayers, M. (1991) *Locke*, 2 vols, London: Routledge.

—— (1993) 'Voluntarism and Naturalism in Physics from Descartes to Hume', *History of Philosophy Yearbook*, vol. 1, Canberra, pp. 41–65.

Bacon, Francis (1857–74) *The Works of Francis Bacon*, (eds) J. Spedding, R. L. Ellis and D. D. Heath, 14 vols, London.

Bacon, J. B., Campbell, K. K. and Reinhardt, L. (eds) (1993) *Ontology, Causality and Mind: Essays in Honour of D. M. Armstrong*, Cambridge: Cambridge University Press.

Barbour, J. (1989) *Absolute or Relative Motion?*, vol. 1 of *The Discovery of Dynamics*, Cambridge: Cambridge University Press.

Barnes, J. (1991) *The Complete Works of Aristotle*, 2 vols, Princeton: Princeton University Press.

Beaufort, L. de (1656) *Cosmopoea Divina*, Lugduni Batavorum.

Bechler, Z. (1991) *Newton's Physics and the Conceptual Structure of the Scientific Revolution*, Dordrecht: Kluwer.

—— (1992) 'Newton's ontology of the force of inertia', in P. M. Harman and A. E. Shapiro, (eds) *The Investigation of Difficult Things*, Cambridge: Cambridge University Press, pp. 287–304.

Bennett, J. (1971) *Locke, Berkeley, Hume: Central Themes*, Oxford: Oxford University Press.

Berkeley, G. (1965) *Berkeley's Philosophical Writings*, (ed.) D. M. Armstrong, New York: Macmillan.

Blair, A. (1992) 'Humanist Methods in Natural Philosophy: the Commonplace Book', *Journal of the History of Ideas*, 53, pp. 541–551.

Boyle, R. (1744) *The Works of the Honourable Robert Boyle*, (ed.) Thomas Birch, London.

—— (1772) *The Works*, (ed.) T. Birch, reprint edition, Hildesheim: Georg Olms, 1965.

—— (1991) *Selected Philosophical Papers of Robert Boyle*, (ed.) M. A. Stewart, Indianapolis: Hackett.

—— (1999–) *The Works of Robert Boyle*, (eds) M. Hunter and E. B. Davis, London: Pickering and Chatto, 14 vols.

Burtt, E. A. (1932) *The Metaphysical Foundations of Modern Physical Science*, 2nd edn, London: Routledge.

Campbell, K. K. (1976) *Metaphysics: An Introduction*, Belmont: Wadsworth.

—— (1990) *Abstract Particulars*, Oxford: Blackwell.

—— (1993) 'David Armstrong and Realism about Colour', in J. B. Bacon, K. K. Campbell and L. Reinhardt (eds) *Ontology, Causality and Mind*, Cambridge: Cambridge University Press, pp. 249–268.

Centore, F. F. (1970) *Robert Hooke's Contribution to Mechanics*, The Hague: Martinus Nijhoff.

Chalmers, A. (1993a) 'The Lack of Excellency of Boyle's Mechanical Philosophy', *Studies in the History and Philosophy of Science*, 24, pp. 541–564.

—— (1993b) 'Galilean Relativity and Galileo's Relativity', in S. French and H. Kamminga, (eds) *Correspondence, Invariance and Heuristics*, Dordrecht: Kluwer, pp. 189–205.

Charleton, W. (1654) *Physiologia Epicuro-Gassendo-Charletoniana*, London: Johnson Reprint Corporation, 1966.

Clagett, M. (1961) *The Science of Mechanics in the Middle Ages*, Madison: University of Wisconsin Press.

Clarke, D. M. (1989) *Occult Powers and Hypotheses: Cartesian Natural Philosophy under Louis XIV*, Oxford: Oxford University Press.

Clericuzio, A. (1990a) 'A Redefinition of Boyle's Chemistry and Corpuscular Philosophy', *Annals of Science*, 47, pp. 561–589.

—— (1990b) 'Robert Boyle and the English Helmontians', in Z. R. W. M. van Martels, (ed.) *Alchemy Revisited*, Leiden: Brill, pp. 192–199.

—— (1993) 'From van Helmont to Boyle: A Study of the Transmission of Helmontian Chemical and Medical Theories in Seventeenth-Century England', *British Journal for the History of Science*, 26, pp. 303–354.

—— (1998) 'The Mechanical Philosophy and the Spring of the Air: New Light on Robert Boyle and Robert Hooke', *Nuncius*, 13, pp. 69–75.

Colie, R. (1963) 'Spinoza in England 1665–1730', *Proceedings of the American Philosophical Society*, 107, pp. 183–219.

Conry, Y. (1980) 'Robert Boyle et la doctrine cartésienne des animaux-machines', *Revue d'Histoire des Sciences*, 33, pp. 69–74.

Copenhaver, B. (1988) 'Astrology and Magic' in C. B. Schmitt and Q. Skinner, (eds) *The Cambridge History of Renaissance Philosophy*, Cambridge: Cambridge University Press, 1988, pp. 264–300.

Cordemoy, G. (1668) *Copie d'une lettre écrite à sçavant Religieux*, Paris.

Cottingham, J. R., Stoothoff, R. and Murdock, D. (1985) trans., *The Philosophical Writings of Descartes*, 2 vols, Cambridge: Cambridge University Press.

Cottingham, J. R., Stoothoff, R., Murdock, D. and Kenny, A. (1991) trans., *The Philosophical Writings of Descartes*, vol. 3, Cambridge: Cambridge University Press.

Crowley, M. E. (1970) 'The notion of nature in the corpuscular philosophy of Robert Boyle', Marquette University Ph.D. thesis.

Cudworth, R. (1678) *The True Intellectual System of the Universe*, 3 vols., trans., J. Harrison, London: Tegg, 1843.

Cumberland, R. (1672) *An Inquiry into the Laws of Nature*, trans. J. Towers, London, 1750.

Curley, E. M. (1972) 'Locke, Boyle and the Distinction between Primary and Secondary Qualities', *Philosophical Review*, 81, pp. 438–464.

Davis, E. B. (1984) 'Creation, contingency and early modern science: the impact of voluntaristic theology on seventeenth century natural philosophy', Indiana University Ph.D. thesis.

—— (1994) '"Parcere nominibus": Boyle, Hooke and the Rhetorical Interpretation of Descartes', in M. Hunter, (ed.) *Robert Boyle Reconsidered*, Cambridge: Cambridge University Press, pp. 157–175.

Deason, G. B. (1986) 'Reformation Theology and the Mechanistic Conception of Nature' in D. C. Lindberg and R. L. Numbers, (eds) *God and Nature*, Berkeley: University of California Press, pp. 167–191.

Des Chene, D. (1996) *Physiologia: Natural Philosophy in Late Aristotelian and Cartesian Thought*, Ithaca: Cornell University Press.

Descartes, R. (1657–1667) *Lettres de Descartes*, 3 vols, (ed.) C. Clerselier, Paris.

—— (1824–1926) *Oeuvres de Descartes*, 11 vols, (ed.) V. Cousin.

—— (1996) *Œuvres de Descartes*, revised edn, 11 vols, (eds) C. Adam and P. Tannery, Paris: Vrin.

Digby, K. (1644) *Two Treatises: Of Bodies and On Man's Soul*, (ed.) R. Wellek, New York: Garland, 1978.

Dijksterhuis, E. J. (1961) *The Mechanization of the World Picture*, London: Oxford University Press.

Dobbs, B. J. T. (1971) 'Studies in the Natural Philosophy of Sir Kenelm Digby', *Ambix*, 18, pp. 1–25.

—— (1975) *The Foundations of Newton's Alchemy, or 'The Hunting of the Greene Lyon'*, Cambridge: Cambridge University Press.

—— (1985) 'Conceptual Problems in Newton's Early Chemistry: a Preliminary Study', in M. J. Osler and P. L. Farber, (eds) *Religion, Science and Worldview: Essays in Honour of Richard S. Westfall*, Cambridge: Cambridge University Press, pp. 3–32.

Drake, S. (1957) *Discoveries and Opinions of Galileo*, trans. S. Drake, New York: Doubleday.

Du Hamel, J. B. (1670) *De corporum affectionibus tum manifestis, tum occultis*, Paris.

Edwards, P. (ed.) (1967) *The Encyclopedia of Philosophy*, 8 vols, New York: Macmillan and Free Press.

Emerton, N. E. (1984) *The Scientific Reinterpretation of Form*, Ithaca: Cornell University Press.

Epicurus (1931) 'Letter to Herodotus', in *Diogenes Laertius*, vol. 2, trans. R. D. Hicks, Loeb Classical Library, Cambridge MA: Harvard University Press.

Field, J. and James, F. (eds) (1993) *Renaissance and Revolution*, Cambridge: Cambridge University Press.

Fracastoro (1546) *De sympathia et antipathia*, in *Operum pars prior*, Lugduni, Apud Franciscum Fabrum, 1591.

Frank, R. G. (1980) *Harvey and the Oxford Physiologists*, Berkeley: University of California Press.

Freeland, C. (1992) 'Aristotle on the Sense of Touch', in M. Nussbaum and A. Rorty, (eds) *Essays on Aristotle's De Anima*, Oxford: Oxford University Press, pp. 227–248.

Friedman, M. (1974) 'Explanation and Scientific Understanding', *The Journal of Philosophy*, 71, pp. 5–19.

Gabbey, A. (1980) 'Force and Inertia in the Seventeenth Century: Descartes and Newton', in S. W. Gaukroger, (ed.) *Descartes: Philosophy, Mathematics and Physics*, Sussex: Harvester Press, pp. 230–320.

—— (1985) 'The Mechanical Philosophy and its Problems. Mechanical Explanations, Impenetrability and Perpetual Motion', in J. C. Pitt, (ed.) *Change and Progress in Modern Science*, Dordrecht: Reidel, pp. 9–84.

—— (1990) 'Henry More and the limits of mechanism', in S. Hutton, (ed.) *Henry More (1614–1687)*, Dordrecht: Kluwer, pp. 19–35.

—— (1992) 'Newton's *Mathematical Principles of Natural Philosophy*: a treatise on "mechanics"?', in P. M. Harman and A. E. Shapiro, (eds) *The Investigation of Difficult Things*, Cambridge: Cambridge University Press, 1992, pp. 305–322.

—— (1993) 'Between *ars* and *philosophia naturalis*: Reflections on the Historiography of Early Modern Mechanics', in J. Field and F. James, (eds) *Renaissance and Revolution*, Cambridge: Cambridge University Press, pp. 133–145.

—— (1998) 'New Doctrines of Motion' in D. Garber and M. Ayers, (eds) *The Cambridge History of Seventeenth-Century Philosophy*, Cambridge: Cambridge University Press, vol. 1, pp. 649–679.

Galileo (1590) *De motu locali*, in *Le opere*, (eds) A Favaro and I. Del Lungo, vol. I, 1890.

—— (1623) *The Assayer*, in S. Drake, trans., *Discoveries and Opinions of Galileo*, New York: Doubleday, 1957.

Garber, D. (1992) *Descartes' Metaphysical Physics*, Chicago: University of Chicago Press.

Garber, D. and Ayers, M. (eds) (1998) *The Cambridge History of Seventeenth-Century Philosophy*, Cambridge: Cambridge University Press, 2 vols.

Gassendi, P. (1658) *Syntagma philosophicum*, in *Opera Omnia*, vols I and II, Lyons.

—— (1972) *The Selected Works of Pierre Gassendi*, trans., C. B. Brush, New York: Johnson Reprint Corporation.

Gaukroger, S. W. (ed.) (1980) *Descartes: Philosophy, Mathematics and Physics*, Sussex: The Harvester Press.

—— (1981) 'Aristotle on the Function of Sense Perception', *Studies in the History and Philosophy of Science*, XII, pp. 75–89.

—— (ed.) (1990) *Antoine Arnauld, 'On True and False Ideas'*, Manchester: Manchester University Press.

—— (1995) *Descartes: An Intellectual Biography*, Oxford: Oxford University Press.

Glanvill, J. (1668) *Plus Ultra*, London.

Grant, E. (1981a) *Much Ado about Nothing: Theories of Space and Vacuum from the Middle Ages to the Scientific Revolution*, Cambridge: Cambridge University Press.

—— (1981b) *Studies in Medieval Science and Natural Philosophy*, London: Variorum Reprints.

—— (1981c) 'The condemnation of 1277, God's absolute power, and physical thought in the late middle ages', article XIII in *Studies in Medieval Science and Natural Philosophy*, London: Variorum Reprints.

Hacking, I. (1975) *The Emergence of Probability*, Cambridge: Cambridge University Press.

Hall, A. R. (1983) *The Revolution in Science 1500–1750*, London: Longman.

—— (1992) 'Newton and the absolutes: sources', in P. M. Harman and A. E. Shapiro, (eds) *The Investigation of Difficult Things*, Cambridge: Cambridge University Press, pp. 261–285.

—— (1993) 'Retrospection on the Scientific Revolution', in J. Field and F. James, (eds) *Renaissance and Revolution*, Cambridge: Cambridge University Press, pp. 239–249.

Hall, A. R. and Hall, M. B. (eds) (1962) *Unpublished Scientific Papers of Isaac Newton*, Cambridge: Cambridge University Press.

Hall, M. B. (1952) 'The Establishment of the Mechanical Philosophy', *Osiris*, 10, pp. 412–541.

—— (1954) 'An Early Version of Boyle's Sceptical Chymist', *Isis*, 45, pp. 153–168.

—— (1970) *Nature and Nature's Laws*, London: Macmillan.

—— (1987) 'Boyle's method of work: promoting his corpuscular philosophy', *Notes and Records of the Royal Society*, 41, pp. 111–143.

Hall, T. S. (1969) *Ideas of Life and Matter*, 2 vols, Chicago: Chicago University Press.

Harman, P. M. and Shapiro, A. E. (eds) (1992) *The Investigation of Difficult Things: Essays on Newton and the History of the Exact Sciences in Honour of D. T. Whiteside*, Cambridge: Cambridge University Press.

Harré, R. (1964) *Matter and Method*, London: Macmillan.

—— (1985) *The Philosophies of Science: An Introductory Survey*, Oxford: Oxford University Press.

Harwood, J. T. (ed.) (1991) *The Early Essays and Ethics of Robert Boyle*, Carbondale: Southern Illinois University Press.

Healey, R. (ed.) (1989) *Reduction, Time and Reality: Studies in the Philosophy of the Natural Sciences*, Cambridge: Cambridge University Press.

Heimann, P. M. and McGuire, J. E. (1971) 'Newtonian Forces and Lockean Powers: Concepts of Matter in Eighteenth-Century Thought', in R. McCormmach, (ed.) *Historical Studies in the Physical Sciences*, vol. 3, Philadelphia: University of Pennsylvania Press, pp. 233–306.

Henry, J. (1986) 'Occult Qualities and the Experimental Philosophy: Active Principles in Pre-Newtonian Matter Theory', *History of Science*, 24, pp. 335–381.

—— (1990) 'Henry More Versus Robert Boyle: The Spirit of Nature and the Nature of Providence', in S. Hutton, (ed.) *Henry More (1614–1687)*, London: Kluwer, pp. 55–76.

Hobbes, T. (*c.*1630) *A Short Tract on First Principles*, printed in R. S. Peters, (ed.) *Body, Man and Citizen: Selections from Thomas Hobbes*, New York: Collier (1962).

—— (1651) *Leviathan*, (ed.) C. B. Macpherson, Middlesex: Penguin, 1968.

—— (1839–1845) *The English Works of Thomas Hobbes*, (ed.) Sir W. Molesworth, 11 vols, London: John Bohn.

—— (1994) *The Correspondence of Thomas Hobbes*, (ed.) N. Malcolm, 2 vols, Oxford: Oxford University Press.

Holland, A. J. (ed.) (1985) *Philosophy, its History and Historiography*, Dordrecht: Reidel.

Hunter, M. (1992) *Letters and Papers of Robert Boyle: A Guide to the Manuscripts and Microfilm*, Bethesda, MD: Bethesda.

—— (1993) 'Casuistry in Action: Robert Boyle's Confessional Interviews with Gilbert Burnet and Edward Stillingfleet, 1691', *Journal of Ecclesiastical History*, 44, pp. 80–98.

—— (ed.) (1994a) *Robert Boyle Reconsidered*, Cambridge: Cambridge University Press.

—— (1994b) *Robert Boyle: By Himself and His Friends*, London: Pickering.

—— (1995a) 'How Boyle Became a Scientist', *History of Science*, 33, 59–103.

—— (1995b) 'How to Edit a Seventeenth Century Manuscript: Principles and Practice', *The Seventeenth Century*, 10, pp. 277–310.

—— (1997) 'Boyle versus the Galenists: a Suppressed Critique of Seventeenth-Century Medical Practice and its Significance', *Medical History*, 41, pp. 322–361.

Hunter, M. and Davis, E. B. (1996) 'The Making of Robert Boyle's *Free Enquiry into the Vulgarly Receiv'd Notion of Nature* (1686)', *Early Science and Medicine*, 1, pp. 204–271.

Hutchison, K. (1982) 'What Happened to Occult Qualities in the Scientific Revolution?', *Isis*, 73, pp. 233–253.

—— (1991) 'Dormitive virtues, scholastic qualities, and the new philosophies', *History of Science*, 29, pp. 245–278.

Hutton, S. (ed.) (1990) *Henry More (1614–1687)*, London: Kluwer.

Jackson, F. and Pargetter, R. (1987) 'An Objectivist's Guide to Subjectivism about Colour', *Revue Internationale de Philosophie*, 41, pp. 127–141.

Jackson, R. (1968) 'Locke's Distinction between Primary and Secondary Qualities', in

D. M. Armstrong and C. B. Martin, (eds) *Locke and Berkeley*, New York: Doubleday, originally published in *Mind*, 38, 1929, pp. 56–76.

Jacobs, S. (1994) 'Laws of Nature, Corpuscles, and Concourse: Non-occasionalist Tendencies in the Natural Philosophy of Robert Boyle', *Journal of Philosophical Research*, 19, pp. 373–393.

Johnson, W. E. (1921) *Logic: Part 1*, *3*, New York: Dover Publications.

Kaplan, B. B. (1993) *'Divulging of Useful Truths in Physick': the Medical Agenda of Robert Boyle*, Baltimore: Johns Hopkins University Press.

Kargon, R. H. (1964) 'William Charleton and Robert Boyle and the Acceptance of Epicurean Atomism in England', *Isis*, 55, pp. 184–192.

—— (1966) *Atomism in England from Hariot to Newton*, Oxford: Clarendon Press.

Keating, L. (1993) 'Un-Locke-ing Boyle: Boyle on Primary and Secondary Qualities', *History of Philosophy Quarterly*, 10, pp. 305–323.

Kirk, G. S., Raven, J. E. and Schofield, M. (eds) (1987) *The Presocratic Philosophers*, 2nd edn, Cambridge: Cambridge University Press.

Koyré, A. (1957) *From the Closed World to the Infinite Universe*, Baltimore: Johns Hopkins University Press.

—— (1965) *Newtonian Studies*, Chicago: University of Chicago Press.

—— (1978) *Galileo Studies*, Sussex: The Harvester Press.

Kroll, R., Ashcraft, R. and Zagorin, P. (eds) (1992) *Philosophy, Science and Religion in England 1640–1700*, Cambridge: Cambridge University Press.

Kuhn, T. S. (1952) 'Robert Boyle and Structural Chemistry in the Seventeenth Century', *Isis*, 43, pp. 12–36.

La Forge, L. (1666) *Traité de L'Esprit de L'Homme*, in *Oeuvres Philosophiques*, (ed.) P. Clair, Paris: Presses Universitaires de France, 1974.

Langton, R. (1993) 'Locke's Mechanism: Relations and God's Good Pleasure', *History of Philosophy Yearbook*, vol. 1, Canberra, pp. 66–88.

Le Grand, A. (1673) *Historia Naturae*, London.

Lewis, D. K. (1993) 'Many, but Almost One', in J. B. Bacon, K. K. Campbell and L. Reinhardt, (eds) *Ontology, Causality and Mind*, Cambridge: Cambridge University Press, pp. 23–38.

Lindberg, D. C. and Numbers, R. L. (eds) (1986) *God and Nature*, Berkeley: University of California Press.

Locke, J. (*c*.1660) *Essays on the Law of Nature*, (ed.) W. von Leyden, Oxford: Oxford University Press, 1958.

—— (1700) *An Essay concerning Human Understanding*, 4th edn, (ed.) P. H. Nidditch, Oxford: Oxford University Press, 1975.

Long, A. A. and Sedley, D. N. (eds) (1987) *The Hellenistic Philosophers*, 2 vols, Cambridge: Cambridge University Press.

Lucretius (1966) *De Rerum Natura*, trans., W. H. D. Rouse, Loeb Classical Library, Cambridge MA: Harvard University Press.

McCann, E. (1985a) 'Lockean Mechanism', in *Philosophy, its History and Historiography*, (ed.) A. J. Holland, Dordrecht: Reidel, pp. 209–229.

—— (1985b) 'Was Boyle an Occasionalist?', in *Philosophy, its History and Historiography*, (ed.) A. J. Holland, Dordrecht: Reidel, pp. 229–231.

McGuire, J. E. (1970) 'Atoms and the "Analogy of Nature": Newton's Third Rule of Philosophizing', *History and Philosophy of Science*, 1, pp. 3–58.

—— (1972) 'Boyle's Conception of Nature', *Journal of the History of Ideas*, 33, no. 4, pp. 523–542.

—— (1977) 'Neoplatonism and active principles: Newton and the Corpus Hermeticum', in R. S. Westman and J. E. McGuire, (eds) *Hermeticism and the Scientific Revolution*, Los Angeles: Clark Memorial Library, pp. 95–142.

—— (1978) 'Existence, Actuality and Necessity: Newton on Space and Time', *Annals of Science*, 35, pp. 463–508.

McGuire, J. E. and Tamny, M. (1983) *Certain Philosophical Questions: Newton's Trinity Notebook*, Cambridge: Cambridge University Press.

Machamer, P. K. and Turnball, R. G. (eds) (1978) *Studies in Perception*, Columbus: Ohio State University Press.

MacIntosh, J. J. (1976) 'Primary and Secondary Qualities', *Studia Leibnitiana*, 8, pp. 88–104.

—— (1983) 'Perception and Imagination in Descartes, Boyle and Hooke', *Canadian Journal of Philosophy*, 13, pp. 327–352.

—— (1991) 'Robert Boyle on Epicurean Atheism and Atomism', in *Atoms, pneuma, and Tranquillity*, (ed.) M. J. Osler, Cambridge: Cambridge University Press, pp. 197–219.

—— (1996) 'Animals, Morality and Robert Boyle', *Dialogue*, 35, pp. 435–472.

Mackie, J. L. (1976) *Problems from Locke*, Oxford: Oxford University Press.

McLaughlin, P. (1993) 'Descartes on Mind-Body Interaction and the Conservation of Motion', *The Philosophical Review*, 102, pp. 155–182.

McMullin, E. (ed.) (1978a) *The Concept of Matter in Modern Philosophy*, Notre Dame: University of Notre Dame Press.

—— (1978b) 'Structural Explanation', *American Philosophical Quarterly*, 15, pp. 139–147.

Mandelbaum, M. (1964) *Philosophy, Science and Sense Perception*, Baltimore: Johns Hopkins University Press.

Martin, C. B. (1993) 'Power for Realists', in *Ontology, Causality and Mind*, (eds) J. Bacon, K. K. Campbell and L. Reinhardt, Cambridge: Cambridge University Press, pp. 175–186.

Martin, C. B. and Armstrong, D. M. (eds) (1968) *Locke and Berkeley: A Collection of Critical Essays*, New York: Doubleday.

Mill, J. S. (1874) *Nature, the Utility of Religion and Theism*, London: Longman.

Millen, R. (1985) 'The Manifestation of Occult Qualities in the Scientific Revolution', in M. J. Osler and P. L. Farber, (eds) *Religion Science, and Worldview: Essays in Honour of R. S. Westfall*, Cambridge: Cambridge University Press, pp. 185–216.

Milton, J. R. (1982) *The Influence of the Nominalist Movement on the Scientific Thought of Bacon, Boyle and Locke*, Ph.D thesis, Imperial College London.

Modrak, D. (1987) *Aristotle. The Power of Perception*, Chicago: University of Chicago Press.

Molière, J.-B. (1673) *Le Malade imaginaire*, Paris: Librairie Larousse, 1958.

More, H. (1653) *Conjectura cabbalistica*, London.

—— (1659) *The Immortality of the Soul*, (ed.) A. Jacob, Dordrecht: Kluwer, 1987.

Mourelatos, A. P. D. (ed.) (1974) *The Pre-Socratics*, New York: Anchor.

Nadler, S. (1994) 'Descartes and Occasional Causation', *British Journal for the History of Philosophy*, 2, pp. 35–54.

Newman, W. R. (1994a) *Gehennical Fire: The Lives of George Starkey, an American Alchemist in the Scientific Revolution*, Cambridge MA: Harvard University Press.

—— (1994b) 'Boyle's Debt to Corpuscular Alchemy' in *Robert Boyle Reconsidered*, (ed.) M. Hunter, Cambridge: Cambridge University Press, pp. 107–118.

—— (1996) 'The Alchemical Sources of Robert Boyle's Corpuscular Philosophy', *Annals of Science*, 53, pp. 576–585.

Newman, W. R. and Principe, L. M. (1998) 'Alchemy vs. Chemistry: The Etymological Origins of a Historiographical Mistake', *Early Science and Medicine*, 3, pp. 32–65.

Newton, I. (1729) *The Mathematical Principles of Natural Philosophy*, trans. A. Motte and F. Cajori, Los Angeles and Berkeley: University of California Press, 1966.

—— (1730) *Opticks*, New York: Dover, 1952, based on 4th edn, London, 1730.

Nussbaum, M. and Rorty, A. (eds) (1992) *Essays on Aristotle's De Anima*, Oxford: Oxford University Press.

Oakley, F. (1961) 'Christian Theology and the Newtonian Science: The Rise of the Concept of the Laws of Nature', *Church History*, 30, pp. 433–457.

—— (1984) *Omnipotence, Covenant and Order: An Excursion in the History of Ideas from Abelard to Leibniz*, Ithaca: Cornell University Press.

Oldenburg, H. (1965–86) *The Correspondence of Henry Oldenburg*, 13 vols, (eds) A. R. and M. B. Hall, Madison, Milwaukee and London: University of Wisconsin Press, Mansell and Taylor & Francis.

Olsen, K. R. (1987) *An Essay on Facts*, Stanford: CSLI.

Osler, M. J. (ed.) (1991) *Atoms, Pneuma, and Tranquillity*, Cambridge: Cambridge University Press.

—— (1992) 'The Intellectual Sources of Boyle's Philosophy of Nature: Gassendi's Voluntarism and Boyle's Physico-theological Project', in R. Kroll, R. Ashcraft and P. Zagorin, (eds) *Philosophy, Science and Religion in England 1640–1700*, Cambridge: Cambridge University Press.

Osler, M. J. and Farber, P. L. (eds) (1985) *Religion, Science and Worldview: Essays in Honour of Richard S. Westfall*, Cambridge: Cambridge University Press.

Oster, M. (1989) 'The Beame of Diuinity: Animal Suffering in the Early Thought of Robert Boyle', *British Journal for the History of Science*, 22, pp. 151–180.

O'Toole, F. J. (1974) 'Qualities and Powers in the Corpuscular Philosophy of Robert Boyle', *Journal of the History of Philosophy*, 12, pp. 295–315.

Park, K. (1988) 'The organic soul' in C. B. Schmitt and Q. Skinner, (eds) *The Cambridge History of Renaissance Philosophy*, Cambridge: Cambridge University Press, 1988, pp. 464–484.

Passmore, J. (1967) 'Boyle, Robert' in P. Edwards, (ed.) *The Encyclopedia of Philosophy*, vol. 1, New York: Macmillan and Free Press, pp. 357–359.

Peters, R. S. (ed.) (1962) *Body, Man and Citizen: Selections from Thomas Hobbes*, New York: Collier.

Pitt, J. C. (1985) (ed.) *Change and Progress in Modern Science*, Dordrecht: Reidel.

Plato (1989) *Plato: The Collected Dialogues*, (eds) E. Hamilton and H. Cairns, Princeton: Princeton University Press.

Power, H. (1663) *Experimental Philosophy*, London.

Principe, L. M. (1995) 'Newly Discovered Boyle Documents in the Royal Society Archive: Alchemical Tracts and His Student Notebook', *Notes and Records of the Royal Society*, 49, pp. 57–70.

—— (1998) *The Aspiring Adept: Robert Boyle and his Alchemical Quest*, Princeton: Princeton University Press.

Pyle, A. (1995) *Atomism and its Critics*, Bristol: Thoemmes Press.

Sargent, R.-M. (1995) *The Diffident Naturalist: Robert Boyle and the Philosophy of Experiment*, Chicago: Chicago University Press.

Sarkar, S. (1992) 'Models of Reduction and Categories of Reductionism', *Synthese*, 91, pp. 167–194.

Schmitt, C. B. and Skinner, Q. (eds) (1988) *The Cambridge History of Renaissance Philosophy*, Cambridge: Cambridge University Press.

Sennert, D. (1636) *Hypomnemata physica*, Frankfurt.

Shanahan, T. (1988) 'God and Nature in the Thought of Robert Boyle', *Journal of the History of Philosophy*, 26, pp. 547–569.

Shapere, D. (1966) 'Plausibility and Justification in the Development of Science', *Journal of Philosophy*, 63, pp. 611–621.

Shapin, S. (1988) 'Robert Boyle and Mathematics: Reality, Representation, and Experimental Practice', *Science in Context*, 2, pp. 23–58.

—— (1993) 'Personal development and intellectual biography: the case of Robert Boyle', *British Journal for the History of Science*, 26, pp. 335–345.

—— (1994) *A Social History of Truth*, Chicago: Chicago University Press.

Skinner, Q. (1969) 'Meaning and Understanding in the History of Ideas', *History and Theory*, 8, pp. 3–22.

Smith, A. D. (1990) 'Of Primary and Secondary Qualities', *The Philosophical Review*, 99, pp. 221–254.

Sorabji, R. (1971) 'Aristotle on demarcating the five senses', in J. Barnes, M. Schofield and R. Sorabji, (eds) *Articles on Aristotle*, vol. 4: Psychology and Aesthetics, London: Duckworth, pp. 76–92.

—— (1988) *Matter, Space and Motion: Theories in Antiquity and Their Sequel*, London: Duckworth.

Spinoza, B. (1670) *Tractatus Theologico-Politicus*, Hamburg.

Stewart, M. A. (1987) Review of Alexander (1985) in *The Locke Newsletter*, 18, pp. 105–118.

—— (ed.) (1991) *Selected Philosophical Papers of Robert Boyle*, Cambridge: Hackett.

Suárez, F. (1597) *Disputationes Metaphysicæ*, Paris, 1866.

Sutton, J. (1998) *Philosophy and Memory Traces: Descartes to Connectionism*, Cambridge: Cambridge University Press.

Tooley, M. (1977) 'The nature of laws', *Canadian Journal of Philosophy*, 7, pp. 667–698.

Turnball, R. G. (1978) 'The Role of the "Special Sensibles" in the Perception Theories of Plato and Aristotle', in P. K. Machamer and R. G. Turnball, (eds) *Studies in Perception*, Columbus: Ohio State University Press, 1978, pp. 3–26.

van Martels, Z. R. W. M. (ed.) (1993) *Alchemy Revisited*, Leiden: Brill.

Vlastos, G. (1950) 'The Physical Theory of Anaxagoras', *Philosophical Review*, 59, pp. 31–57, reprinted in A. P. D. Mourelatos, (ed.) *The Pre-Socratics*, New York: Anchor, 1974, pp. 459–488.

Warton, T. (1761) *The Life and Literary Remains of Ralph Bathurst, M. D.*, London.

Webster, C. (1965) 'The Discovery of Boyle's Law, and the Concept of the Elasticity of Air in the Seventeenth Century', *Archive for History of Exact Sciences*, 2, pp. 441–502.

—— (1967) 'Henry Powers' Experimental Philosophy', *Ambix*, 14, pp. 150–178.

—— (1986) 'Puritanism, Separatism, and Science', in D. C. Lindberg and R. L. Numbers, (eds) *God and Nature*, Berkeley: University of California Press, pp. 192–217.

Weinberg, J. R. (1965) *Abstraction, Relation and Induction*, Madison: University of Wisconsin Press.

Westfall, R. S. (1956) 'Unpublished Boyle Papers Relating to Scientific Method', *Annals of Science*, 12, pp. 63–73, 103–117.

—— (1971a) *Force in Newton's Physics*, London: Macdonald.

—— (1971b) *The Construction of Modern Science*, Cambridge: Cambridge University Press.

—— (1973) 'Circular Motion in Seventeenth-Century Mechanics', *Isis*, 63, pp. 184–189.

—— (1986) 'The Rise of Science and the Decline of Orthodox Christianity: A Study of Kepler, Descartes, and Newton', in D. C. Lindberg and R. L. Numbers, (eds) *God and Nature*, Berkeley: University of California Press, pp. 218–237.

Westman, R. S. and McGuire, J. E. (eds) (1977) *Hermeticism and the Scientific Revolution*, Los Angeles: Clark Memorial Library.

Whitehead, A. N. (1933) *Adventures of Ideas*, New York: Cambridge University Press.

Wiener, P. P. (1932) 'The Experimental Philosophy of Robert Boyle (1626–91)', *Philosophical Review*, 41, pp. 594–609.

Williamson, J. (1990) 'Boyle and Locke on Material Substance', in P. Gilmour, (ed.) *Philosophers of the Enlightenment*, Edinburgh: Edinburgh University Press, pp. 31–46.

Wilson, M. D. (1979) 'Superadded Properties: The Limits of Mechanism in Locke', *American Philosophical Quarterly*, 16, pp. 143–150.

Wojcik, J. (1997) *Robert Boyle and the Limits of Reason*, Cambridge: Cambridge University Press.

Woolhouse, R. S. (1983) *Locke*, Minneapolis: University of Minnesota Press.

Wotton, W. (1697) *Reflections upon Ancient and Modern Learning*, 2nd edn, London.

Yolton, J. W. (1970) *Locke and the Compass of Human Understanding*, Cambridge: Cambridge University Press.

—— (1984) *Perceptual Acquaintance from Descartes to Reid*, Minneapolis: University of Minnesota Press.

Index